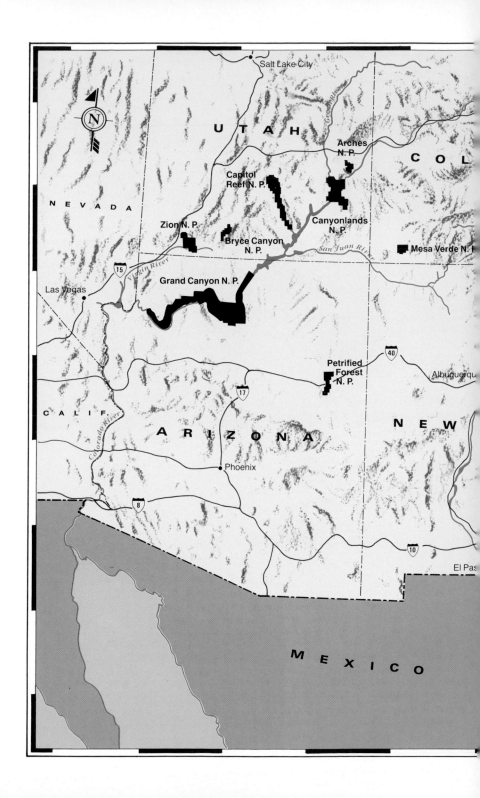

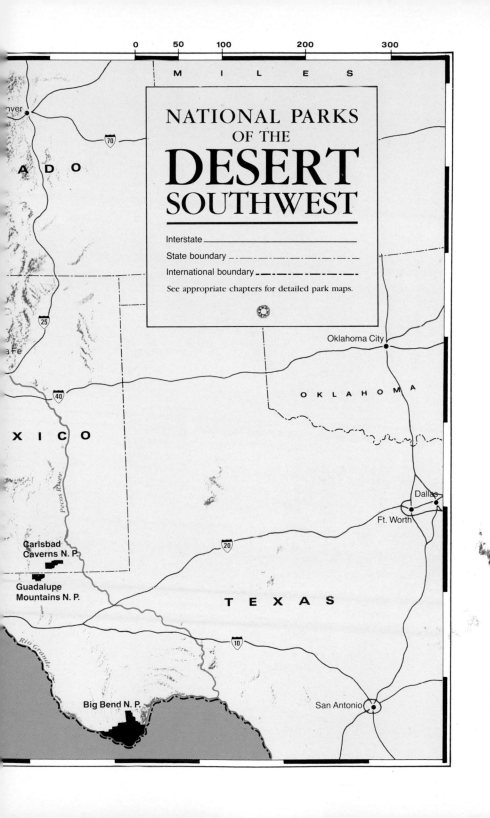

NATIONAL PARKS
OF THE
DESERT
SOUTHWEST

Interstate ———————————
State boundary ——————————
International boundary ———————————

See appropriate chapters for detailed park maps.

THE SIERRA CLUB GUIDES
TO THE
NATIONAL PARKS
OF THE
DESERT
SOUTHWEST

Published by

Stewart, Tabori & Chang

Cover photograph: Grand Canyon National Park
(© Jeff Gnass)

Frontispiece: The Golden Throne, Capitol Reef
(© Jim Shotwell/Tom Stack & Assoc.)

Back cover: Double Arch, Arches National Park
(© Frank Mendonca/Tom Stack and Assoc.)

Text by:

Conger Beasley, Jr.—Grand Canyon and Petrified Forest
Michael Collier—Mesa Verde
Frank Deckert—Big Bend
Robert Gildart—Bryce Canyon and Zion
Daniel Murphy—Carlsbad Caverns and Guadalupe Mountains
Stephen Trimble—Arches, Canyonlands, and Capitol Reef

Consulting Editor James V. Murfin

Project Editor: Irene Pavitt

Designer: J. C. Suarès

Photo Editor: Christine A. Pullo

Illustrations and maps © Bill Russell

Library of Congress Cataloging in Publication Data
Main entry under title:

Sierra Club guide to the national parks of the desert Southwest.

Includes index.
1. National parks and reserves—Southwest, New—
Guide-books. 2. Southwest, New—Description and
travel—1981   —Guide books. I. Beasley, Conger.
II. Murfin, James V. III. Pavitt, Irene. IV. Sierra
Club. V. Title: Guide to the national parks of the
desert Southwest. VI. Title: Desert Southwest.
F787.S56 1984   917.9   83-9310
ISBN 0-394-72488-7 (Random House)

Created and published by Stewart, Tabori & Chang, Inc.
Text pp. 13–34, 37–72, 75–98, 101–130, 133–162, 165–184, 187–218, 221–246,
249–274, 277–300, 303–325 copyright © 1984 Stewart, Tabori & Chang, Inc.
740 Broadway, New York, N.Y. 10003.

Photographs, drawings, and maps copyright © 1984 Stewart,
Tabori & Chang, Inc. and as indicated on this page and in
the photo credits on pp. 344 and 345.

Printed and bound in Japan.

P R E F A C E

THIS COUNTRY'S FORTY-EIGHT NATIONAL PARKS CONtain natural wonders more varied and extraordinary than those found in any other nation on earth. Embodied and preserved in them is the beauty of a vast land, which only a few centuries ago was wilderness. Every year, 50 million people visit these parks, testifying to a deep appreciation of the treasures they offer.

Recognizing the need for park guide books that are practical as well as beautiful, Stewart, Tabori & Chang is proud to present *The Sierra Club Guides to the National Parks*. These books have been created with the cooperation of the Sierra Club, which has been committed to conservation since 1892, and with the participation of the National Park Service and Random House. The five regional guides planned for the series—the Desert Southwest, the Pacific Southwest and Hawaii, the Rocky Mountains and the Great Plains, the Pacific Northwest and Alaska, and the East and Middle West—take you through each of the national parks of the United States.

Leading nature writers and photographers, experts in their fields, have provided text and photographs that work together as a tour of the parks. One chapter is devoted to each park, beginning with its discovery and use by man, moving on to its natural and geological history, its animal and plant life, and finally exploring its sites, trails, and trips. Each chapter also includes an up-to-date facilities chart, trail guides, and park and trail maps created especially for the book. An extensive full-color appendix of the most commonly seen animals and plants is included at the end of each book.

M A P S

C O N T E N T S

ARCHES
NATIONAL PARK

Delicate Arch, only 45 feet high, appears much taller.

ARCHES NATIONAL PARK, 125 WEST 200 SOUTH
MOAB, UTAH 84532, TEL.: (801) 259-8161

Highlights: Delicate Arch □ Double Arch □ Landscape Arch □ Fiery Furnace □ Devil's Garden □ Herdina Park □ Klondike Bluffs □ Courthouse Towers □ Park Avenue □ Balanced Rock □ Garden of Eden

Access: From Moab take U.S. 191 North for 5 miles to park entrance. See map on pages 15–16.

Hours: Daily, 24 hours, year-round. Visitor Center, 8 A.M.–4:30 P.M.; extended hours in summer; closed Thanksgiving, Christmas Day, and New Year's Day.

Fees: Entrance $5/vehicle, $2/person; Golden Age and Golden Eagle passes honored. Camping, $5/per night.

Parking: Adequate parking at each public-use point.

Gas, food: In Moab.

Lodging: In Moab.

Visitor Center: Arches Visitor Center, at main entrance, offers slide show, books, maps, and posters for sale.

Museum: In Arches Visitor Center. Offers geological and historical displays.

Pets: Not permitted in backcountry roadless areas or on hiking trails. All pets outside vehicles must be on leash. Horseback riding permitted in specific backcountry areas. Permit required for all horseback trips. All riders should first stop at Visitor Center. No grazing; no rentals; no stables.

Picnicking: At Visitor Center, Balanced Rock, and Devil's Garden.

Hiking: Trails available. Carry water.

Backpacking: Backpack camping permitted in wilderness area with free permit, but at least 5 miles off roads and trails and out of sight of the Arches. Carry water. If in backcountry; inform rangers about trip plans.

Campground: Devil's Garden, 53 sites, both tent and trailer. First-come basis. Fires only in fire grates; gathering wood forbidden. No showers, no hookups. $5 fee.

Tours: Through Fiery Furnace daily in spring, summer, fall. In English only; other tours depend on season and staff.

Other activities: Extensive interpretive activities during high season. Sightseeing flights at airport outside park.

Facilities for disabled: Arches Visitor Center, campground restrooms, and a campsite.

For additional information, see also Sites, Trails, and Trips on pages 26–32.

A RCHES NATIONAL PARK CONTAINS THE GREATEST known concentration of natural stone arches. The park is a jewel—a scattering of sandstone spires perched above the Colorado River canyon on a highland that feels like a formal garden, decorated with twisted piñon and juniper trees and natural statuary of arches, buttes, towers, and hoodoos. The La Sal Mountains—more than 12,000 feet and snow-capped most of the year—form a tantalizing background of evergreen and aspen forest.

Arches introduces the unique rock landscapes of the Colorado Plateau. Its story is straightforward: a collapsed salt dome cracking rocks on its flanks, eroding to fins of sandstone ideal for arch formation. The park is big enough to feel wild—73,379 acres—but small enough to be enjoyed in a day. An 18-mile paved road penetrates to its heart and leads past most major features. Easy and moderate trails lead to many arches, including the monumental buttresses of Double Arch, Landscape Arch (longest natural span in the world), and exquisite Delicate Arch.

This is high desert country, ranging from 3,960 to 5,653 feet. Shrubs dominate, with cottonwoods along washes the only trees other than the tough dryland junipers and piñons. Practically nothing grows on some shales, but hanging gardens luxuriate at seeps. Animal life is typical of rugged plateau country: deer, jack rabbit, gray fox, raven, mourning dove, white-throated swift, toad, collared lizard, rattlesnake. Dry, achingly hot in summer and sometimes frigid in winter, Arches makes a challenging home for these living things, but their evolutionary success matches the feel of the park landscape—spare, careful, quiet, and elegant.

Near this complex of fins lies Sand Dune Arch.

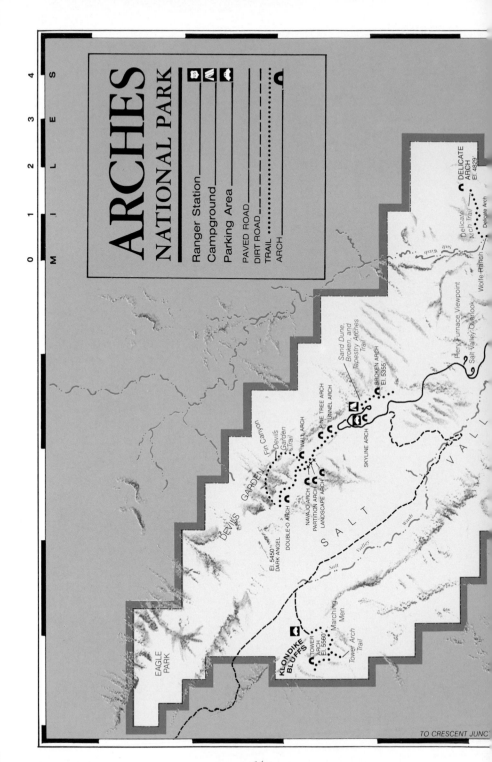

ARCHES
NATIONAL PARK

Ranger Station
Campground
Parking Area

PAVED ROAD
DIRT ROAD
TRAIL
ARCH

EAGLE
PARK

KLONDIKE
BLUFFS

TOWER
ARCH
El. 5560

Marching
Men

Tower Arch
Trail

El. 5450
DARK ANGEL

DEVILS GARDEN

Fin Canyon

Devils
Garden
Trail

DOUBLE-O ARCH

NAVAJO ARCH
PARTITION ARCH
LANDSCAPE ARCH

WALL ARCH

PINE TREE ARCH
TUNNEL ARCH

Sand Dune,
Broken, and
Tapestry Arches
Trail

BROKEN ARCH
El. 5355

SKYLINE ARCH

SALT VALLEY

Salt Valley Wash

Fiery Furnace Viewpoint

Salt Valley Overlook

Delicate
Arch Trail

Wolfe Ranch

Delicate Arch

DELICATE
ARCH
El. 4829

Salt Wash

TO CRESCENT JUNC

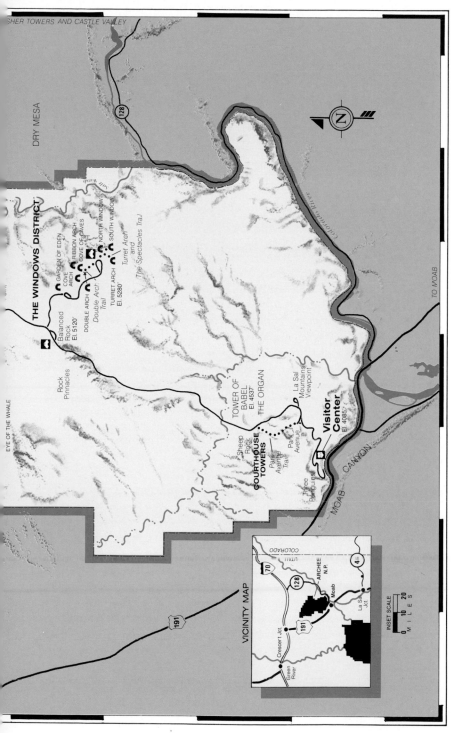

SHER TOWERS AND CASTLE VALLEY

DRY MESA

EYE OF THE WHALE

THE WINDOWS DISTRICT

Salt Wash

GARDEN OF EDEN
COVE ARCH
RIBBON ARCH
COVE OF CAVES
NORTH WINDOW
SOUTH WINDOW

Balanced Rock
El. 5120'

Turret Arch
and
The Spectacles Trail

Double Arch Trail

TURRET ARCH
El. 5280

Rock Pinnacles

TOWER OF BABEL
El. 4537

THE ORGAN

La Sal Mountains Viewpoint

Visitor Center
El. 4085'

Sheep Rock

COURTHOUSE TOWERS

Park Avenue

Park Avenue Trail

Three Gossips

MOAB CANYON

Colorado River

TO MOAB

128

N

VICINITY MAP

UTAH
COLORADO

70

128

ARCHES N.P.

Moab

191

Crescent Jct.

Green River

La Sal Jct.

4

INSET SCALE

0   10   20
MILES

191

A thousand years back in canyon-country prehistory, two powerful cultures had developed in the Arches region, the Fremont and the Anasazi. Arches National Park straddles the boundary between them, an open territory used from about A.D. 1000 to 1300 as a marginal agricultural and hunting area by the Anasazi from the south, and as a hunting area and shrine for magical rock art by the Fremont from the north.

The Prehistoric Frontier

Anasazi corn farmers must have regarded Arches as a barely usable frontier. The Fremont favored hunting and gathering, and probably used the park seasonally. The finest rock-art site—with Fremont, Anasazi, and Barrier Canyon-style figures—tragically was vandalized in 1980.

On this fine line of agriculture, where just enough rain fell to support life, a minor drought evidently pushed the people past an invisible threshold between success and failure, bringing regional abandonment about 1300. The ultimate fate of the Fremont remains a mystery. The Anasazi migrated farther and farther south; today their descendants live in the Hopi and Rio Grande pueblos.

The Ute Indians were living across all of western Colorado and eastern Utah when whites arrived. The Ute hunters took so well to horses in the early 1800s that they carried their hunts and raids from the buffalo plains in the east to the Navajo and Paiute country in the south and west. The Utes, too, left petroglyphs at Arches.

Trails and Trappers

Most of the whirl of nineteenth-century exploration passed north of Arches, on the same easy path that Interstate 70 and the railroad follow today. But one historic trail came up from New Mexico, bound for California, to cross the Colorado River at Moab and head north right past the present-day park. The trappers and traders called it the Old Spanish Trail, although it was used most heavily by Mexicans and Americans in the 1830s and 1840s.

One mountain man left his cryptic signature on a number of cliffs in the area, including one at Arches dated June 9, 1844. We know little about this mysterious Denis Julien, but his inscriptions in Canyonlands hint that he may have been the first to travel down the Colorado and Green rivers by boat.

Opposite: The Arch-in-the-Making (now Skyline Arch) c. 1935.

Canyon Conquest

As the Mormons pushed out from Salt Lake City, they chose the present site of Moab for their Elk Mountain Mission in 1855. But the Utes whom they sought to convert rebelled, and three Mormon deaths forced abandonment that same year. Not until the late 1870s did settlers return to the east side of the Colorado River. By 1883, Moab had a post office, and the Denver and Rio Grande Railroad between Denver and Salt Lake City passed by just 30 miles north.

In 1888, Arches got its first settler in the person of John Wesley Wolfe, a Civil War veteran who went west from Ohio for his health, and until 1910 lived with his family on the bank of Salt Wash below Delicate Arch. His cabin still stands, counterpart in pioneer spirit to the broken spear points and pictographs of the vanished Native Americans.

Establishment of the Park

The father of Arches National Park was a prospector who in 1923 suggested to the managers of the railroad that they develop Klondike Bluffs as a tourist attraction. Alexander Ringhoffer guided the officials through the remarkable sandstone maze, and the impressed railroad men contacted Stephen Mather, first director of the National Park Service. Mather initiated the political process that created the small Arches National Monument in 1929. Over the years, Moab groups, led by Dr. J. W. Williams and Loren L. Taylor, pushed through major additions to the monument, and in 1971 their work culminated in the establishment of Arches National Park.

G E O L O G Y

Unlikely as it seems, common salt is the creative force behind the features of Arches National Park—the densest cluster of natural stone arches on earth. A roundabout story, however, leads to this realization, and to the landscape of today's park.

Arches and Salt

The main thread of the tale began 300 million years ago, when a huge basin developed in southeastern Utah and southwestern Colorado. Oceans filled the basin, and a neighboring highland shed into it vast quantities of sediment. As the ocean shrank, salts, gypsum, and other "evaporites" crystallized from the brine under the hot rays of the Pennsylvanian period sun. This basin is called the Paradox Basin, and the 3,000 feet of salt deposits, the Paradox Formation.

Balanced Rock, near The Windows, teeters on its pedestal.

Arches went through hundreds of millions more years of deposition, uplift, and erosion. But the ancient salt remained a major character in its story. Later formations that overlie the Paradox salt came to Arches as sediments that rippled the tidal flats of shallow seas, from rivers and lakes, and as the wind-blown sand dunes of deserts. Two hundred million years of rocks, in thirteen distinct layers, lie exposed in the park. Once you learn to recognize these formations, their names resonate with the sense of the place: Paradox, Honaker Trail, Cutler, Moenkopi, Chinle, Wingate, Kayenta, Navajo, Entrada, Summerville, Morrison, Dakota, and Mancos.

As these heavier layers piled on the lighter underlying salt, they forced the salt upward where the rock cover was thinnest, squeezing it in slowly moving "plastic" flows along areas of weakness in long parallel cores. More and more salt flowed into the rises as new sediments weighed heavier and heavier on the troughs. The rising salt domed up the overlying rocks in folds, cracking rocks along their sides.

Then, less than 10 million years ago, regional uplift further cracked the flanks of these folds in a series of joints paralleling each long salt dome. Finally, as erosion ate down through the rising stack of ancient sedimentary rocks, ground water reached the salt, dissolving out dome foundations, which collapsed. Exactly such events led to the landscape seen today in Salt Valley.

Arches and Water

Thus this rather nondescript valley slowly gave rise to the spectacular Entrada Sandstone ridges where the arches form. Water dissolves cement between sand grains in the rock, and grinds down along joints, isolating narrow "fins." Winter brings a trickle of snowmelt freezing in cracks, wedging the fins to rubble. Slabs pop off when cliffs release ancient pressures built up when they lay buried under thousands of feet of other rock. Cleansing summer thunderstorms sweep away "waste" rock to the Colorado.

And sometimes, a block wedged from a wall deepens an alcove just enough to pierce the fin, a pothole grinds through a cliff edge, and a last rockfall leaves behind a natural, free-standing stone span—an arch.

Joints along both sides of Cache and Salt valleys provided the blueprint for the groups of arches and spires: Eagle Park, Devil's Garden, Fiery Furnace, and Delicate Arch on the east; Klondike Bluffs, Herdina Park, and The Windows on the west. The miniature Monument Valley of Courthouse Towers formed along a second major fold in the earth's surface. Underlying these Entrada rock gardens, the Navajo Sandstone lies exposed as a rolling floor of "petrified sand dunes."

Golden eagle.

In the prairies and in tropical rain forests, ecological communities remain the same for hundreds of miles; but in the American West, abrupt changes in elevation create banded life zones, from low desert flats to tundra-crowned mountains—all visible in a single glance.

At Arches, elevation varies little —from 3,960 feet to 5,653 feet. Precipitation averages a puny 8.5 inches over the entire park. Yet vegetation changes abruptly in a single stride—from grassland to desert scrub, from oak thickets to piñon and juniper woodland. Why so much variety?

Plant Communities: The Desert Mosaic

The biological story of Arches is grounded in rock. On Navajo Sandstone slickrock and on either side of Salt Valley along ridges studded with clusters of Entrada fins and spires, Utah juniper and piñon pine form a sparse woodland that covers nearly half the park. Juniper is more tolerant of arid conditions than is piñon, and since Arches is near the low-elevation limit of woodland, juniper predominates.

These trees grow in unlikely-looking cracks where moisture accumulates and underwrites life not possible otherwise. Cliffrose, squawbush, single-leaf ash, and serviceberry take advantage of the same cracks.

In areas with a few inches of sandy "soil," shrubs take over. Blackbrush dominates in Arches, its roots sunk where moisture "perches" just above bedrock, allowing slow uptake of water. Once sand accumulates beyond 18 inches, ground water percolates too deep for blackbrush, and grassland thrives—most notably in Salt Valley, where bunch grasses like galleta, Indian rice grass, and sand dropseed grow.

Salt Valley once may have been pure grassland. After nearly a century of heavy grazing by sheep and cattle, however, shrubs like Mormon tea and snakeweed crowd the grasses. Not until 1982 was grazing finally eliminated from the most recent additions to Arches National Park.

Clockwise, from top: A golden eagle in flight. The kangaroo rat survives without water. The spadefoot toad digs deep below dry earth to find moisture. Columbine in bloom.

Where deep wind-blown sand piles in orange dunes, wavy-leaf oak and feathery old-man sage stabilize the loose grains. The shales of the Mancos and Morrison formations support only a sparse cover of saltbush, shadscale, and astragalus. In alkali-ridden bottom lands along Salt Wash, salt-tolerant shrubs like greasewood, seepweed, and pickleweed survive.

And where water works its magic full-time, along streams and at seeps, the plant world runs wild with luxuriance, free from desert restraints. Tamarisk (introduced from Eurasia years ago), cottonwoods, and willows line Salt and Courthouse washes. Shielded by alcoves, hanging gardens festoon seeps with columbine, monkey flower, primrose, and maidenhair fern. No need here to contrive waxy coverings for tiny leaves, grow enormous spreading roots, or maintain thick fleshy stems for water storage—at seeps and streams plants can relax.

Animal Life: Coping with the Desert

The animals of Arches National Park take advantage of each plant community in myriad ways, and they have evolved their own means of coping with desert extremes. Kangaroo rats, for example, burrow in sand dunes, relying only on the moisture that is contained in the dry seeds they eat and on an incredibly efficient water metabolism. Piñon jays flock through piñon groves in ridiculously noisy groups, feeding on (and caching for winter) the nutritious pine nuts. Spadefoot toads dig as deep as 20 inches below dry potholes to wait for moisture, while the hardened mud crust above them bakes in summer and freezes in winter, its ground temperature fluctuating through almost 200 degrees.

With luck, in daytime at Arches you will see an antelope ground squirrel race across the road, white tail held suavely over its back; or a collared lizard might sprint between rocks, rearing up on its hind legs to obtain top speed.

Birds liven up the sunlit sky as well. Golden eagles nest in the cliffs of Arches, soaring high on midday updrafts in search of a jack rabbit lunch. A black-throated sparrow calls from a perch in blackbrush. Trilling house finches answer from juniper snags. And from the cliffs above, the down-scale lilt of a canyon wren seems the song of the rock itself.

Night comes. Hunters range out from their dens—mountain lions after deer, gray foxes after rodents and birds, midget faded rattlesnakes after mice, coyotes after absolutely anything.

Arches may be a tough place to make a living, but to several hundred species of vertebrates and to thousands of species of invertebrates, Arches is home.

Overleaf: The fragile and wondrous Landscape Arch, spanning 291 feet, is the world's largest known natural arch.

Arches lends itself to relaxed, prowling drives through bonsai slickrock gardens and to easy strolls past awesome arcs of stone. The park entrance lies just 5 miles north of Moab, but it leads into a wild rock landscape that could be continents or centuries away from the pavement and plastic of town.

Park Headquarters and the Colorado River Canyon. From the Visitor Center, and the road winding up into the park behind it, you get a good look at the Moab Fault. Rocks across the valley are 100 million years older than formations behind the Visitor Center; the valley here follows a 30-mile fault that has dropped rocks on the Arches side 2,500 feet below corresponding layers on the opposite side of the canyon. This panorama makes for good practice in geological thinking.

Back toward Moab, the road follows the park boundary between the Visitor Center and the Colorado River. Then up the Colorado for 10 miles on Utah 128, you remain just across the river from the park. This lovely drive leads to Fisher Towers, and eventually to Cisco, on Interstate 70. The wide, gentle curve of the Colorado River beneath Navajo Sandstone walls is reminiscent of what Glen Canyon must have looked like before being drowned by Lake Powell.

Park Avenue and Courthouse Towers. The main park road leaves the Visitor Center and winds through Arches for 18 miles to Devil's Garden. In its first mile, it zigzags up the abrupt escarpment of Entrada Sandstone along the Moab Fault, an instant initiation into slickrock balds, hanging gardens in alcoves, and sculptured stone.

In just 2 miles, the road reaches Park Avenue, an open canyon that is lined with great skyscraper slabs of Entrada. A 1-mile trail leads down through scattered junipers to meet the road at a second parking area. Park Avenue makes a good place to begin to fine-tune your eye for distinguishing rock formations.

The Entrada has three members, and throughout the park their different natures control the course of erosion. The soft, lower Dewey Bridge Member erodes quickly. It supports many of the park's fins, which are formed by remnants of the higher, harder Slick Rock Member. Capping some monuments is the uppermost, white Moab Member. The "buildings" of Park Avenue are Slick Rock Entrada sitting on foundations of the Dewey Bridge Member. Toward the end of the walk, Navajo Sandstone (beneath the Entrada) forms the floor of the canyon—the avenue's sidewalk.

Just beyond Park Avenue is Courthouse Towers, a jumble of small buttes and towers whittled off a huge arching slab of Entrada by Courthouse Wash and its tributaries—in much the same way that the larger buttes of Monument Valley, Arizona, are remnants of a continuous mesa. Several arches, balanced rocks, and towers here have names that match their whimsical shapes—the Three Gossips, Sheep Rock, Baby Arch.

Just a bit farther, a huge expanse of cross-bedded Navajo Sandstone, "the petrified sand dunes," stretches away to the east toward the La Sal Mountains. Great buttresses of Entrada guard the mountain like circling battleships, flaring orange at sunset.

The Windows. Nine miles from the Visitor Center lies Balanced Rock, which guards the spur road to The Windows section. This is the halfway point on the road, and was the park entrance when the main approach to Arches was a dirt road winding in from farther north on U.S. 191.

Near Balanced Rock was the trailer in which Edward Abbey lived as he kept the journal of his Arches park-rangering experience that became the classic book *Desert Solitaire.* Near here, too, was Abbey's favorite juniper tree: "there is a kind of poetry, even a kind of truth, in simple fact....If a man knew enough he could write a whole book about the juniper tree. Not juniper trees in general but that one particular juniper tree which grows from a ledge of naked sandstone near the old entrance to Arches...."

Find a juniper of your own to watch. Abbey is right; they have much to teach.

Along the 3-mile side road to The Windows lie buttes and hoodoos—rocks shaped like hams, golf balls, and elephants—and several of the park's finest arches. Short trails of a few hundred yards lead from the end of the road to Turret Arch, North and South Window (together forming the Spectacles), and famed Double Arch.

These are open, approachable spans. They have formed on spurs of the highest butte in the park, and here you feel the sweep of the country—to the La Sals, to Courthouse Towers across the field of slickrock of the petrified dunes. This is a good place for wildflowers. Watch for larkspur, yucca, evening primrose, sand verbena, Indian paintbrush, and orange-red dock.

Panorama Point. Back on the main road, just past Balanced Rock, begins the descent toward Salt Valley. At its rounded rim is Panorama Point, where nearly the whole park is visible.

A counterclockwise 360° view during an evening storm starts at the south: Balanced Rock, The Windows, and the Garden of Eden—black silhouettes and blinding lightning strikes; behind them, the La Sals,

Trails of Arches National Park

Park Avenue Trail: Starts at Park Avenue viewpoint; ends at Courthouse Towers viewpoint; 2 miles round trip; .75 hour; 320-foot ascent; open canyon with "skyline" of sandstone fins; usually hiked one way (hikers picked up at lower trail head).

Double Arch Trail: Starts at Windows parking area; ends at Double Arch; .5 mile round trip; .5 hour; 80-foot ascent; easy walk through piñon and juniper woodland to two-buttressed Double Arch.

Turret Arch and The Spectacles Trail: Starts at Windows parking area; ends at The Spectacles; .6 mile round trip; .75 hour; 150-foot ascent; right branch of easy trail leads to Turret Arch; left branch leads to North and South Windows (The Spectacles); can stand under arch.

Delicate Arch Trail: Starts at Wolfe Ranch; ends at Delicate Arch; 3 miles round trip; 2 hours; 500-foot ascent; steep climb up natural ramps of slickrock to the arch, which is perched on the edge of a sandstone bowl, framing the La Sal Mountains; magnificent views.

Tower Arch Trail: Starts at Klondike Bluffs parking area; ends at Tower Arch; 3 miles round trip; 2 hours; 80-foot ascent; primitive trail through dunes, piñon, and juniper into high bluffs with imposing towers; return trail loops past the Marching Men.

Sand Dune, Broken, and Tapestry Arches Trail: Starts at parking area at 16-mile mark on park road; ends at campground; 1.5 miles round trip; 1 hour; 50-foot ascent; crosses open meadows and threads its way between high fins and through Broken Arch, with spurs to Sand Dune Arch and Tapestry Arch.

Devil's Garden Trail: Starts at end of park road; ends at Dark Angel; 4.5 miles round trip; 5 hours; 320-foot ascent; leads to seven arches (including Landscape Arch, longest natural span in the world), and views of several more arches; overlooks Fin Canyon; best to photograph sites in early morning; primitive trail beyond Landscape Arch (at .8 mile); carry water and food.
See map on pages 14–15.

Skyline Arch in Devil's Garden.

with fresh snow over golden autumn aspen, wisps of rain trailing out of a cloud cap, a slash of orange Entrada at their base. The great red walls up toward Castle Valley and the Colorado River canyon; a rise of slickrock around Delicate Arch, red rock turned glistening wet silver by rain. Beyond, "biscuits" of the uppermost Entrada, the white Moab Member, form a flat field in front of the distant Book Cliffs (which look like real mountains); the forest of fins in the Fiery Furnace—a dense pack of sandstone slices; then Devil's Garden running back behind, up the flank of the salt dome, more and more distant fins ending at the faraway mysterious spire of Dark Angel. The open flat bowl of Salt Valley—Klondike Bluffs sitting nicely above it on the left, presiding in style. Lightning striking due west, thunder rolling around behind it.

And then the full moon comes out from behind clouds, high and crisp over the Garden of Eden and the La Sals.

Delicate Arch and Wolfe Cabin. Twelve miles from the Visitor Center, a gravel road leads to Wolfe Cabin and the Delicate Arch Trail and viewpoint. This is one of the finest trails in the canyon country, 1.5 miles long, a 500-foot climb that can be a scorcher in midsummer, but is worth every panting step.

The trail begins at Wolfe's 1906 Bar-DX Ranch cabin, crosses Salt Wash on a suspension bridge (look for seeps and springs upstream), and winds up Entrada slickrock where junipers pose in suggestive elegance. They foretoken the elegance of the arch itself, which bursts on you from around a corner at the end of the trail with unconscious drama—perched on the edge of a graceful bezel of stone. The span of Delicate Arch reaches just 45 feet high, but appears much bigger in its setting.

It is difficult to photograph Delicate Arch; the classic view is so famous that it no longer captures the thrill of this place. For a less predictable image, try the viewpoint across the canyon, which can be reached by a short spur road from Wolfe Ranch. Beyond, wilderness in upper and lower Salt Wash makes for good backpacking.

Fiery Furnace. The Fiery Furnace is the densest array of fins in the park, named for their red glow at sunset. Deep slots separate spires in a maze that hides at least eighteen arches and one natural bridge. Tortuous routes through the Furnace make it tricky for route-finding, and most hikers see this area only in the summer, when rangers lead 2-hour walks through it.

Opposite: The Organ is a red sandstone monolith in the Courthouse Towers section of the park. To many visitors it resembles a massive pipe organ.

Devil's Garden. The park road enters Devil's Garden, where a series of trails lead to major arches; finally, the drive ends at the campground. The first trail in Devil's Garden is a short walk to Broken and Sand Dune arches. At the extreme north end of the Fiery Furnace, Sand Dune Arch hides low in a slot between two fins; a dune beneath it almost buries its abutments. Try to be there early in the morning, when the sand still preserves nighttime tracks of beetle, kangaroo rat, and gray fox.

A bit farther along is Skyline Arch, which is famous for its pair of "before November 1940" and "after November 1940" photographs. During that winter, a large block fell from the arch, doubling its size.

The main Devil's Garden Trail leads from the end of the road to Landscape Arch (.8 mile), Double-O Arch (2 miles), and Dark Angel (2.4 miles). Branches lead to several arches along the way, and one trail loops back through isolated Fin Canyon. Beyond Landscape Arch, the trail is unimproved.

Devil's Garden contains most of the known arches in the park, sixty-four by one count. Landscape Arch is its jewel, at 291 feet the world's longest known natural stone span.

Beyond lie the quiet ramps of stone leading deeper into Devil's Garden, good country for backpacking. Listen for black-throated sparrows and canyon wrens; sound carries so well that footfalls thud in soft sand at 150 yards. In its peace and grace, this truly is a garden.

Klondike Bluffs. Klondike Bluffs lies 9 miles down a dirt road across Salt Valley from Devil's Garden. The first cluster of spires at Arches to be publicized, it is now the least visited area of the park accessible by passenger car. The Tower Arch Trail runs through the high bluffs, in dune sand and through piñon and juniper woodland, about 1.5 miles to a fine arch. A rougher return is possible past the playful Marching Men.

Not so linear as Devil's Garden, Klondike Bluffs almost feels like the big, complex landscapes of Canyonlands National Park. The sense of isolation is powerful; here, if anywhere in the park, mountain lion tracks might turn up, imprinted in the kneaded sand.

Four-Wheel-Drive Roads

Rough roads lead from Balanced Rock through Herdina Park to Klondike Bluffs, and on through Salt Valley to Eagle Park. Check with park rangers on current road conditions. In Herdina Park, an arch stares through a humpback of slickrock: The Eye of the Whale.

Opposite: Double Arch, one of sixty-four arches in The Windows.

BIG BEND
NATIONAL PARK

Rime coats trees and grass at Panther Pass.

BIG BEND NATIONAL PARK, TEXAS 79834
TEL.: (915) 477-2251

Highlights: Sotol Vista □ Castolon □ Boquillas Canyon □ Lost Mine Trail □ Santa Elena Canyon □ Hannold Grave Homesite Fossil Bone Exhibit □ Dagger Mountain □ Dagger Flat □ Old Sam Nail Ranch □ The Basin

Access: From Alpine, 108 miles to park headquarters on Texas 118. See map on pages 38–39.

Hours: Daily, year-round. Most Visitor Centers and ranger stations, 8 A.M.–5 P.M. daily.

Fees: Entrance, $5/vehicle for 7 days or $15/annual permit; $2/person entering on foot or by bus for 7 days. Daily fee for camping in developed areas.

Parking: Ample throughout park.

Gas: At Panther Junction, Rio Grande Village, and Castolon (unleaded only).

Food: At Chisos Mountain Lodge, The Basin.

Lodging: At Chisos Mountain Lodge, The Basin. Call (915) 477-2291 for reservations.

Visitor Centers: At Panther Junction, Rio Grande Village, The Basin, and Persimmon Gap.

Museum: Lajitas Museum and Desert Garden outside park.

Gift shop: At Chisos Mountain Lodge.

Pets: Permitted on leash, except in public buildings and on trails. Horseback riding permitted; rentals at Chisos Remuda.

Picnicking: At various areas throughout park.

Hiking: Permitted. Spring water available, but best to carry it.

Backpacking: Permitted with free permit. No wood fires. Carry water.

Campgrounds: Concession operates trailer park with full hookups and showers. Park has 3 campgrounds, 198 sites, no hookups.

Other activities: River trips and fishing.

Facilities for disabled: Restrooms, Panther Path Nature Trail.

For additional information, see also Sites, Trails, and Trips on pages 54–70 and the map on page 57.

DEEP LIMESTONE CANYONS CARVED BY THE RIO GRANDE; barren desert flats and rugged mesas; mountains nearly 8,000 feet high where Douglas fir, ponderosa pine, and white-tailed deer exist in a last stronghold against encroaching aridity: this is Big Bend National Park. Containing 1,100 square miles of Chihuahuan Desert country on the Mexican border, Big Bend nestles in the downward arc of the Rio Grande that gave the region—and the park—its name. Colorful geologic formations, as well as fossils of sea creatures, dinosaurs, and early mammals, reveal much of the earth's history. Plants and animals from Mexico reach the northern extreme of their ranges at Big Bend, and some from the United States are uncommon this far south. Some species occur *only* here. Nearly 400 kinds of birds have been seen in Big Bend, more than in any other national park.

The beauty is often subtle but sometimes overwhelming: sweeping vistas with horizons 100 miles away, displays of desert wildflowers, the cathedral-like ambiance at the bottom of a river canyon. There is mystery and magic as well. The weird, stark appearance of the country coupled with the romance of the Mexican border gives visitors the feeling that a last frontier lingers on and that they are a part of it.

H I S T O R Y

Beginnings

Scant evidence exists of the prehistoric big-game hunters who roamed the Big Bend region 10,000 or more years ago. They were replaced about 6,000 B.C. by a group of Indians who led a seminomadic existence, taking advantage of the seasonally available desert resources. This life style of hunting and gathering, known as the Desert Culture, continued until the Spanish influence began.

Spanish and Indians

In the early 1500s, Spanish explorers moved into the area in their quest for riches. Seldom did they penetrate the Big Bend region, but preferred to detour around this harsh country, which they termed *El Despoblado*—"the uninhabited land." Spanish settlements were raided frequently by Indians who retreated to the safety of *El Despoblado*, but eventually these groups of Indians were overwhelmed and dispersed by the Spanish. Pressured by the Comanches, the Apaches moved into

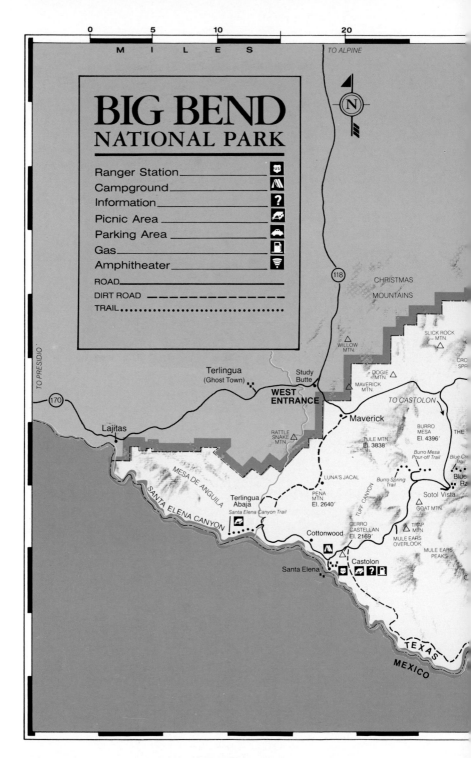

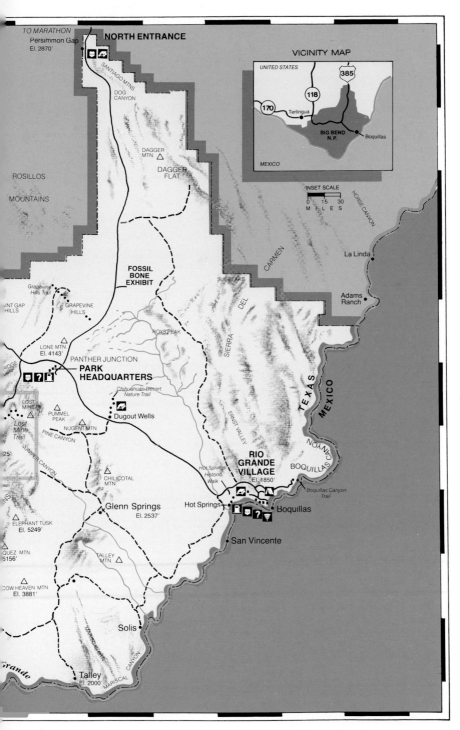

VICINITY MAP

UNITED STATES

385

118

170

Terlingua

BIG BEND N.P.

Boquillas

MEXICO

INSET SCALE

0   15   30
M I L E S

TO MARATHON

Persimmon Gap
El. 2870'

NORTH ENTRANCE

SANTIAGO MTNS

DOG CANYON

DAGGER MTN. △

DAGGER FLAT

ROSILLOS

MOUNTAINS

La Linda

FOSSIL BONE EXHIBIT

SUE PEAKS

CARMEN

SIERRA DEL

Adams Ranch

HORSE CANYON

Grapevine Hills Trail

INT GAP HILLS

GRAPEVINE HILLS

ROYS PEAK

LONE MTN. El. 4143'

PANTHER JUNCTION

PARK HEADQUARTERS

Chihuahuan Desert Nature Trail

LOST MINE PK.

Lost Mine Trail

PUMMEL PEAK

NUGENT MTN.

PINE CANYON

Dugout Wells

ERNST VALLEY

TEXAS

MEXICO

BOQUILLAS

JUNIPER CANYON

CHILICOTAL MTN.

Hot Springs Historic Walk

RIO GRANDE VILLAGE
El. 1850'

Boquillas Canyon Trail

Glenn Springs
El. 2537'

Hot Springs

Boquillas

ELEPHANT TUSK El. 5249'

QUEZ MTN 5156'

TALLEY MTN. △

San Vincente

COW HEAVEN MTN. El. 3881'

Solis

Talley
El. 2000'

MARISCAL MTN.

MARISCAL CANYON

Grande

the Big Bend country from the north to fill the void and assumed the role of harrassing the Spanish. By the early 1800s, the Spanish decided that riches were not to be had in the region, and they left. As Anglo-Americans pressed westward, the Comanches were forced south into the Big Bend and eventually drove out most of the Apaches. The great Comanche War Trail sliced through the heart of the Big Bend, and as Americans continued to move into and through the Big Bend, forts were built to protect them from the Indians. By the mid-1800s, the army had greatly reduced the Comanche influence in the Big Bend. Except for some increase in Indian activity during the Civil War, when frontier forts were abandoned, the Comanche era was over.

Explorers and Surveyors

Much of the early American exploration of the Big Bend was conducted by parties traveling on and along the Rio Grande. The first such group to traverse the entire southern boundary of the present-day park was part of the international boundary survey. The exploration was led by Marine Tyler W. Chandler and Lieutenant Duff C. Green in 1852. They traveled by land and water and chose to go around Santa Elena Canyon and Boquillas Canyon, both of which appeared too dangerous from their peripheral observations.

Attempting to complete the boundary survey in 1881, Texas Ranger Captain Charles L. Nevill and four surveyors succeeded in navigating through Santa Elena Canyon. (At least, the Nevill *expedition* succeeded. Captain Nevill, who had nearly drowned in a boat accident upriver, chose to direct operations from the cliffs above.) Finally, in 1899, Robert T. Hill of the U.S. Geological Survey led an expedition into this land of tall tales (and, perhaps, taller realities) to squelch or confirm the rumors about this last frontier of Texas. In only three weeks, Hill and his party successfully navigated 350 miles of the Rio Grande, including the three great canyons that are now within Big Bend National Park.

The Camel Corps

Lumbering across the Chihuahuan Desert in the summers of 1859 and 1860 were two of the oddest expeditions to venture into the heart of the Big Bend. The army, seeking the most efficient means of transportation on the western frontier, chose the Big Bend area as one place to test camel power. In the first expedition, led by Second Lieutenant

William H. Echols of the Topographical Engineers, two dozen camels carrying 400 pounds each marched south from Fort Davis. The caravan probably passed through Dog Canyon and down Tornillo Creek to the Rio Grande and returned by a similar route. The following summer the Camel Corps explored the area west of the Chisos Mountains. The camels had proved themselves under scorching skies and over rugged terrain, leaving horses and mules in their dust.

The promise of camel transportation across the western United States was to be unfulfilled, however. The Civil War halted the experiment, and after the war the railroad made camels obsolete.

Ranching

Relatively lush grasslands around the Chisos Mountains attracted ranchers to the Big Bend in the late 1800s. Cattle, horses, sheep, and goats grazed the region until the park was established in 1944. Overgrazing was especially devastating between 1942 and 1944, when the state of Texas granted free grazing privileges to the ranchers whose land it had purchased. Recovery of the grasses has been slow, but revegetation appears to have accelerated in recent years. Because of erosion of topsoils, however, some areas, such as Tornillo Flat and along Terlingua Creek, may never recover.

Settlers, Miners, Waxmakers, and Revolutionaries

The Big Bend is not a land to support a large human population. But as the Indians faded into legend and the ranchers made inroads, other groups filtered into the area around the turn of the century. Mexicans migrated northward to farm the flood plain of the Rio Grande. Working for themselves or for American landlords, they raised cotton as well as food crops to help supply the nearby mines.

In 1909, an ore tramway began carrying loads of silver, lead, and zinc ore from the Corte Madera mine above Boquillas to the ore terminal in Ernst Valley. Mariscal Mine on Mariscal Mountain near the very tip of the Big Bend yielded 894 flasks of mercury between 1917 and 1919. Candelilla, or waxplant, was commercially harvested from Big Bend's limestone soils, and factories to extract the high-quality wax from the plant sprang up at McKinney and Glenn Springs in 1911.

When the Mexican Revolution broke out in 1911, it spilled across the Rio Grande to involve Big Bend's early settlers. Bands of revolutionaries roamed the border, and fearful settlers on both sides of the river left their homes to seek security farther north in the United States. After revolutionaries attacked the villages of Glenn Springs and Boquillas on the night of May 5, 1916, President Woodrow Wilson called up the National Guard. By the end of July, more than 100,000 men had gathered in Texas and Arizona to guard the border. Other raids occurred in the surrounding country, but not within the area of the present-day park. After a decade of tension and border unrest, peace finally returned to the Big Bend.

Establishment of the Park

The National Guardsmen who had been stationed in the Big Bend spread the word about its rugged beauty and supported efforts to create a national park there. The man who really got the ball rolling was Everett Ewing Townsend, a former Big Bend lawman turned Texas state legislator. Through Townsend's efforts and influence, Santa Elena, Mariscal, and Boquillas canyons were included in Texas Canyons State Park, which was established in May 1933. Later that year the Chisos Basin was added as a site for a Civilian Conservation Corps camp, and the name of the park was changed to Big Bend State Park. National-park proponents were still not satisfied with this piecemeal approach and continued to push for a larger, more complete park. With private donations and state funds, more land was purchased until the state of Texas donated 1,100 square miles of land to the people of the United States. On June 12, 1944, Big Bend National Park was established.

G E O L O G Y

So jumbled, mixed, inverted, extruded, and intruded are the rocks of Big Bend National Park that some geologists wryly refer to this conglomeration as the "eggbeater formation." Yet it *is* decipherable, and the rocks are usually well exposed. Geology classes from throughout the United States travel to Big Bend to study the earth's history in stone.

Some Paleozoic era rocks are exposed at Persimmon Gap, but most of the rocks in the park are from the Cretaceous period or later. Lower Cretaceous seas covered the Big Bend area, and as sea creatures died over millions of years, their shells and skeletons piled up to form massive layers of limestone that are thousands of feet thick. Close examination of the huge cliffs of the Sierra del Carmen and Mesa de Anguila reveals sea-shell fragments embedded in the solid limestone. As the sea grew shallower, lime mud deposits formed layers that are now exposed in the flagstone formations that are easily seen at Hot Springs.

Opposite: Fascinating colors and textures are evident on numerous Big Bend rocks.

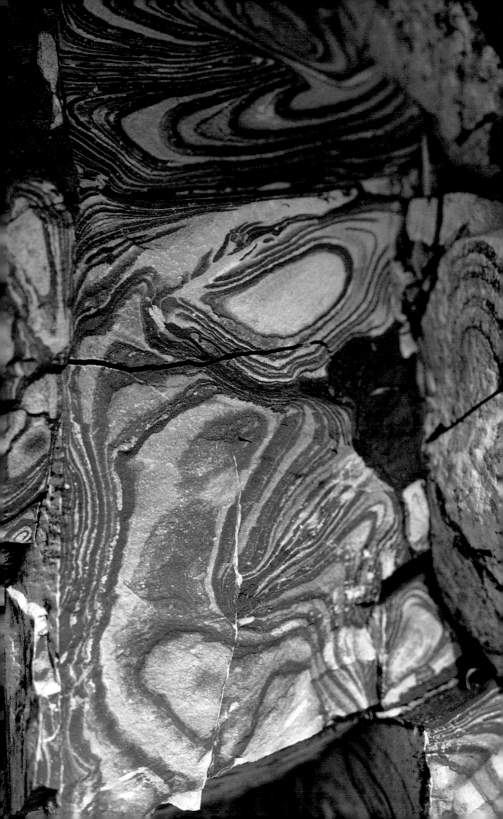

The Age of Dinosaurs

Plesiosaurs and other marine reptiles swam in the increasingly shallow waters. As the land rose and the sea receded, the succession of plant and animal life changed with the environment. Dinosaurs, flying reptiles, a huge crocodilelike creature, and other reptiles of all sizes slogged, splashed, and swam through or soared over lush forests and swamps. Their fossilized bones are still being found in the park's badlands formations, such as those near the Maverick entrance and on Tornillo Flat. Perhaps the most famous park fossil is from this period: the Big Bend pterosaur. This flying reptile, which had a wingspan of 51 feet, was the largest animal ever to fly over the surface of the earth. At the end of the Mesozoic era, the giant reptiles vanished from the Big Bend country (as they did worldwide) for reasons that are still unclear. At about the same time—give or take a few million years—a 40-mile-wide trough, known as the Sunken Block, formed between Mesa de Anguila and the Sierra del Carmen.

Mammals and Mountains

Now began the Age of Mammals, the Cenozoic era. The land rose higher, and a milder climate produced lush grasslands and forests. A wide variety of now-extinct mammals flourished. Some were similar to today's rhinoceros, horse, camel, deer, dog, and cat.

This was a time of mountain building, erosion, deposition, and igneous activity that deposited molten rock underground and left layers of lava and volcanic ash across the earth's surface. In the center of the Sunken Block, the Chisos Mountains were born. The rounded peaks of the Chisos began as molten underground masses that have since been exposed by erosion. The blocklike peaks and the South Rim were formed by successive lava flows that also have eroded into their characteristic shapes. One collapsed volcano, or caldera, has been found in the Chisos, and others are suspected. From these spewed the volcanic ash that settled and hardened in various sections of the park.

Geology Today

In this place of little water, aqueous signatures are scrawled across the land. Canyons cut through solid rock, dichotomous erosion patterns on the flats, arroyos that lead into mountain canyons—water has been at Big Bend. And visitors can watch it work as a summer thunderstorm creates a flash flood that can move tons of rock in mere minutes to a place a little closer to the river. Pieces of Emory Peak, the highest point in the park, can be found along the Rio Grande. The face of Big Bend National Park is always changing.

N A T U R A L   H I S T O R Y

Climate and Precipitation

Big Bend National Park is near the northern end of the Chihuahuan Desert, four-fifths of which is in Mexico. The Big Bend climate is gradually becoming more arid. Ten thousand years ago, trees and other vegetation covered what today is desert. Reduced precipitation forced this vegetation and associated animals to retreat to higher, moister elevations in the Chisos Mountains, where they now exist on mountain islands surrounded by a sea of aridity.

Annual precipitation varies from less than 4 inches near Castolon to 25 inches in the High Chisos, where two or three light snowfalls may occur each winter. (True desert conditions exist in areas that receive less than 10 inches of rainfall annually.) Summer temperatures in the river canyons can exceed 115° F.

With park elevations ranging from 1,800 feet to more than 7,800 feet, the stage is set for a wide variety of plant and animal habitats in relatively close association. If they are so inclined, del Carmen white-tailed deer meandering through piñon pines and junipers on Emory Peak can gaze at desert flats 6,000 feet below where kangaroo rats hop among cactus and creosote bush. The diversity of environments enables Big Bend to support more than 1,000 kinds of plants.

Trees and Shrubs

The warm, moist river flood plain encourages the growth of many plants that are not usually found in the desert. Several are exotics, or not native to the area. Among these are tree tobacco and the bamboolike giant reed. Perhaps the most significant of these newcomers is the salt cedar, which grows not only on the flood plain but also at desert springs that it often dries up with its spendthrift use of water. Native plants and animals suffer as a result. Exotic cottonwoods have been planted at Rio Grande Village and Castolon Campground, but the only native lance-leaf cottonwoods are in a grove between Castolon and the river. Trees in the legume (pea) family are abundant along the river, and some species such as catclaw acacia and honey mesquite follow the washes and arroyos into the foothills. The desert willow, with its lovely orchidlike flowers, is often a companion of these trees in the arroyos.

While the vegetation often looks sparse and sometimes monotonous across the desert, a surprising variety of plants reveal themselves to those who walk among them. One must use some care, though, as emphasized by an old cowboy who said, "Everything out there either sticks, stings, or stinks." One of the "stickers" is lechuguilla, the indicator plant of

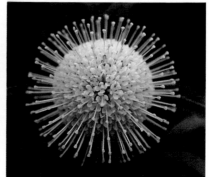

Left: A family of collared peccaries.
Top: Buttonbush flower.
Above: Desert millipede.

the Chihuahuan Desert. A small agave that is related to the century plant, lechuguilla blooms and dies after about fifteen years of growth.

Plants here exhibit interesting strategies for desert survival. The ocotillo sheds its leaves during dry periods and grows them again after rains. Flowers cover the ceniza, or barometer bush, soon after a rainstorm; they then wither, die, and fall to the ground a few days later. Four yuccas grow in the park. The Torrey yucca is the most common, but the giant dagger yucca is the most spectacular. Every three or four years, the display of flowering stalks at Dagger Flat is breath taking. Flowering shrubs that color the desert and grasslands include feather dalea, skeleton-leaf goldeneye, damianita, and yellow trumpet flower.

Two classic desert plants that thrive in Big Bend are the creosote bush and the century plant. The creosote bush is common throughout the desert, and its yellow blossoms can be seen somewhere in the park at almost any time of year. To the true desert lover, the aroma of creosote bush after a summer thunderstorm is heaven-scent. Growing for perhaps fifty years with little or no fanfare, the century plant suddenly one spring begins to shoot up a huge stalk that is tipped with platters of nectar-rich flowers. Insects and birds flock to the banquet and feast on the nectar, or on one another. Then, having used up fifty years' worth of stored energy, the plant dies and gradually is decomposed.

The Chisos Mountains are a north-meets-south environment for trees. The flaccid-foliaged drooping juniper is primarily a tree of Mexico, while ponderosa pine and quaking aspen are more common to the north. Some plants grow *only* in the Chisos Mountains. One, the mountain sage, with its dark green leaves and brilliant brick-red flowers, is a hummingbird's delight. The Chisos also are host to at least nine kinds of oaks.

Wildflowers and Cacti

March and April are the best months for viewing both wildflowers and blooming cacti, but some spectacular wildflower displays also may occur after summer thunderstorms. Seeds that have lain dormant for years may germinate if moisture and temperature are just right. A profusion of thyme-leaf dogweed can turn sun-baked Tornillo Flat into a golden plain. Every year brings splashes of color from the ubiquitous Big Bend bluebonnet (lupine to non-Texans).

Narrow-leaf globemallow brightens the river flood plain, while yellow rocknettle drapes nearby limestone cliffs. Both are common at Hot Springs. Prickly poppy, with its huge white flowers, and bicolor mustard occur from the river to the foothills. The wildflowers are more scattered in the mountains than in the desert, but they are no less beautiful. Longspur columbine, Mexican campion, and cedar sage decorate mountain slopes and secluded springs.

Big Bend is home to more than sixty kinds of cacti, several of which are rare and threatened by illegal collecting. Cacti range in size from the button cactus, which can be shaded by a silver dollar, to massive prickly pears, which cover many square feet of desert. Near Rio Grande Village, the brownspine prickly pear glows as sunlight is diffused by its translucent spines. Purple-tinged prickly pear is both abundant and striking, as is the tasajillo, or Christmas cactus, which retains its red fruits throughout the winter holiday season. On limestone hillsides the livingrock cactus grows flush with the soil surface until a pink flower dares new heights of an inch or so above the ground.

The hedgehog cactus flowers vary from yellow to red with many colors in between. And the strawberry cactus tastes as good as it looks. The summer-ripe fruit are luscious. Even the High Chisos supports a cactus population. Growing out of rocky outcrops on the highest peaks, the claret-cup cacti, with their brilliant red flowers, are fitting jewels to adorn the crown of mountaintops on the skyline.

Wildlife

When watching for wildlife in the desert, it is important to scan the nearby ground surface as well as the horizon. While a desert mule deer is bounding over a hilltop, a snake or a scorpion may be sneaking by at your feet.

The "creepy crawlies," or arthropods, of the desert take fascinating forms and are fun to watch. Sunspiders, tarantulas, and vinegarroons are predators that may be seen capturing beetles and moths. During the day, cicadas buzz; at night, crickets and katydids chirp and trill. Big Bend has more than 100 kinds of grasshoppers!

Catfish are common in the Rio Grande, and a variety of smaller fish live in the waters near the mouths of Terlingua and Tornillo creeks. The Big Bend gambusia is an endangered species. The entire population of this 1-inch-long mosquito fish lives in a man-made pond near Rio Grande Village.

Spadefoot toads often bide their time underground for months before a summer thunderstorm brings them popping from the ground like a spontaneous generation of life. They feed on termites and other insects, lay eggs in temporary ponds, and then dig back into the earth with the spades on their hind feet. The eggs hatch, and the tadpoles quickly mature into toads before the ponds dry up (if they are lucky). Thirty kinds of snakes and twenty-one kinds of lizards live in Big Bend.

Some snakes, such as the Trans-Pecos rat snake and the gray-banded kingsnake, are west Texas specialties. Four kinds of rattlesnakes and one kind of copperhead are here, but if you watch where you put your feet and hands and use a flashlight after dark, they will not be a problem. Able to withstand higher temperatures than most snakes, the western coachwhip is a large pink snake that often slithers across the path of surprised park visitors.

Big Bend is a bird watcher's paradise. The Colima warbler nests in the Chisos Mountains and nowhere else in the United States. Foothill canyons are nest sites for the Lucifer hummingbird, which, although fairly common in the park, can be observed in few other places in the United States. The endangered peregrine falcon has been successful in the river canyons and in the Chisos Mountains in recent years. And, of course, the roadrunner, symbol of the desert, may be seen nearly any day of the year chasing lizards or snapping up grasshoppers.

Two kinds of deer make their homes in the park. In the Chisos Mountains, the diminutive del Carmen white-tailed deer lives as a sub-species confined to these and other island mountaintops of west Texas and adjacent Mexico. The larger desert mule deer has moved into the lower, drier elevations, where it is often seen browsing on roadside plants. Both of these deer are a major part of the diet of Big Bend's top predator, the mountain lion. Called "panther" locally, this big cat has made a remarkable comeback from the days when intensive predator control around the park greatly reduced its numbers.

The coyote, another symbol of the Southwest, is occasionally seen, but more often heard as a howl across the desert night. Its prey species —black-tailed jack rabbits, eastern and desert cottontails, kangaroo rats and other rodents—are common.

One mammal that draws a great deal of attention, perhaps because it is relatively large and yet unfamiliar to many park visitors, is the col-lared peccary, or javelina. These piglike animals live throughout the park and travel in herds of from ten to twenty individuals. They are tough critters that eat cactus and lechuguilla, but they are not danger-ous to humans.

Opposite: A rainbow grasshopper perches on a prickly pear. This insect can leap twenty times the length of its body and is a voracious eater of green leaves and plants. The "tobacco" it spits helps drive away enemies.

SITES, TRAILS, AND TRIPS

The Rio Grande at Santa Elena Canyon.

A visitor to Big Bend has a selection of several ways to travel through the park and discover its diverse attractions and secrets. Paved roads lead to the major developed areas and to many sites of interest along the way; backcountry roads go to lesser used park areas; trails and primitive routes range from short self-guided walks to mere lines on a map that show a general route through some of the park's most remote wilderness; float trips can take boaters on quiet, open stretches of river and into the depths of the three great canyons of the park.

Paved Roads

Persimmon Gap to Panther Junction (26 miles). Driving south from Marathon, Texas, on U.S. 385, you will enter the park at Persimmon Gap, the same point at which the Comanche War Trail passed through the Dead Horse Mountains. Continuing south, the road passes Dog Canyon, Devil's Den, Dagger Mountain, and the improved dirt road that leads to Dagger Flat, with its concentration of giant dagger yuccas. For several miles the road stretches across Tornillo Flat, one of the areas in the park with the least vegetation. At the Fossil Bone exhibit are displayed fossil skulls and other bones of early mammals that roamed this country 50 million years ago. Just south of this exhibit a bridge spans Tornillo Creek, which drains most of the north and east sides of the park. (If you have ever seen a desert flash flood, you will understand why the bridge has a wide span.) The road finally climbs up a long, gentle slope past Hannold Grave and pioneer homesite to park headquarters and the Visitor Center at Panther Junction.

Maverick to Panther Junction (22 miles). Entering the park from the west at Maverick, this road immediately passes through Big Bend's painted desert, a beautiful badlands area that was a lush environment 70 million years ago when dinosaurs roamed the land and pterosaurs flew above. Just past the top of a steep hill, the north end of the Old Maverick Road turns off. Farther on, the Christmas Mountains can be

54

viewed just outside the park to the north, and Tule Mountain is to the south. The road swings around the northern end of Burro Mesa, a huge fault block that was once at the same elevation as Emory Peak, the highest point in the park, but that is now 3,500 feet below. After passing the Santa Elena Junction, the road passes three backcountry roads that lead to the north: Croton Spring, Paint Gap, and Grapevine Hills. Between the Basin Junction and Panther Junction, the road crosses a series of washes in a good wildlife-viewing area. Watch for javelina, mule deer, and coyotes along this stretch.

Panther Junction to Rio Grande Village (20 miles) *and Boquillas Canyon* (23 miles). This road is downhill most of the way from foothill grasslands through typical Chihuahuan Desert to the banks of the Rio Grande. The majestic Sierra del Carmen cliffs are visible to the southeast throughout the journey. A few miles below Panther Junction, the Glenn Springs Road angles off; about 1 mile beyond along the main road, a short improved gravel road leads to Dugout Wells, where a schoolhouse stood in the early 1900s. As the road continues its gradual descent, Chilicotal Mountain can be seen to the southwest. The road levels out, and just beyond the turnoff of the east end of the River Road, it crosses the Lower Tornillo Creek Bridge and climbs into rolling hills. After passing the Hot Springs Road and the south end of the Old Ore Road, the main road passes through a tunnel and drops down onto the Rio Grande flood plain.

Straight ahead is Rio Grande Village, which includes a visitor center, campground, picnic area, store, service station, and trailer facilities. The Boquillas Canyon Road leads off to the east. About 1 mile down the road, a dirt road goes to the International Crossing, where a villager from Boquillas, Mexico, ferries visitors across the river in a rowboat for a fee. They may then walk or ride a burro (again, for a fee) .75 mile into the village. Beyond Boquillas Crossing, the road leads to Boquillas Canyon parking area, where the Boquillas Canyon Trail begins.

Basin Junction to the Chisos Basin (7 miles). This road goes into the heart of the Chisos Mountains. Because of the steep grades and switchbacks, trailers longer than 20 feet are not allowed on this road.

The road begins at the Basin Junction, 3 miles west of Panther Junction. As the road climbs through Green Gulch, the rounded intrusive igneous rocks of Pulliam Ridge are to the right, and the blocklike extrusive igneous rocks of Panther and Lost Mine peaks are to the left. Desert plants give way to woodland species such as oaks, juniper, and piñon pine as the land rises. The road crests at 5,800 feet at Panther

Trails of Big Bend National Park

Chihuahuan Desert Nature Trail: Starts at Dugout Wells; ends at parking area; .5 mile round trip; .5 hour; introduction to Chihuahuan Desert ecology; fine point for photographs of Chisos Mountains and Sierra del Carmen; evidence of historic human occupation of desert; self-guiding. See map on pages 38–9.

Hot Springs Historic Walk: Starts at Hot Springs parking area; ends at Hot Springs; 2 miles round trip; 1 hour; must for history buffs; excellent view of Rio Grande; good photographic opportunities for old rock and adobe buildings; hot springs flow out of limestone at ruins of bath house. See map on pages 38–9.

Tuff Canyon Trail: Starts at Tuff Canyon parking area; ends at canyon bottom; .8 mile round trip; .5 hour; water-carved route between walls of tuff; harder lava flows farther into the canyon often contain pools of water; interesting contrast between views from overlook and from canyon bottom.

Burro Spring Trail: Starts along Burro Mesa Pour-off spur road; ends at Burro Spring; 2.2 miles round trip; 2 hours; overlook above Burro Spring provides good opportunities for viewing and photographing wildlife. See map on pages 38–9.

Burro Mesa Pour-off Trail: Starts at end of Burro Mesa Pour-off spur road; ends at Burro Mesa Pour-off; 1 mile round trip; .75 hour; cross sections of ancient lava flows form canyon walls; desert blooms in spring. See map on pages 38–9.

Boquillas Canyon Trail: Starts at end of Boquillas Canyon spur road; ends at Rio Grande; 1 mile round trip; 1.5 hours; 30-foot ascent; first 50 yards steep, then easy walking; Indian-made bedrock mortar holes in limestone shelf at river edge; huge sandslide formed by down-canyon winds; excellent view of canyon entrance. See map on pages 38–9.

Grapevine Hills Trail: Starts at Grapevine road; ends at a "window" of balanced boulders; 2.2 miles round trip; 50-foot ascent at the end of trail; probably prettiest desert hike in park; fascinating rock formations; good trail for children. See map on pages 38–9.

Santa Elena Canyon Trail: Starts at end of Santa Elena Canyon road; ends inside canyon; 1.7 miles round trip; 2 hours; dramatic walk into mouth of Santa Elena Canyon; fossil sea shells and 1,500-foot-high canyon walls; excellent photographic point looking out of canyon at Chisos Mountains. See map on pages 38–9.

Lost Mine Trail: Starts at Panther Pass; ends at Lost Mine Overlook; 4.8 miles round trip; 4 hours; 1,250-foot ascent; excellent introduction to plants and animals of the Chisos Mountains; views of Pine Canyon, Juniper Canyon, and East Rim; colorful rock formations at end of trail; self-guiding leaflet.

Window View Trail: Starts and ends at Basin trail head; .3 mile round trip; .5 hour; excellent stroll in evening; view of sun setting through the Window is a unique photographic opportunity; benches along trail.

Window Trail: Starts at Basin trail head; ends at pour-off; 5.3 miles round trip; 4 hours; 800-foot ascent; wide variety of plants and birds; one of the best photographic points for Casa Grande in the late afternoon; pools of water near pour-off contain aquatic insects and may attract large wildlife.

THE BASIN TRAIL MAP

Ranger Station _____ 🏛
Campground _____ 🏕
Amphitheater _____ 🎭
Horse Stable _____ 🐎

ROAD _____
TRAIL •••••••••••••••••••••••

M   I   L   E   S
0   1   2   3   4

High Chisos Complex: Starts at Basin trail head; ends at various points; up to 14.5 miles round trips; 1 hour to overnight; 1,800-foot ascent; extensive complex of trails in Chisos Mountains between 5,400 and 7,200 feet; passes Laguna Meadow and moist woodland in Boot Springs Canyon; dramatic panorama of Sierra del Carmen, Sierra Quemada, and the mouth of Santa Elena Canyon from the South Rim; check map at trail head.

Blue Creek Trail: Starts .2 mile south of Laguna Meadow; ends at Blue Creek Ranch overlook; 5.5 miles one way; 2 hours one way; 2,400-foot ascent; several plant zones; fine photographic opportunity for colorful geologic formations in Red Rocks Canyon; buildings from ranch at lower end.

Juniper Canyon Trail: Starts .2 mile above springs; ends at Juniper Canyon road; 4 miles one way; 2 hours one way; 300-foot ascent; ascends to a high pass and then drops into Juniper Canyon; Upper Juniper Springs has old concrete water trough, but spring is undependable in dry years.

Emory Peak Trail: Starts at Pinnacles Pass; ends at Emory Peak; 2 miles round trip; 2 hours; 600-foot ascent; ascends to highest point in park (7,835 feet); 360° panorama with views deep into Mexico and Texas; last few yards require a scramble over rock.

Pass, where there is a parking area at the head of the self-guiding Lost Mine Trail.

Dropping into the Chisos Basin, the road winds around a series of switchbacks with massive Casa Grande Peak looming above. About 1 mile from Panther Pass, a paved road leads off to the lower Basin, where a campground, an outdoor amphitheater, and the Chisos Remuda are located. Horses may be rented at the Remuda for guided horseback trips to the Window and into the High Chisos. Straight ahead in the upper Basin are the Chisos Mountains Lodge, a store, and a ranger station. This is also the head for trails within the Chisos Basin and into the High Chisos.

Santa Elena Junction to Santa Elena Canyon (30 miles). Beginning at the Santa Elena Junction, 13 miles west of Panther Junction, this road (the newest in the park) comes close to some of the park's geological formations, historic sites, and spectacular views.

The road stretches south along the east side of Burro Mesa; a few cottonwood trees are visible along Cottonwood Creek. The Chisos Mountains are to the left, and soon Casa Grande Peak comes into view through the Window. A short trail leads from the Old Sam Nail Ranch parking area to the adobe ruins of a ranch house surrounded by an oasis of vegetation. A windmill still pumps water that attracts birds and other wildlife. Beyond the ranch, dikes run across the hillsides like random rock walls. The road climbs a hill and arrives at the Blue Creek Ranch parking area, from which a trail leads into the Blue Creek drainage to a stone building that was a line camp on the Homer Wilson Ranch.

Just past Blue Creek Ranch, a short road goes to Sotol Vista, which is perhaps the finest view accessible by paved road in the park. The road now drops out of the Sotol grasslands back into the true desert at the southern base of Burro Mesa. Soon a paved road turns off and curves 3.5 miles back to a dead end near an arroyo that comes out of Burro Mesa. Along this road is the head of the Burro Spring Trail, and at the end of the road is the head of the Burro Mesa Pour-off Trail, which leads to a huge dry waterfall, or pour-off.

The road now winds through one of the most geologically spectacular areas of the park, passing such volcanic and igneous features as Goat Mountain, Mule Ears Peaks, Tuff Canyon, and Castolon Peak.

About 1 mile past Castolon Peak is the village of Castolon, which has retained the flavor of a turn-of-the-century border trading post. Built and used briefly as an army post, Castolon has been a frontier trading post since the early 1900s. A store and ranger station are here, and gasoline is available. Immediately past Castolon, a dirt road leads to the International Crossing across from the Mexican village of Santa Elena.

The road is now on the Rio Grande flood plain, where cotton and other crops were grown until 1959. Along the road is the oldest building in the park, an adobe structure in an area called Old Castolon. The road now parallels the Rio Grande, and the 1,500-foot cliffs of the Sierra Ponce across the river in Mexico dominate the scene. Several historic buildings are scattered between here and Santa Elena Canyon. Near the canyon, at a parking area, is an impressive view of the canyon mouth.

Just past the parking area, the south end of the Old Maverick Road turns off, and the road to the canyon changes from pavement to dirt. At the end of the dirt road is the beginning of the self-guiding Santa Elena Canyon Trail, which leads into the awesome canyon mouth.

Backcountry Roads

None of these roads is paved, but some are improved so that normal passenger cars can be driven on them. The primitive roads should be driven only in a high-clearance vehicle. Visitors should check at park headquarters or with a park ranger for road conditions before driving any backcountry road.

Improved Dirt Roads

Old Maverick Road (14 miles). The Old Maverick Road, which connects Santa Elena Canyon with Maverick, may be taken to avoid retracing the route over the paved road to Santa Elena Canyon. Starting at the canyon end, the road follows Terlingua Creek for a few miles; a side road leads down to the creek at Terlingua Abaja, the site of a small farming village in the early 1900s.

The road then crosses normally dry Alamo Creek. To the right is Peña Mountain, and just beyond is Luna's Jacal, former house of Gilberto Luna, who raised a family in what may appear to be an inhospitable environment. The road skirts around the right side of Rattlesnake Mountain and overlooks an eroded badlands area that is especially colorful in morning or evening light. The junction with the paved road at Maverick is just beyond the badlands.

Croton Spring Road (1 mile). The short Croton Spring Road starts about 3 miles east of the Santa Elena Junction. The area around the spring at the end of the road shows evidence of use by Indians, and the spring

---

Overleaf: The Chisos Mountains tower 6,000 feet above the Rio Grande.

itself was developed to some extent by ranchers. Look for mortar holes in the rocks where Indians ground mesquite seedpods and for patches of dark gray earth where their campfires burned.

Grapevine Hills Road (8 miles). Beginning just west of the Basin Junction, the Grapevine Hills Road turns north and immediately passes Government Spring, a good place to watch for wildlife at twilight. In a few miles the road curves around the Grapevine Hills and arrives at a parking area, which is the trail head for the Grapevine Hills Trail. The road continues to curve around the hills and eventually ends at the Grapevine Hills Ranch Site. Some large trees, a spring, a rock water tank, and other remains of the ranch make this an interesting area for exploration.

Dagger Flat Road (7.5 miles). The Dagger Flat Road turns off the road to Panther Junction about 10 miles south of Persimmon Gap. Signs along the way, visible from a car, identify Chihuahuan Desert plants. The road ends at Dagger Flat, a small valley filled with giant dagger yuccas. These 10- to 15-foot-tall yuccas are impressive even unadorned, but they provide a majestic floral display during a good blooming year, when hundreds of flowering stalks crown the plants.

Hot Springs Road (2 miles). About 1 mile below the Lower Tornillo Creek Bridge, the Hot Springs Road turns south and travels through rolling limestone hills until it squeezes through a narrow canyon and ends near the confluence of Tornillo Creek and the Rio Grande. J. O. Langford homesteaded at Hot Springs in 1909 and built a health resort. The store and motor court buildings remain standing, and the foundation of the bathhouse still collects 105° F water that flows out of the rocks on the bank of the Rio Grande.

Primitive Roads

The *Paint Gap Road* is 5 miles long, passes through the Paint Gap Hills, and ends at an old ranch site at Dripping Spring. The *Old Ore Road* follows part of the route of the ore wagons that hauled their loads from the ore terminal in Ernst Valley to Marathon, Texas. This 25-mile road winds along the west side of the Deadhorse Mountains. The 15.5-mile *Glenn Springs Road* has an elevation range of about 1,100 feet and travels through both grassland and lowland desert. It passes the site of the tragic 1916 Glenn Springs raid. The *Pine Canyon Road* and *Juniper Canyon Road* are spurs into these canyons off the Glenn Springs Road. The longest backcountry road in the park is the 51-mile

River Road, which extends across the southern end of the park. Several side roads lead south off this road to fishing camps on the Rio Grande and to historic sites, including Mariscal Mine.

Self-Guiding Trails and Walks

These seven trails provide a good introduction to the varied environments and historical features of Big Bend National Park. Each trail is described in an interpretive leaflet or on signs along the way. Except for the Lost Mine Trail, which is somewhat strenuous, all are easy walking.

Rio Grande Village Nature Trail (signs) winds through lush floodplain vegetation and then climbs onto a desert hill with excellent views of the Rio Grande and Mexico. *Santa Elena Canyon Trail* (signs) enters the mouth of Santa Elena Canyon and dead ends at a dramatically claustrophobic point where the river is squeezed wall-to-wall between sheer 1,500-foot cliffs. *Panther Path* (leaflet), a short walk through a desert garden at park headquarters, and *Chihuahuan Desert Nature Trail* (signs), at Dugout Wells, provide a close-up look at some common desert plants and their remarkable adaptations to this arid environment. *Lost Mine Trail* (leaflet) begins at Panther Pass and climbs to 6,850 feet to reveal superb views of Green Gulch, Pine Canyon, Juniper Canyon, and the East Rim. This is the quickest access to the plants and animals of the High Chisos Mountains. *Hot Springs Historic Walk* (leaflet) and *Castolon Historic Compound* (leaflet) let you follow in the footsteps of Big Bend's pioneers as you learn about their lives and visit the structures they left behind.

Developed Trails

Boquillas Canyon Trail. The Boquillas Canyon Trail climbs over fossil-shell-encrusted limestone rock that is 100 million years old and then drops down to the Rio Grande near a group of Indian bedrock mortar holes. Along the river in the canyon, displacement of the limestone layers along faults in the canyon wall can be seen on the Mexican side. Near the entrance to the canyon, a large sand slide appears to have poured out of a shallow cave high up on the Texas side, but it is actually formed by down-canyon winds. The sand slide is a wonderful renewable resource for children of all ages to play on.

The trail begins at the Boquillas Canyon parking area, and is 1.4 miles round trip.

Grapevine Hills Trail. The magical and mysterious qualities of this park are nowhere more apparent than among the weirdly shaped rocks along the Grapevine Hills Trail. Formed from a dome-shaped underground lava flow that has since been exposed and shaped by erosion, the Grapevine Hills offer hikers the opportunity to walk through an enchanted jumble of rocks. The trail follows an arroyo through boulder-covered hillsides to a small pass. A series of metal stakes to the right of the pass leads to a large "window" formed by boulders.

The trail begins 1 mile from the end of the Grapevine Hills Road, and is 2.2 miles round trip.

Burro Spring Trail. In the desert, where there is water there is wildlife. Burro Spring is a good place to see signs of wildlife activity. The Burro Spring Trail curves around a small mountain to an overlook above the spring. Sit quietly, and javelina, mule deer, or coyote may come to drink. Drop down to the spring and look for tracks and droppings.

Aquatic insects and sometimes tadpoles can be found in the small pools. Here the contrast of aquatic life juxtaposed with cacti and ocotillo is dramatic. To avoid retracing your steps, follow the wash below the spring, turn left around the end of the mountain, and turn left again at the next wash to return to the starting point.

The trail begins at the parking area along the Burro Mesa Pour-off spur road, and is 2.2 miles around trip.

Burro Mesa Pour-off Trail. The Burro Mesa Pour-off Trail leads around a small hill and up the right fork of an arroyo. Sand and gravel are underfoot as the trail continues past graceful desert willow and Mexican buckeye trees, which are covered with pinkish-purple blossoms in

The 3,000-foot-high volcanic cores of Mule Ears Peaks are aptly named.

the spring. A box canyon is formed at the end of the trail, with the pour-off standing as a huge dry waterfall. The power of erosion is evident on the polished black rock on the upper part of the pour-off.

The trail begins at the parking area at the end of the Burro Mesa Pour-off spur road, and is 1 mile round trip.

Tuff Canyon Trail. At Tuff Canyon, water has carved through relatively soft layers of hardened volcanic ash, or tuff. Before taking the trail into the canyon, stop at the overlooks on the canyon rim to get a different perspective on the gray-white canyon walls. The trail goes south down the hillside to the canyon mouth. From there the route is through the canyon until the harder rocks and terraces formed by lava flows are reached. The semicircle of the upper terrace resembles a miniature, dry Niagara Falls. The soft tuff and loose rock on the canyon walls are dangerous to climb, so the safest return trip is along the same route. The trail begins at the Tuff Canyon parking area, and is .75 mile round trip.

Window View Trail. The short Window View Trail can provide a leisurely walk in the heart of the Chisos Basin. It circles a small hill and has benches along the way that encourage relaxation and contemplation. The trail is a good place to watch for del Carmen white-tailed deer in the evening as the sun sets through the Window.

The trail begins at the Basin trail head, and is .3 mile.

Chisos Basin Loop Trail. The two trails that lead out of the Chisos Basin into the High Chisos are linked in the Basin to form this short loop trail. Most of the mountain peaks that encircle the Basin are visible from points along the way. Grasses, oaks, juniper, piñon pine, century plant, and other typical mountain plants grow here. Since summer temperatures in the upper Basin rarely climb higher than 80° to 90° F, this is a pleasant hike during most of the year.

The trail begins at the Basin trail head, and is 1.6 miles round trip.

The Window Trail. All surface water that may occasionally flow out of the Chisos Basin must exit through a V-shaped notch in the west side known as the Window. The Window Trail descends through an open area of grasses and chaparral into shaded Oak Creek Canyon. A variety of birds may be seen and heard in these different habitats. The canyon narrows, and the trees eventually give way to polished bedrock. Usually a few pools of water are present and populated by aquatic insects such as water boatmen, backswimmers, and water striders. On the return hike, Casa Grande forms an impressive backdrop, especially when it seems to glow in the warm afternoon light. The Chisos Remuda provides guided horseback trips to the Window.

The trail begins at the Basin trail head or at the Basin Campground, and is 5.2 miles round trip from the trail head and 4 miles round trip from the campground.

High Chisos Trails Complex

South Rim Trail. A long loop hike with many interesting highlights, the South Rim Trail is one of the finest in the park. In a counterclockwise direction, the trail ascends out of the Chisos Basin through woodland until it reaches a chaparral area near the Basin rim that is covered with Coahuila scrub oak. The trail then levels out, and just beyond is Laguna Meadow, an open area covered with stipa grass, and a favorite haunt of the uncommon yellow-nosed cottonrat. Watch for the Colima warbler in the woodlands around the meadow. Mescalero Apaches probably baked the hearts of sotol and agave in the pit at the north end of the meadow.

As the trail leaves the meadow, look uphill to the left for a grove of about 100 quaking aspens growing on the talus slope below Emory Peak. Soon Blue Creek Trail turns off to the right, and beyond that the Colina Trail leads off to the left and reaches Boot Spring in about 1 mile. Continuing toward the South Rim, hikers will see new vistas open up to the southwest. Finally, the trail abruptly reaches the cliffs of the South Rim, with the desert spread 2,500 feet below and a classic panorama of mountains—some nearly 100 miles away in Mexico.

The trail continues along the edge of the South Rim past the Boot Spring "short-cut" trail. Either turn left on this trail or proceed to the East Rim, which provides more lovely vistas and is a marvelous place to watch a sunrise. From the East Rim, the trail drops down past the junction with the Juniper Canyon Trail to Boot Spring, a moist woodland environment that harbors an interesting assemblage of plants and animals. Another good spot to look for the Colima warbler or hear the flammulated owl, Boot Canyon contains tall Arizona cypress and Douglas fir. After leaving Boot Spring the trail passes the area's namesake, the "Boot," a spire of volcanic rock that is shaped like an inverted cowboy boot. Past the junction with the Emory Peak Trail, the trail descends back into the Basin on the Pinnacles Trail, which is steep and rocky and has several switchbacks. Nonetheless, it is beautiful; cliffs, spires, woodland, and meadows can be seen along the way.

The trail begins at the Basin trail head, and is 13 miles round trip or 14.5 miles if the East Rim is included. The Chisos Remuda provides guided horseback trips to the South Rim and Boot Spring via the Laguna Meadow Trail.

Other High Chisos Trails. Just south of Laguna Meadow, the *Blue Creek Trail* descends through Blue Creek Canyon to Blue Creek Ranch and parking area on the road to Castolon. The trail passes through several plant zones and among some colorful rock formations in Red Rocks Canyon. The *Juniper Canyon Trail* begins above Boot Spring, ascends to a high pass, and then drops down to the end of the Juniper Canyon primitive road. The *Emory Peak Trail* begins near Pinnacles Pass and in 1 mile attains the 7,835-foot summit of Emory Peak, the highest point in the park. The 360° view of the Big Bend country is breathtaking.

Primitive Routes

Sometimes little more than an imaginary line between two geographic features, a primitive route is not for the novice desert hiker. About twenty of these routes exist in the park, and other unnamed cross-country routes offer similar opportunities to explore the wildest parts of Big Bend. Consult with a park ranger before attempting any hikes of this type.

Float Trips

Float trips on the Rio Grande offer visitors a means of exploring the park at a leisurely pace in a canoe, a kayak, or an inflatable raft. The river flows for 107 miles along the southern boundary of the park, but the most popular float trips are through the river-carved canyons. Outfitters outside the park conduct guided trips, or you may obtain a permit from the National Park Service and go on your own.

Hot Springs Canyon. A good place to get your feet wet and to whet your appetite for longer Rio Grande float trips is the 2.5-mile Hot Springs Canyon trip. Put-in is at the site of the historic Hot Springs resort, where Tornillo Creek joins the Rio Grande. No difficult sections are encountered, and the canyon walls provide a feeling of remoteness even on this short trip. Watch for cliff swallow nests stuck to the canyon walls overhanging the water and for turkey vultures soaring high above near the canyon rim. Several take-out points are available in the Rio Grande Village area.

Santa Elena Canyon. This 17-mile river segment provides a challenging and inspiring 1- or 2-day trip. Put-in is near Lajitas on the west side of the park. The first 11 miles are through rugged desert mesa country with colorful interfaces of limestone and igneous rocks. Just past Arroyo San Antonio, which enters from the Mexican side, the river makes a right turn and slips into a deep, narrow slot in Mesa de Anguila: Santa Elena Canyon. Not far inside the entrance, the Mirror Canyons face each other from either side of the river. Soon the roar of the Rockslide can be heard echoing off the canyon walls. At the Rockslide a huge piece of limestone cliff on the Mexican side crashed down into the canyon, creating a slope of boulders that extends into and across the river. These house-size chunks form a maze that is decipherable only from above. River runners must stop on the Mexican shore above the Rockslide, climb up the slope, memorize a route, and then hope their memory does not fail as they paddle through the labyrinth. The Rockslide can be portaged, or rafts and canoes can be guided through with ropes at certain water levels. All but the most experienced boatmen should follow these procedures, and even experienced boatmen should scout it before running it.

The South Rim Trail through the Chisos Mountains is one of the finest hikes in the park.

Past the Rockslide the river is gentle, but the blue-gray vertical canyon walls that rise 1,500 feet to a slit of sky make floating this section an awesome and humbling experience. Arch Canyon and Fern Canyon on the Mexican side are fragile jewels that may be carefully explored, perhaps accompanied by the downward spiraling song of the canyon wren. The canyon mouth eventually appears, revealing the Chisos Mountains far in the distance. The take-out is just outside the mouth, where Terlingua Creek enters the Rio Grande at the Santa Elena Canyon parking area.

Mariscal Canyon. This 7-mile trip can be done in 1 day, but because of the amount of driving time involved, boaters may want to spend the night at the put-in or take-out or within the canyon itself. The usual put-in is at Talley, and the usual take-out is at Solis, both of which are accessible only via the River Road using a high-clearance vehicle.

The open country around Talley quickly becomes more confining until the river is squeezed into the crack of the canyon entrance. There the river extends across the width of the canyon, and not far ahead a small rockslide requires scouting and maneuvering to get through without upsetting. About .5 mile beyond, a large flat-topped block of limestone sits in the middle of the river forming the Tight Squeeze. At normal water levels, the 10-foot-wide gap between this boulder and the Mexican shore can be run with care. Stay near the Mexican side, and turn sharply left after clearing the slot to avoid being pushed into a rock dead ahead. The Tight Squeeze is easily portaged.

About 1.5 miles downriver a large arroyo enters from the Mexican side. A wax camp is sometimes in operation here, extracting wax from the candelilla plant, which has been gathered nearby. Also look for Indian petroglyphs and mortar holes on rocks on the right side of the arroyo. The canyon is more open through this stretch and then becomes confined again briefly before breaking out into desert again. The take-out at Solis is about 2 miles from the canyon mouth.

Boquillas Canyon. Floating through Boquillas Canyon offers different opportunities from those on the Santa Elena and the Mariscal trips. There are no difficult spots, the canyon is more eroded and open, and several side canyons await exploration. With a put-in at Rio Grande Village and a take-out at La Linda, this trip is about 30 miles long, so 2 to 3 days should be planned to enjoy it fully. This is an excellent trip for canoeing and for photographing the eroded geological formations along the river and in the side canyons.

Opposite: Mescalero Apaches roasted and ate the tender heart of the agave.

BRYCE CANYON
NATIONAL PARK

BRYCE CANYON NATIONAL PARK
BRYCE CANYON, UTAH 84717, TEL.: (801) 834-5322

Highlights: Fairyland Point □ Rainbow Point □ Sunrise Point Sunset Point □ Inspiration Point □ Yovimpa Point □ Bryce Natural Bridge □ Agua Canyon □ Navajo Trail □ Queen's Garden Trail

Access: From west, take U.S. 89 from Bryce Junction, south of Panguitch. Turn east at this junction and follow Utah 12 and 63 to entrance. See map on pages 76–77.

Hours: Daily, 24 hours, year-round, except for roads to Fairyland Point and Rainbow Point, which close at sundown.

Fees: Entrance, $5/vehicle, $2/person; senior citizens and disabled Americans, free. Camping, $5/vehicle.

Parking: At Visitor Center and each viewpoint. Limited in summer.

Gas, food: In park from late May to September 30. Rest of year, surrounding area (within 7 miles).

Lodging: In park at Bryce Canyon Lodge from late May to September 30.

Visitor Center: On main road, 1 mile from park boundary, by entrance station. Publications; 7-minute slide program. Closed Christmas Day.

Museum: Exhibits in Visitor Center.

Gift shop: In Bryce Canyon Lodge from late May to September 30.

Pets: Permitted on leash, but not within the canyons or in public buildings. Horseback riding from spring through fall; rentals available in park and at motels in area.

Hiking: Permitted only on designated trails because of crumbly rock. Water must be carried. Maps available at Visitor Center.

Backpacking: Permitted in southern portion with a permit. Water availability varies, carry it. Camping at designated sites only. No fires.

Campgrounds: 218 campsites in North or Sunset Campground. $5/vehicle. From late May through September 30, showers available in park. Some sites year-round. First-come basis. Reservations taken only for organized groups. Senior citizen discount. Some sites for trailers; no hookups.

Tours: From May to September 30, guided walks and talks; van tours; in winter, with special arrangements, snowshoe tour.

Other activities: Cross-country skiing; sightseeing flights.

Facilities for disabled: Most park buildings, rim trail, restrooms, and viewpoints accessible.

For additional information, see also Sites, Trails, and Trips on pages 89–96 and the map on page 91.

EIGHTEEN MILES LONG, UP TO 5 MILES WIDE, AND, IN places, 800 feet deep, Bryce Canyon is an example of unique erosional patterns. More properly called an amphitheater because of its configuration, Bryce Canyon is the largest of the many horseshoe-shaped canyons that radiate from the eastern rim of the high Paunsaugunt Plateau. The canyons and the tableland make the park a 36,010-acre wonderland of forests, mountain meadows, and bizarre rock formations that have been sculpted primarily from a weak silt stone.

Bryce Canyon National Park ranges in altitude from 6,600 to 9,100 feet. Between these elevations are situated three distinctly different plant communities that strongly influence where the park's approximately 50 species of mammals and more than 450 species of plants are most apt to be seen. The 164 recorded bird species of Bryce Canyon are also dependent to a large extent on these plant communities, but they, of course, can fly to other areas where food may be more abundant.

The thirty-mile-long Pink Cliffs are part of the Wasatch Formation.

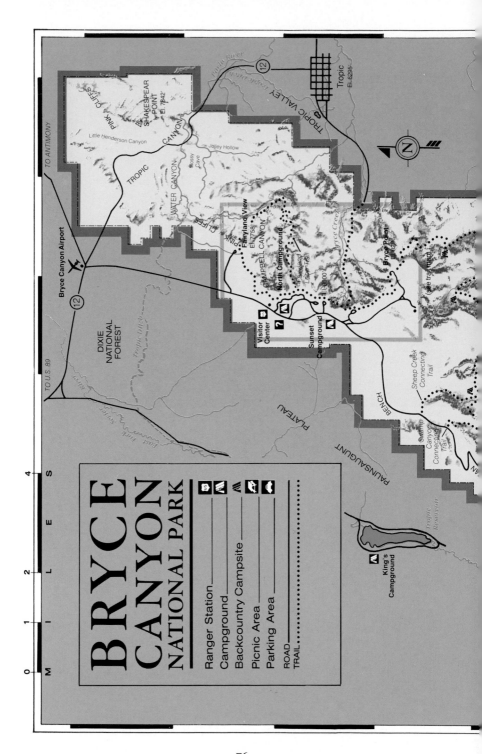

VICINITY MAP

BRYCE CANYON N. P.

Cannonville

Hatch

INSET SCALE

0   5   10
M I L E S

H   I   S   T   O   R   Y

Early Inhabitants

The first people to venture near Bryce were an ancient group of Indians known as the Anasazi. For hundreds of years these Indians inhabited the areas that are now incorporated into many southwestern national parks. There is also evidence that they were in the Bryce area as early as A.D. 1, although no tangible evidence of that early presence exists within the park itself. Evidence, however, of another group of Indians is available.

As the Anasazi Indians departed from the Bryce area about 1,000 years ago, the nomadic Paiutes began moving in. Visitors occasionally may find arrowheads that attest to the presence of these nomads, who left no remains of permanent structures. Bryce apparently was used only as a hunting ground during the summer months, when the Paiutes migrated into the park to hunt deer, elk, and small game such as rabbits. They also gathered edible foods such as piñon nuts and the bulb of the sego lily. The Paiutes were a peaceful though superstitious people. The somewhat familiar shapes that they found among the weathered Bryce Canyon rocks gave rise to several legends that were. passed down through the years. For example, Paiutes described the rock forms with a word that when translated means "red rocks standing like men in a bowl-shaped recess." According to their legends, birds, animals, and lizards that once had lived in the canyon had the power to make themselves look like people. For some reason, their conduct did not please Shin-Owav—a Paiute demigod of great power—and he turned them into rocks. Imaginative visitors to the park will be able to see these human forms. Look for them, and try to discern individuals standing erect, groups gathering in a row, or hunters stalking game.

Explorers

The first recorded travel near Bryce Canyon occurred in 1866, when a Mormon militia pursued marauding Indians south of the park area. Scouts were undoubtedly sent out by the Church of the Latter-Day Saints between 1851 and 1860 in search of agricultural lands, but there is no written record of such exploration. It is believed that these explorers entered the Paria Valley, which lies to the east of Bryce and is the recipient of many of the park's tributaries.

In 1872, a one-armed explorer, Major John Wesley Powell, climbed the Pink Cliffs. Accompanying Powell on this and on several other explorations was Captain C. E. Dutton. Dutton, a man of eloquence, wrote in *Geology of the High Plateaus of Utah* that "the upper tier of the vast

An early party of tourists explores Bryce Canyon on horseback.

amphitheater [the Bryce Amphitheater] is one mighty ruined colonnade. Standing obelisks, prostrate columns, shattered capitals... all bring vividly before the mind suggestions of the work of giant hands, a race of genii now chained up in a spell of enchantment, while their structures are falling in ruins through centuries of decay." Prose such as this was later used to excite the imagination of visitors, but it did little to lure the hard-working Mormon ranchers and farmers who were intent on earning a living from the "badland" of Bryce.

Around 1875, Ebenezer and Mary Bryce homesteaded on land that penetrated the main canyon of the present-day park. They raised sheep and cattle, built a road for hauling timber, and dug an irrigation ditch from Pine Creek. Soon the canyon became known as Bryce's Canyon. But in 1880, Ebenezer and Mary departed the arid lands for Arizona, summarizing their feelings for the canyon in far less laudatory terms than those of Dutton. Said Bryce, "It's a hell of a place to lose a cow."

In 1892, the last of the early settlers established a community near the site of the Bryces' former cabin. Because of the mild climate, the town was called Tropic. The town still exists essentially because water was diverted to it from the East Fork of the Sevier River, whose headwaters originate in Bryce.

Establishment of the Park

The earliest reports of this extraordinary region to reach the general public were penned in the early 1900s. Of these authors, J. W. Humphrey may have been the most instrumental in attracting visitors to the area. In 1915, Humphrey, a forest supervisor in the old Sevier National Forest, was coerced into accompanying a friend to the rim of the Paunsaugunt Plateau, from which Bryce National Park has been carved. Later, Humphrey wrote, "You can imagine my surprise at the indescribable beauty that greeted us, and it was sundown before I could be dragged from the Canyon view." Humphrey then began to promote Bryce through articles that glorified the beauties of the area. He even offered to pay one skeptic ten dollars if he was disappointed with Bryce.

Enthusiasm grew, and national recognition followed. Bryce Canyon National Monument was created on June 8, 1923. One year later, the monument was redesignated Utah National Park. Eventually, on September 15, 1928, the area was doubled in size and given the name by which it is known today.

Opposite: Fantastic rock shapes, known as hoodoos, form an eerie landscape below Inspiration Point.

G E O L O G Y

Bryce Canyon National Park is an exemplary result of three major geological forces—deposition, uplift, and erosion.

Deposition

The foundations of Bryce Canyon National Park were laid down by a shallow sea that existed about 150 million years ago. Although these sedimentary layers can be seen in Zion National Park, they cannot be seen in Bryce.

The depositions that form Bryce began to be laid down about 70 million years ago. Helping to delineate these sediments were a series of mountains. One group, the north–south ranging Rockies, began rising to the east. They eventually were joined by unnamed east–west ranging mountains that existed close to the present location of the Grand Canyon of the Colorado. Simultaneously, yet another mountain range began to rise along what is now the Idaho border. These three chains merged to form a bowl-shaped series of mountains that trapped a huge body of water referred to by geologists as Lake Flagstaff.

During the existence of Lake Flagstaff, waters ranged from one huge lake to a chain of large lakes. Siltstone, which is extremely soft, was

the primary sediment in these lakes. Also brought in by the various rivers and streams that fed into Lake Flagstaff was the compound calcium carbonate, which acts as a binding agent and helps add strength and rigidity to the rocks with which it becomes associated. Alternating layers of hard and soft rock, which geologists call differential hardness, contribute directly to some of the unique formations in Bryce Canyon National Park. Coloring these structures are minute amounts of iron and manganese, which were deposited in Lake Flagstaff. Iron creates the reds; manganese, the blues and lavenders.

Uplift

In some areas of the world, similar sediments undoubtedly were deposited, and they have lain undisturbed through the eons. But 25 million years ago, deep within the earth beneath southern Utah and northern Arizona, powerful forces were at work. Gradually, over millions of years, the Colorado Plateau was uplifted until parts of it were 2 miles above sea level. Lake Flagstaff disappeared at about the same time that the land was uplifted, but it left sediments that eventually contributed to the Wasatch Formation—the portion of Bryce Canyon National Park that is visible today. Because of its vivid coloration, this 30-mile-long formation is also called the Pink Cliffs.

The pressures exerted on the Colorado Plateau were so great that the uplifted land broke into huge chunks along fault lines—breaks in the continuity of a body of rock. Southwestern Utah is dominated by seven of these masses. Bryce Canyon has eroded from one of them, the Paunsaugunt Plateau, while Cedar Breaks and Zion National Park have been formed from another, the Markagunt Plateau.

Concurrent with the pressures that created the Colorado Plateau and its subsequent fault lines was the creation of joints, or weak areas of fracture within an individual rock or a group of rocks. The existence of many such areas has contributed substantially to some of the park's major geological formations.

Erosion

Bryce Canyon is the result of deterioration on a grand scale. While deposition and uplift occurred many millions of years ago, erosion maintains its relentless onslaught against the Colorado Plateau.

In Bryce, it is water—"time and raindrops, time and snow, time and ice," as naturalists frequently say—that creates the spires and pinnacles. Wind plays a very insignificant part in forming these imposing hoodoos. A study of the weather records has indicated that a cycle of freeze and thaw occurs in Bryce more than 200 times a year. During the day, snowmelt drips into the cracks in rocks and is held fast. Then during the night, the water cools, freezes, and expands. The expanding ice exerts such a strong force that it widens the cracks and joints in the rocks. Over a period of a few years, massive rocks are pushed, shoved, and broken down by the action of ice; indeed, freeze–thaw action is probably the most important way bedrock is broken down into successively finer fragments. Eventually, whole sections of wall may fall, windows may collapse, and the rim of the canyon is pushed back.

This hoodoo, near Bryce Creek, has been christened Queen Victoria.

NATURAL HISTORY

Vegetation

The vegetation of Bryce is arranged in tiers, or zones. Because the higher elevations of the park receive more rain than the lower areas, the plant life changes with the altitude.

The lowest tier is the Piñon–Juniper Zone, which occurs at elevations below 7,000 feet—areas usually found below the canyon rim. This zone receives about 12 inches of precipitation a year. One of the most common species growing in this zone is the Utah juniper, which is more a shrub than a tree. Two other common trees in the piñon and juniper forest are the Gambel oak and the piñon pine. Both produce floral parts that provide deer and birds with an abundance of food. In the autumn, when its leaves turn a rich golden-brown, the Gambel oak gives additional color to the already brilliant canyon.

At about 8,000 feet, the forest complex changes into the Ponderosa Pine Zone. Increased rainfall, which averages about 16 inches a year, supports a more luxuriant growth of trees. Because of the greater variety of vegetation, wildlife is attracted to this zone.

One of the most abundant shrubs that is associated with trees characteristic of the 8,000-foot elevation is the green-leaf manzanita. Growing in profusion along the canyon rim, it often carpets the slopes beneath the towering ponderosa pine. Leaves of this shrub tend to be vertically oriented with respect to the ground. Furthermore, they often face in a north–south direction. These features permit the stronger rays of the sun to strike only a small surface of the leaf, which thus conserves water. Winter snows also protect the leaves from freezing; as a result, the manzanita has evolved to grow no higher than the snows that surround it in winter.

The highest tier is the Spruce–Fir–Aspen Zone, which is located above 9,000 feet. One tree that is often found in the more exposed portions of this zone is the bristlecone pine. This species is named for the long, slender, bristlelike prickles that grow on the end of each cone scale. Unlike most trees, the bristlecone pine can eke out a living under extremely adverse climatic conditions because small sections of the tree remain alive, although the greater part dies off. With the return of clement weather, the tree rebounds and growth resumes. Because of its unique ability, the bristlecone pine is the longest-lived organism on earth; the oldest pine in Bryce Canyon is estimated to be 1,700 years old.

Interspersed between bush and trees in the Spruce–Fir–Aspen Zone

Opposite: A limber pine at canyon rim. The buttressed roots indicate heavy erosion.

is a profusion of wildflowers whose brief existence complements the beauty of the understory. These species add vivid coloration to the drab brush, which is predominantly green or brown.

One of the first flowers to herald the approach of spring is the star lily, which dots the high forest floor. The tufted, grasslike leaves of this flower surround one or more small, fragrant white flowers. Blossoms begin to open while patches of snow remain in the May forest.

Another lily that thrives in the park's fir forest is the sego lily, which is the state flower of Utah.

Other flowers common to the park are the Indian paintbrush, penstemon, wild iris, and columbine. Rabbitbrush is another abundant plant; when cool air turns its green leaves a radiant yellow, residents know that autumn cannot be far away.

Wildlife

Prairie dogs have long been controversial animals. Ranchers and farmers detest them because they dig holes into which horses occasionally

Opposite: The shy bobcat spends its days hidden among rocks or perched in trees. Above: The wily coyote prowls for food through deep snow.

step and because they consume vast amounts of vegetation. But they are vital contributors to the ecology of their natural habitats. Their presence is a key to the existence of other species of wildlife. For instance, some of their communities attract burrowing owls and snakes.

Although prairie dogs are native to Bryce Canyon, they had been eliminated by the early 1950s. In 1974, the National Park Service began to reestablish this rodent in sites near the Visitor Center and Sunset Campground. By 1978, a few successful breeding colonies had been established. These colonies have flourished, and prairie dogs again inhabit the park in relatively stable numbers.

Three chipmunk species live in Bryce. The most prevalent is the Uinta chipmunk, which abounds on the plateau and along the rim. In the canyon, the least and cliff chipmunks may sometimes be seen. The only animal with which chipmunks may be confused is the golden-mantled ground squirrel, which is particularly abundant along the rim and at automobile turnouts along the road. It can be differentiated from chipmunks by its markings: its body stripes do not extend along the face, but stop near the base of the neck.

Mule deer are common on the plateau and are frequently seen in summer in meadows at dawn or dusk. During the winter, should heavy snows blanket their food supplies, these animals may drift down from the plateau to lower elevations outside the park.

Many mammals that make their homes in Bryce are secretive and seldom seen. Examples include the bobcat, the gray fox, and the striped skunk.

Many resident birds soar among the park's hoodoos or flit from branch to branch. Among these are the Steller's jay, the golden eagle, the raven, the red-tailed hawk, the Clark's nutcracker, the pygmy nuthatch, a variety of woodpeckers, and the engaging blue grouse. Blue grouse, which are common in the spruce-fir-aspen community, conduct courtship displays in the spring that add interest to them as a species.

Another resident is the white-throated swift, which may dive at speeds of up to 200 miles per hour when foraging for insects. The vividly colored western tanager is a frequent visitor.

Most reptiles find Bryce too cold, however, the skink, a small-scaled lizard, is seen occasionally, and the short-horned lizard is found in abundance. The skink darts among the rocks for protection, while the short-horned lizard, unusual among reptiles in that it gives birth to live young, relies on changing coloration to evade its predators, which are legion. These reptiles are active during the day, and sharp-eyed visitors may see one basking in the sun on a rock or against a fallen tree.

SITES, TRAILS, AND TRIPS

Highway

"Window" rocks.

Bryce Canyon National Park can be entered only from the north. The dead-end road terminates in 20 miles and could easily be driven in an hour were it not for the numerous enticing viewpoints. Each offers a different perspective of the varied domes, temples, spires, pinnacles, and arches of the park. The highway passes along a slightly canted plateau that ascends to the south through the Ponderosa Pine Zone to the Spruce–Fir–Aspen Zone. The Piñon–Juniper Zone lies below the rim and is best appreciated by hiking one of the trails.

Overlooks

Fairyland View. The first view of the Canyon is from Fairyland View. Nothing has prepared visitors for the array of colors and for the bizarre shapes that erosion has wrought. This viewpoint brings onlookers extremely close to the spires and pinnacles.

Sunrise and Sunset Points. Spur roads that lead to the next pulloffs go to the canyon that is specifically referred to as Bryce Canyon. These spurs terminate at Sunrise and Sunset points and provide expansive views of this canyon. Of the two viewpoints, only one has been appropriately named. Sunrises can be seen from Sunrise Point, but for a view of a sunset, go to Inspiration Point, which is higher than the Paunsaugunt Plateau.

From these points, areas more than 100 air miles away can be seen. Off in the distance and outside the park is the Aquarius Plateau, the highest plateau in North America. It rises to elevations of more than 10,000 feet. Sunset Point also offers views of Boat Mesa, an area that is described by naturalists as an ellipse. Approximately 320° of the mesa is exposed, and cliff faces plummet 800 feet. During the summer, the park is frequently assaulted by lightning strikes, and Boat Mesa is not a safe place to be during a summer thunderstorm.

Bryce Natural Bridge View. One of the pulloffs, located about three-quarters of the way along the drive, offers a view of Bryce Natural

Trails of Bryce Canyon National Park*

Rim Trail: Starts at Fairyland Point; ends at Bryce Point; 11 miles round trip; 3.5 hours; 550-foot ascent; easiest trail in park skirts Bryce Amphitheater; numerous access points; unmaintained side trails to Boat Mesa; spectacular panorama of amphitheater.

Queen's Garden Trail: Starts and ends at Sunrise Point; 1.5 miles round trip; 1-2 hours; 320-foot ascent; one of the most colorful trails into Bryce Canyon; "natural stucco" coats and colors rocks; views of Queen Victoria and Gulliver's Castle.

Navajo Trail: Starts at Sunset Point and ends in Wall Street where the 1984 rock slide is visible; 2.2 miles round trip; 1–2 hours; 521-foot ascent; moderately strenuous.

Queen's Garden and Navajo Trail: Starts and ends at Sunrise or Sunset Point; 3 miles round trip; 2–3 hours; 521-foot ascent; strenuous hike with some of park's most diverse scenery; climb more gradual from Sunset Point; luxuriant plant life.

Peek-a-boo Loop Trail: Starts and ends at Bryce, Sunset, or Sunrise Point; 5–6.5 miles round trip; 3–4 hours; 500–800-foot ascent; strenuous foot and horse trail; abrupt switchbacks and unexpected tunnels; view of the Wall of Windows and other examples of erosion.

Fairyland Loop Trail: Starts and ends at Sunrise Point or Fairyland View; 8 miles round trip; 5 hours; 900-foot ascent; strenuous; views of the Chinese Wall, Tower Bridge, the remains of Oastler's Castle, and Boat Mesa; passes bristlecone pine and piñon-juniper forest; shuttle to Fairyland View eliminates 2.5-mile hike along Rim Trail.

Hat Shop Trail: Starts and ends at Bryce Point; 3.8 miles round trip; 4 hours; 900-foot ascent; little-used, strenuous trail to area of many pillars, each capped by a "hat," or caprock; very steep climb back.

Under the Rim Trail: Starts at Bryce Point; ends at Yovimpa Point; 22.5 miles round trip; 2 days (minimum); 1,500-foot ascent; remote hike through older sections of Bryce; numerous elevation changes with marked transition in vegetation and abundant wildlife; panoramic views; registration required for primitive camping on trail; no fires; shuttling a vehicle recommended.

Riggs Spring Loop Trail: Starts and ends at Yovimpa Point; 8.8 miles round trip; 4-5 hours; 1,675-foot ascent; drops below rim through ponderosa pine forest; easy hike if follow sign to Yovimpa Pass; backcountry camping. See map on pages 76–7.

Bristlecone Loop Trail: Starts at Rainbow Point; 1 mile round trip; 1 hour; 100-foot ascent; easy; dramatic views of canyons and cliffs.

*All trails negotiate areas high above sea level. With exception of the Rim Trail, trails in Bryce commence with an abrupt descent. The return ascent can tax the most physically fit.

TO UTAH 12

**FAIRYLAND
VIEW**
El. 7758'

FAIRYLAND

Trail

PINK

ENTRANCE

**Visitor Center and
Ranger Station**

Rim

△ BOAT MESA
El. 8076'

CAMPBELL

**North
Campground**

Campfire
Programs

Fairyland Loop Trail

CHINESE
WALL

Store
Showers
Laundry

Nature Center

El. 8015'

Campbell Creek

SUNRISE POINT

△ TOWER
BRIDGE

Corral

Horse Trail
(Horses Only)

Lodge

Queen's
QUEEN'S
GARDEN

Garden Trail

**Sunset
Campground**

SUNSET POINT
El. 8000'

Navajo Loop Trail

Campfire
Programs

SILENT
CITY

FAIRY
CASTLE

B R Y C E
AMPHITHEATER
TRAIL MAP

THE
CATHEDRAL △
El. 7660'

**INSPIRATION
POINT**
El. 8143'

Peek-a-boo Loop Trail

Rim

WALL OF
WINDOWS

Ranger Station	
Campground	
Picnic Area	
Amphitheater	
Gas	
Information	

ROAD
TRAIL ....

Trail

**BRYCE
POINT**
El. 8269'

Under-the-Rim Trail

N

PARIA VIEW

M O   I   L   E   S
½   1

Bridge. This structure is not really a bridge, but rather an arch that is 95 feet high and 54 feet wide. Geologically speaking, a bridge spans a streambed, while an arch is created when a hole is worn through rock by the erosive action of weathering.

Running water played only a minor part in the formation of the Bryce Natural Bridge. The arch is the direct result of a recess that developed thousands of years ago in the soft underlying layers of the cliff area; the strong, weather-resistant top layer remains as the bridge. Initially, particles were pried away from the softer portion of the wall by mechanical weathering. Gradually, the indentation worked backward and upward, aided by underground water, until the arch isolated itself from the main rim of the plateau. Enlargement of the recess continues as surface water widens and deepens the channel by moving material away from beneath the arch. The structure is becoming less secure, and someday it will fall.

Agua Canyon Viewpoint. Another interesting point along the highway is Agua Canyon. Located at an elevation of 8,800 feet, the canyon is appropriately named. *Agua* is the Spanish word for "water," and Agua Canyon marks a divide in the region's water table. Water draining eastward joins the Paria River, then flows to meet the Colorado River, and eventually enters the Gulf of California. Water draining westward (just across the highway) goes down Puma Hollow, then joins the East Fork of the Sevier River, and eventually flows northward via the Sevier River into the Great Basin.

From the Agua Canyon Viewpoint can be seen two prominent monoliths that have been given familiar names, The Hunter and The Rabbit. Recognizing them may require a little imagination, but none is required to appreciate the brilliantly colored walls of orange and gold. Following a rain shower, or when the sun is at an appropriate angle, this is one of the most vividly colored areas in the park.

Yovimpa and Rainbow Points. The last highway overlooks are Yovimpa Point and Rainbow Point, which are separated by only a few hundred yards. At 9,105 feet, these pulloffs are located at the park's highest elevation. From either of these points, visitors may embark on a hike of less than 1 mile and reach an area where bristlecone pines may be seen. At Yovimpa Point is found the oldest (1,700 years) specimen of these long-lived trees within the park.

The view from Yovimpa is spectacular and appears endless. From the relatively young rocks on which Yovimpa Point now reposes, the eye can journey back 136 million years to the Jurassic period, when

The erosion of shale and sandstone sculpted the pinnacles in Fairyland.

dinosaurs roamed over some of the upper sediments near Zion National Park. The land continues to fall away to the Kaibab Plateau, site of the Grand Canyon of the Colorado.

Hikes

Bryce Canyon is worthy of a more intimate acquaintance than can be gained from standing on the plateau rim. There is a rare fascination in threading one's way through a bewildering multitude of marvelously carved figures.

Sixty-one miles of trails wander through the park; although not impressive in total miles, even short hikes can sap your energy. Remember that virtually all hikes start from the rim and descend distances that sometimes total 1,700 vertical feet. Also keep in mind that hikes are made at altitudes ranging between 7,000 and 9,000 feet. Climbing back up in the heat of the day can be an excruciating experience. Water is generally scarce and when found may not be potable, so hikers should carry canteens. One gallon per person per day is the recommended quantity, particularly if any cooking is to be done.

Backpack stoves are required equipment if any cooking is contemplated. For several reasons, it is illegal to build fires. One, of course, is to prevent forest fires. Another is to prevent the burning of downed logs, which, as they rot, recycle essential organic compounds into the particularly thin topsoil of the park.

Most trips into the depths of Bryce are best made as day excursions. A number of loop trails that can be hiked in a single day offer the intrigue of continuously changing views. It is difficult to provide an estimate of the time involved for any of these trips, because that depends entirely on the individual's physical condition.

Fairyland Loop. One of the most spectacular of the park's trails is the Fairyland Loop. It begins at the Fairyland View overlook. The loop is 8 miles long and drops 850 feet. Many of the prominent features of the park can be seen by the hiker along this path. Look for the Chinese Wall, Tower Bridge, and views of Boat Mesa. A few ancient bristlecone pines dot the trail, and occasionally a hiker's shadow may send a skink scurrying among the rocks. In dry sites near or on Boat Mesa, hikers may also find the short-horned lizard. (In early August, take a naturalist-conducted trip to Boat Mesa to see the 1- to 2-inch-long young of the short-horned lizard. They will have just been born and are still clinging to limbs and twigs.) Rim Trail continues on to Bryce Point, which is the jumping-off point for another of the park's loop trails.

Peek-a-boo Loop. Peek-a-boo Loop, which begins at Bryce Point, wanders for 5 miles through the Bryce Amphitheater. The amphitheater is the main showpiece of the park. It contains the headwaters of several branches of Bryce Creek, and in some areas manzanita grows in profusion. Rock formations in the amphitheater resemble minarets, camels, turtles, and humans. If you are there in the early morning, elongated shadows play tricks with your imagination, and you may find that curiosity will lure you almost unknowingly down into the recesses of the amphitheater.

Take a topographical map and see if you can pinpoint The Cathedral, the Wall of Windows, and the Silent City. At the Silent City, standing on a rise overlooking the "city," you may be reminded of the onion-domed churches of medieval Russia. In early morning, you may hear sounds from a few of the "city's" residents. But as you climb back up to the rim, you will be jolted back to reality and realize that the hum of the "city" may actually have been the shriek of a hawk.

Navajo Trail. Another fascinating 1-day hike is that along the Navajo Trail, which begins at Sunset Point. This trail drops 520 feet in .75 mile. Along the way are examples of the various types of erosion that have made Bryce what it is today.

Wall Street is a prime example of a geological oddity that exists because of the park's unique system of joints. When the land began to be pushed up almost 25 million years ago, areas of stress were created that weakened the rock along vertical lines. Water freezing in cracks enlarged these areas of weakness, and over a period of several million years, widened the gap to such an extent that an eastern traveler probably looked up and, remembering a familiar sight, christened the area "Wall Street." At several points along the base the walls of the "street" are a mere 25 feet apart and several hundred feet high.

Another feature along the Navajo Trail that is illustrative of geological formations in Bryce is Thor's Hammer. Sediments laid down by ancient Lake Flagstaff varied in their degree of hardness. Thor's Hammer is one of those structures that has a layer of hard rock overlying a layer of soft rock. Because of the resistance of the harder cap rock to erosion, the structure has assumed the appearance of a mushroom. Twin Bridges, which also is seen along this trail, is another example of differential hardness. If it were not for the presence of a hard layer of rock on top of each of these structures, the canyon that houses these bridges would be an uninterrupted pair of walls.

Queen Garden Trail. Not all structures that exhibit differential deposition retain their original forms. A path that joins the Navajo Trail is referred to as the Queen Garden Trail, along which hikers see a structure that many believe looks much like Queen Victoria. Older photographs, however, reveal that the "queen's" crown has eroded dramatically in the past twenty-five to thirty years.

Rim Trail. In addition to the park's loop trails, there are others that offer a further variety of experiences. Of these, the Rim Trail is the easiest to negotiate. Beginning at Fairyland View, this trail progresses along the rim without either rising or dropping appreciably. Six miles later, after passing both Sunrise and Sunset points, the trail terminates at Bryce Point. Chipmunks and golden-mantled ground squirrels are constant companions. Occasionally hikers see a nuthatch.

The Rim Trail offers an excellent opportunity to assess the park's rate of erosion. Hikers should look for trees that appear to be raised on buttressed roots. Such trees not only show that the rim of the canyon is gradually receding, but they also provide a means for determining the rate of recession. Two measurements are needed for the computation. First, an increment borer is used by park scientists to ascertain the age of the tree. Then, measurements are made to determine where the soil should be and where it actually is. The difference between the two extremes of soil levels divided by the age of the tree gives the rate at which the rim of the canyon is slipping away or, as naturalists like to say, it reports "the time involved before Bryce Canyon Lodge will have to be replaced."

The foregoing calculations indicate that the rim of the canyon is eroding at an average rate of 1 foot every 50 years. Geologically, that is a rather rapid rate, although by human standards it is virtually imperceptible. Bryce Canyon Lodge, which is situated at a distance of about 200 feet from the rim, will be with us for another 10,000 years. Bryce Canyon National Park will last a little longer! Because many sections of the narrow band comprising Bryce Canyon are about 15 miles wide, the process of erosion, which both creates and destroys, will continue for many more millions of years. There is creation in destruction, and as old spires and pinnacles crumble, new ones will appear.

Under-the-Rim Trail and Riggs Spring Loop. For those who wish to undertake hikes longer than day trips, overnight camping is available. The 23-mile Under-the-Rim Trail and the 9-mile Riggs Spring Loop are recommended for backpacking. Both trails pass through the park's three plant communities and offer skyline views of the Pink Cliffs. Prior to embarking on such outings, a backcountry permit must be obtained. (Hikers using any of these trails are advised to watch where they place hands and feet, as the Great Basin rattlesnake is occasionally sighted.)

Special Walks. In addition to the hikes that are marked by signs, a series of special walks is sometimes offered by Bryce naturalists. Since the areas that are visited on these walks may be either fragile or difficult to locate and dangerous if the correct route is not chosen, the hikes are not advertised in the park's standard pamphlets. Nevertheless, visitors who are interested are welcome to register for these hikes; the total number that may compose each group is controlled. Hikers who would like more information should request the handouts that describe the purpose of each trip and state the hour and day of the week on which the trips will be conducted.

Opposite: Thor's Hammer at sunrise as seen from the Navajo Trail.

CANYON LANDS
NATIONAL PARK

CANYONLANDS NATIONAL PARK
125 W. 200 SOUTH, MOAB, UTAH 84532
TEL.: (801) 259-7164

Highlights: The Needles □ The Maze □ The Grabens □ Tower and Keyhole Ruins □ Salt Creek Ruins □ Doll House □ White Rim Island in the Sky □ Grand View Point □ Land of Standing Rocks Cataract Canyon □ Mesa Arch □ Upheaval Dome □ Angel Arch Fortress Arch.

Access: From Moab, 32 miles on U.S. 191 and Utah 313 to Island in the Sky; 76 miles on U.S. 191 and Utah 211 to The Needles. See map on pages 102–103.

Hours: Daily, 24 hours. Information stations, 8 A.M.–4:30 P.M.; extended hours in summer.

Fees: Entrance, $5/vehicle, $2/person; $5/individual sites; $2/person for group sites (10 person minimum).

Parking: At major points.

Gas, food: In Moab, Monticello, Green River, and Hanksville. Gas stations relatively rare. Gas and limited supplies at Needles Outpost near entrance to Needles District.

Lodging: In Moab, Monticello, Green River, and Hanksville.

Visitor Center: Information Office in Moab. Year-round, 8 A.M.–4:30 P.M. weekdays. Information stations are located in each district of the park, year-round 8 A.M.–4:30 P.M., with extended summer hours.

Pets: Permitted on leash, except on trails. Horseback riding; bring own feed and water.

Picnicking: Facilities available at several points in park.

Hiking: Permitted; many trails available. See ranger for information.

Backpacking: Permitted with free permit. Carry extra water.

Campgrounds: In Needles and Island in the Sky: fee only at Needles from April 1 to September 30. First-come basis. No hookups. Groups, 3 sites in Needles district; reservations accepted. No wood gathering. Primitive backcountry campgrounds on 4-wheel drive routes.

Tours: Commercial river trips and four-wheel drive trips.

Other activities: Sightseeing flights, river trips (with permit), commercial bus tours.

Facilities for disabled: Restrooms, surface pathways (limited).

For additional information, see also Sites, Trails, and Trips on pages 116–128.

FOR DIVERSITY, CANYONLANDS NATIONAL PARK GIVES even the Grand Canyon a run for its money. Its 337,570 acres range in elevation from 3,700 feet at the head of Lake Powell to more than 7,000 feet at the highest point on the south boundary above Salt Creek. Like the Grand Canyon, Canyonlands protects a great inner gorge carved by the Colorado River, with a rim high above that offers awesome views. But here, too, are flats studded with slickrock needles and spires, an intricate system of side canyons decorated with massive stone arches, and rich archeological resources famous for fine rock art.

Two rivers slice Canyonlands into three districts. Between the Green and Colorado rivers lies the Island in the Sky mesa, with expansive vistas from its rims, and midway down toward the rivers the 100-mile White Rim jeep road encircling it. On the east bank of Cataract Canyon lies The Needles, spires and canyons that include Salt Creek's arches, ruins, and rock art. To the west of the rivers lies The Maze, the most isolated and least visited area of the park. The rivers themselves form a fourth district—lovely flat water on the upper Colorado and Green, and the twenty-four of Cataract Canyon's fifty-two rapids that remain undrowned by Lake Powell.

Canyonlands vista, with the Green River in the distance.

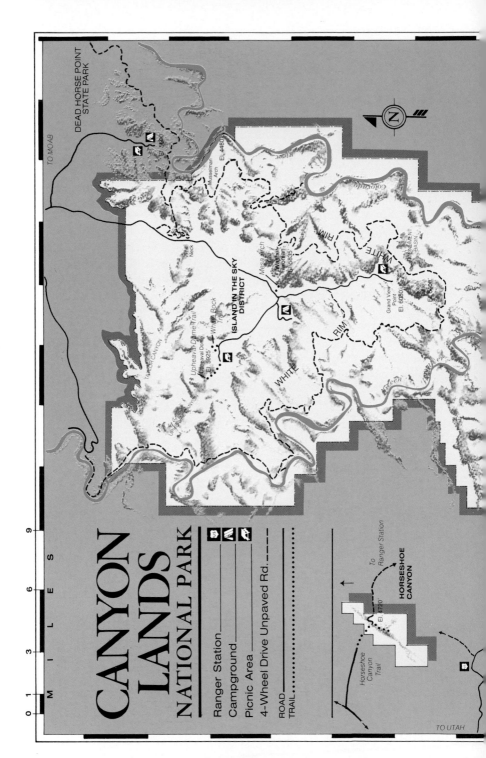

CANYON
LANDS
NATIONAL PARK

Ranger Station
Campground
Picnic Area
4-Wheel Drive Unpaved Rd.
ROAD
TRAIL

MILES
0   1   3   6   9

TO MOAB

DEAD HORSE POINT
STATE PARK

El. 5800

Musselman
Arch

El. 4480

Colorado

Mesa Arch

Washer
Woman
El. 5835

WHITE   RIM

Grand View
Point
El. 6080

MONUMENT
BASIN

Standing
Rock
El. 5400

Vine
Neck

White Rock
Trail

ISLAND IN THE SKY
DISTRICT

Upheaval Dome Trail

Upheaval Dome
El. 5925

Taylor Canyon

Upheaval Canyon

WHITE   RIM

Green

N

TO UTAH

Horseshoe
Canyon
Trail

El. 4720'

HORSESHOE
CANYON

To
Ranger Station

102

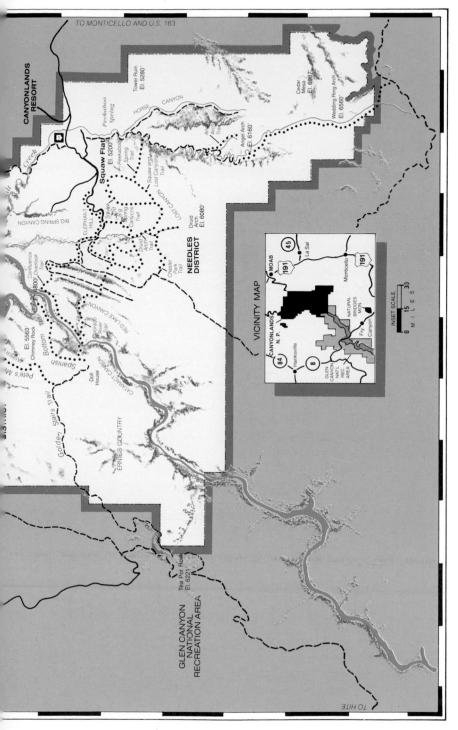

TO MONTICELLO AND U.S. 163

CANYONLANDS
RESORT

Squaw Creek

BIG SPRING CANYON

Peekaboo
Spring

HORSE CANYON

Tower Ruin
El. 5280'

Cedar
Mesa
El. 6987'

Wedding Ring Arch
El. 6560'

Squaw Flat
El. 5200'

Peekaboo
Spring
Trail

Angel
Arch
Trail

Angel Arch
El. 6160'

ELEPHANT
HILL

Squaw
and
Lost Canyon
Trail

Squaw
and
Big
Spring
Canyons
Trail

LOST CANYON

Druid
Arch
El. 6080'

NEEDLES
DISTRICT

Druid
Arch
Trail

Chesler
Park
Trail

Confluence
El. 4800' Overlook
Trail

Bottom

THE GRABEN

RED LAKE CANYON

Colorado River
Trail

Spanish

Chimney Rock

El. 5563'

CATARACT CANYON

Pete's Mesa

MASTER

Bottom Trail

Golden Stairs Trail

Doll
House

ERNIES COUNTRY

DISTRICT

Tea Pot Rock
El. 6221'

GLEN CANYON
NATIONAL
RECREATION AREA

TO HITE

VICINITY MAP

CANYONLANDS
N. P.

MOAB

191

45

La Sal

191

Monticello

Hanksville

84

8

GLEN
CANYON
NATL.
REC.
AREA

NATURAL
BRIDGES
MON.

Fry
Canyon

INSET SCALE

0   15   30

M I L E S

Canyonlands has living things—high desert shrubland, piñon and juniper woodland, and the animals that are tied to such plant communities. Desert bighorn sheep roam its cliffs; rodents scale its sheer mesas. Wildflowers bloom after rains. But this is mostly a landscape of rock. The sheer immensity, the sweep, of the stone impresses as much as anything. From the Island, The Needles, The Maze, or the rivers, Canyonlands puts life in perspective against a background both reassuring and suggestive, an immense reach of silence and wilderness, endless time and unfathomable rock.

H   I   S   T   O   R   Y

The earliest Canyonland peoples hunted and gathered for thousands of years in the land that would become the park, but left few marks of their passage. Not until just before A.D. 1000 did the two great prehistoric nations of Utah, the Fremont and the Anasazi, come to Canyonlands.

Prehistoric Peoples: Canyon Frontier

The Anasazi moved north into Canyonlands when the San Juan-Mesa Verde country to the south began to get crowded. Here on the skimpy outer limits of essential resources, perhaps 1,000 people lived in stone pueblos. Not many canyons had enough bottom land for corn fields and for bean and squash patches to support more than a few families. The people supplemented crops with every imaginable local food—from tiny rice-grass seeds to nutritious piñon nuts, from pocket gophers and frogs to bighorn sheep.

The Fremont people migrated to Canyonlands from the north and west. They relied more on hunting than on sedentary farming, and left behind few artifacts. One aspect of their culture remains strong and communicative, however. Fremont pictographs and petroglyphs are truly art—huge, hollow-eyed human figures wearing great shields, headdresses, and necklaces. Perhaps the best rock art in North America covers the walls of Horseshoe Canyon at Canyonlands; "The Great Gallery" is believed by some archeologists to be the work of a separate culture—the Barrier Canyon people—even older than the Fremont.

The Salt Creek area has the densest concentration of Anasazi ruins at Canyonlands—pueblos perched in alcoves, and granaries. Right next to Anasazi ruins, enigmatic Fremont faces guard the silent side canyons. Scholars have not yet untangled the relationship of the two cultures.

Even this central core of Anasazi activity in Canyonlands seems to have been abandoned by 1250. Perhaps a drought or a change in weather patterns that brought arroyo-cutting flash floods destroyed the capability of the land to support even marginal agriculture. The fragile success of the farmers was ended by something in the unforgiving cycle of nature.

When the Anglo-Americans arrived, Ute and Navajo peoples were using the future park as hunting grounds. These peoples, too, allowed the obstacle of the barren canyons to form the frontier of their territories, a buffer between mounted Ute raiders of the north and Navajo sheepherders of the south.

Trappers, Surveyors, and the Man with One Arm

As in so many places in the West, the beaver men were the first Americans to explore this country. One trapper, Denis Julien, left his signature, accompanied by dates in 1836, on cliffs throughout the canyons of the Green and Colorado rivers. We know little more of him, but with Julien began not only the history of Canyonlands, but also the evident onset of Colorado River running.

In 1859, Captain John Macomb tried to reach the confluence, and became the first explorer overland into the future park. His journal-keeper, geologist John Strong Newberry, gives us our first glimpse of The Needles. He was impressed with the "battlemented towers of colossal but often beautiful proportions, closely resembling elaborate structures of art," but he judged the land "worthless and impracticable."

Next came John Wesley Powell. Newberry's report remained unpublished when Major Powell began his historic river trip in 1869. His work on the Colorado Plateau in the next few years, with that of his brilliant cohorts and rivals, filled in the last great blank on the United States map. Powell's river trips in 1869 and 1871 took him down the Green and through Cataract Canyon, and the canyons owe most of their place-names to the one-armed major and his men.

Near the confluence, Powell looked out at the heart of the future park and declared: "Wherever we look there is but a wilderness of rocks, deep gorges where the rivers are lost below cliffs and towers and pinnacles, and ten thousand strangely carved forms in every direction, and beyond them mountains blending with the clouds."

Nothing has changed.

Powell was followed by other river runners, including the disastrous Brown–Stanton party of 1889, which surveyed the canyon for a water-level railroad from Colorado to the sea. Stanton spent a month in Cataract Canyon, enduring near-starvation for his dream, but the railroad was never built.

Cattle Raising and Rustling

Large cattle herds worked down toward the rims as early as 1874, and in the next two decades tens of thousands of cattle grazed The Needles. By 1940, the Scorup and Somerville brothers' Indian Creek Cattle Company was the largest cattle outfit in Utah and one of the largest in the West.

With the cattle came rustlers, and the canyons were the perfect place to fatten up stolen herds in secrecy, or to hide out after a bank robbery. Robber's Roost, just west of the park, was headquarters in the 1880s and 1890s for Butch Cassidy and his Wild Bunch, and their

Outlaw Trail crossed the Green River near Fort Bottom. Few lawmen would risk following Butch and his boys into the Canyonlands. The outlaws knew the box canyons and ambush points by heart, and the lawmen were greenhorns.

In the 1950s, uranium prospectors searched the length of every outcrop in Canyonlands for hot spots; nearly all the area's jeep roads began as prospector's tracks. Charlie Steen's incredible Mi Vida strike just east of the park touched off a boom that has never quite died.

Left: Cattle herds grazed in the Canyonlands area until the park was established in 1964. Above: Major John Wesley Powell with a Paiute Indian guide.

Establishment of the Park

Canyonlands was included in the vast Escalante National Park, which conservationists proposed in the 1930s. It would have preserved 7,000 square miles of southeastern Utah, including Glen Canyon, which has since been lost under Lake Powell. But this park never made it to fruition, and only the isolation and limited resources of Canyonlands saved it from development in the following decades.

Finally, in the early 1960s two men combined their efforts to create Canyonlands National Park. Stewart Udall, Secretary of the Interior under President John F. Kennedy, took a flight along the Colorado River to examine a proposed dam site at the confluence, looked out at the spectacle of The Needles and the Doll House, and said to himself, "My God, that's a national park down there!" Arches National Monument Superintendent Bates Wilson also recognized Canyonlands' potential. Wilson proceeded to feed Udall the information he needed in Washington, and, between them, they propelled Canyonlands National Park into existence in 1964.

G   E   O   L   O   G   Y

Canyonlands National Park surrounds the confluence of the Green and Colorado rivers, the isolated focal point of the Canyonlands section of the Colorado Plateau. The park takes its name from this official geography: it is a dazzling sample of the best of the Canyonlands.

Deep canyons slice through high mesas; isolated buttes tower over mazes of needles and fins; natural

Angel Arch.

stone arches grace side canyons; and island mountains stud the cardinal points of the horizon. Canyonlands is a bedrock landscape; rock defines the place, with only a few spare touches of soft, gentling plants.

The River and the Rocks

As at the Grand Canyon, the Colorado River reigns in this world. The river has rasped down through 300 million years' worth of rocks, and as its tributaries eat back into surrounding mesas to keep pace, the grand rock stair-steps of the canyonlands evolve.

The Colorado and Green rivers divide Canyonlands in a great Y. In the center lies Island in the Sky Mesa, isolated 2,000 feet above the two rivers with its wide ledge of White Rim Sandstone halfway between the mesa top and the rivers. East of the Colorado, The Needles and the twisting canyons of Salt Creek lie below Hatch Point Mesa and the Abajo Mountains. The Orange Cliffs rim the western Canyonlands basin—The Maze and Land of Standing Rocks.

Underneath Canyonlands lies the Paradox Formation, 300 million years old, which is exposed only in the deepest reaches of Cataract Canyon. With this oldest rock begins the stack of formations that reads like a sorcerer's chant: Paradox, Honaker Trail, Elephant Canyon, Halgaito, Cutler, Cedar Mesa, Organ Rock, White Rim, Moenkopi, Moss Back, Chinle, Wingate, Kayenta, Navajo.

The rocks of Canyonlands span just 125 million years of the earth's history. Those of the most recent 175 million years already have been eroded off the top, and the early rocks—the first 4 billion years of earth records—still lie hidden below the Paradox. Thirty-five hundred feet of sandstones, siltstones, mudstones, shales, limestones, salt, gypsum, and jasper spread beneath the viewpoints at the tips of the high mesas in an extravaganza of sedimentary variety. A whit more diversity, and comprehension of this place might pass beyond reach.

A Few Characters in the Stratigraphic Drama

Each layer reads in several ways—cause and effect, color and texture, age and strength. At the top of the stack, the Navajo Sandstone—monarch of the plateau's cross-bedded dune-deposited sandstones—remains in a few buttes and domes on mesa tops. The mesas themselves stand on walls of Wingate Sandstone—the orange-brown "Great Wall" of Canyonlands, instantly recognizable columnar cliffs tapestried with lustrous desert varnish.

Midway through the walls of Canyonlands is a complex of rocks from the Permian period, which began about 270 million years ago and lasted for a changeable 45 million years. In the higher walls of Cataract Canyon, The Needles, The Maze, and on up to the White Rim, confusing evidence remains of the swiftly cycling environments of this period. Most of these Permian rocks belong to the Cutler Formation, whose complicated interfingerings (described by one geologist as a "stratigraphic nightmare") record the sweeps of the Permian ocean across Canyonlands.

Conspicuous red and white bands layer The Needles. The red beds were deposited by Permian rivers when Canyonlands lay above the sea. Cedar Mesa Sandstone forms the white layers, which were laid down in near-shore sand bars of the Permian ocean and as wind-blown dunes along its coast.

Salt: The Director

The old underlying Paradox beds have a firm grip on all that happens above them. These beds contain thousands of feet of salt, which was deposited by a deep but evaporating ocean in Pennsylvanian time. As the ocean shrank, salts—vast amounts of gypsum, "table" salt, and other "evaporites"—crystallized from its briny waters.

Under pressure, salt flows like plastic, and since it is less dense than other rocks, it tends to rise. The thousands of feet of rock above the Paradox Formation have weighed down on the salt beds for 300 million years, giving the salt ample time to push upward. The salt seeks the easiest path—where cover is thinnest—doming up the overlying rocks, usually without breaking the surface.

Such salt domes mark Canyonlands with landforms that are enigmatic to those who do not know about the Paradox salt oozing about deep underground. The Colorado River follows one such salt dome, its path evidently controlled by the long crest of the fold. Upheaval Dome on the Island in the Sky is a sharply folded circular salt dome that has been breached by erosion. And salt flowing from under the Needles region toward the river has dragged with it ("rafted") the overlying layers, which have broken under this stress along faults in The Grabens and in parallel cracks (joints) in The Needles themselves.

Water: The Stage Changer

Such joints provide a rough sketch that blocks out the slabs that water can erode into fins, and the cubes that can be carved into spires and needles.

And it is water that has created the Canyonlands landscape. The river carves no wider than its course; it sets the gradient—the tempo—for its tributaries, which each year edge farther back into mesas and benches. Undercut cliffs collapse in crashes of dust and stone. Flash floods tumble the debris downstream, scouring clean the canyons and widening the Canyonlands basin by a boulder's width each time a slab ruptures.

The fine details of erosion create everyone's favorite small-scale wonders. Arches pierce fins of sandstone as alcoves retreat; potholes scattered across mesa rims grind downward; ice expands inside a crack and wedges off a chunk of sandstone to transform a spire.

The rock landscape of Canyonlands continues to crack, crumble, and roll away down its master, the river, toward the sea.

Opposite: Snowfall on the Cedar Mesa fins and the distant La Sal Mountains.

At the first sweeping look from the Island in the Sky, Canyonlands seems barren of life. The weather, too, runs to extremes; San Juan County boasts a 144° annual temperature range—from −29°F to 115°F—one of the widest in the world. A single day may pass through 50° of variation. Grassy green is not a color that comes to mind when you picture the Canyonlands; rather, the colors are those of the rocks— red, cream, brown, orange, black.

Down in the canyons, however, there is plenty of greenery. Not the smug, profligate greens of endless mountains and meadows, but the careful, wise, singular greens of desert plants that have adapted to both severe summer water stress and winter cold.

The Sometimes-Green Desert: Plant Communities

In cracks and joints on exposed slickrock grow piñon pine and Utah juniper. Unable to survive on the 8 inches of precipitation that reaches the park yearly, these canny trees have gotten around the problem by growing in fissures that concentrate runoff and provide much greater effective moisture.

Other shrubs also take advantage of such cracks, with their pockets of silt and moisture, forming a rich plant community. Here small mammals reach their greatest diversity: Colorado chipmunk, rock squirrel, and several species of mice and wood rats. This woodland-shrubland also provides important resting cover for deer.

Under these trees and in open patches among the shrubs grows a unique complex of lichens, algae, moss, and fungi, which covers the ground surface like a skin disease or a carpet of lumpy black crud. This unflattering description may suit its appearance, but the importance of this "cryptogamic" soil crust cannot be overestimated. It soaks up water, ponding runoff to encourage absorption and slow erosion. Its algae convert atmospheric nitrogen into a form that can be used by higher plants. But it is so fragile that light grazing or even a single footstep can destroy tens of years of growth.

Rocks in Canyonlands will not hold still long enough for soils to develop; flash floods are too busy sweeping erosional debris away to the rivers. Sandy debris does accumulate in places, and if it is uniformly shallow, blackbrush grows in vast stands. Blackbrush "perches" its roots just above the bedrock, where ground water also perches, ready for slow uptake. This humble shrub covers 1 million acres in southeastern Utah. But its small leaves, which drop in drought, and tiny yellow blossoms have not inspired poets in search of symbols or even botanical researchers; this is a poorly studied plant community.

Where soils deeper than 18 inches cover bedrock, blackbrush scrub gives way to grassland. Galleta, needle-and-thread, Indian rice grass, and blue grama sway in spring green and summer golds in meadows in The Needles and on top of the Island. Here flourish seed-eating animals and birds, typified by Ord's kangaroo rats and horned larks and black-throated sparrows.

These three communities cover 80 percent of the park area. Lesser plant communities include saltbush and shadscale on Chinle shales; sage and four-wing saltbush on thick alluvial deposits on benches above arroyos with seasonal access to the water table; cottonwood-, willow-, and tamarisk-banked river bottoms; and hanging gardens at seeps.

During the last century, The Needles area has been heavily grazed; inaccessibility luckily softened the impact on The Maze and the Island. Overgrazing tramples the cryptogamic soil cover, and allows exotic plants such as cheatgrass, halogeton, and Russian thistle to replace native grasses in disturbed areas. In the 1880s and 1890s, in particular, tens of thousands of cattle grazed southeastern Utah. Uranium exploration has taken its toll, too, particularly on the White Rim. The lightly grazed Maze district preserves the park's most pristine vegetation.

Canyons and Mesas: Challenge to Dispersal

The rivers dictate to the living world of Canyonlands, just as they rule the rockscape. They harbor unusual fish in their turbid waters: the endangered Colorado River squawfish and the humpback chub. Their drainage system maps out the mosaic of park ecosystems. Their powerful currents and deep canyons form monumental barriers to dispersal for most terrestrial vertebrates.

The greatest contrast among the three park districts can be seen in their rodents, which total one-third of the Canyonlands mammal list. Only three of twenty-five rodents—the beaver, piñon mouse, and Colorado chipmunk—show no geographic subspecies variation in the park.

The harsh environment of Canyonlands seems to limit the total populations of mammal species, allowing several similar animals (for example, three species of wood rats in The Needles; four species of white-footed mice throughout the park) to coexist even where they compete for the same resources. Cover provided by an infinite number of cracks, crannies, and ledges seems to ease competition. Bats flourish; nearly all Utah species summer in this metropolis of roosting sites, with its warm air and abundant insects. The Needles have been described as "wood rat heaven," with more species living together there than anywhere else on earth.

Slickrock can form a significant barrier, too, when standing vertically in Wingate walls. Recent research on isolated buttes in Canyonlands has answered some tantalizing questions about the kinds of animals that live on top of these sheer-walled mesas. A number of small mammals are capable of climbing the 400-foot cliffs to colonize these buttes. But habitat preferences make many species unlikely colonizers; they simply do not live near enough to the cliffs. Wood rats, piñon mice, and chipmunks climb well, but they require moist vegetation and cover, which are absent on the ascent route. Other mammals might be capable of climbing the cliffs, but could not succeed in the habitat on top.

The canyon mouse is the slickrock-dweller *par excellence* of Canyonlands, and it is this beautiful little animal that turns up on every isolated butte so far examined. On The Jug, an island mesa off the "mainland" of the Island in the Sky, the canyon mouse is the only mammal found on the 20-acre mesa top. Other buttes have bushy-tailed wood rats, chipmunks, and other mice species. Isolated mesa tops seem to resemble true islands; they support fewer species of both small mammals and reptiles than do mainland areas like the Island in the Sky, but they allow for more individuals of each kind.

Romance and Radioactivity

Cliffs also are crucial to Canyonlands' most romantic mammal, the desert bighorn sheep. Canyonlands has the fastest-growing desert bighorn population in the West. Sheep clamber about in broken bench lands of the White Rim, in The Needles, and (as of 1982) in The Maze, where they have been reintroduced. Rams wander seasonally right up to the rim of the Island. And in dry periods, when potholes are empty, the sheep come down to the rivers for water.

Cliffs form more than mere background for the sheep—more than shelter for lambing, or range for feeding on their preferred blackbrush and galleta grass. The cliffs are absolutely essential escape cover; in one long-term study on the White Rim, 99 percent of all bighorn spotted were within .6 km (just over .37 mile) from rough escape terrain. They carefully avoid venturing farther into open country and thus never waste their incredible cliff-climbing ability when danger threatens.

Some threats to the sheep—and the park—will not be so easily escaped. Tar sands in Elaterite Basin form an attractive source of potentially developable oil where asphalt seeps naturally from the White Rim. And a Paradox salt dome beneath Davis Canyon in The Needles has been proposed as a national high-level nuclear waste repository, just 11 miles upgroundwater from Cataract Canyon.

The ecology of Canyonlands seems simple—it is "only a desert,"

Clockwise, from top:
Fishhook cactus. Whiptail lizard. Cottonwood with catkins. Horned lark.

after all. But connections—real, if invisible—lead outward from the park to the entire lower Colorado River basin and beyond. They can snap without our knowing, even when treated with respect.

If we are lucky, and if we are wise, we will come to understand these intricacies that tie Canyonlands to the life on earth while its bonds still remain taut, not when they lie smoking in radioactive ruin.

SITES, TRAILS, AND TRIPS

There are many ways of being in a canyon landscape. Drivers can travel through it—at 55 miles per hour on pavement; at 30 miles per hour on smooth dirt roads; or at a grinding, bone-jolting 5 miles per hour on barely drivable four-wheel tracks. Loiterers can perch on a high mesa and look down, or lie in a shaded crack and look up. The more adventurous can ride horseback, walk marked trails, or navigate wilderness cross-country. And boaters can travel by raft or kayak through thrilling rapids and along peaceful flat water on rivers.

Canyonlands National Park offers all these ways of seeing canyon landscapes. Sample several; each has its own rewards. And each of the three sections of the park protects unique resources; Canyonlands, in a way, is three separate parks.

Island in the Sky District

Between the Green and the Colorado rivers lies an enormous mesa that is accessible by car only across The Neck, which is not much wider than the road itself. The entrance road to the Island leaves U.S. 191 about 10 miles north of Moab. Seventeen miles in, the pavement veers off to Dead Horse Point State Park, a developed viewpoint that overlooks a stretch of the Colorado River canyon known as the upper Grand Canyon. Straight ahead, a dirt road leads toward bolder experiences in Canyonlands itself.

Over The Neck, the Island in the Sky road leads another 12 miles to the tip of the mesa at Grand View Point. The flat top of the Island makes a great natural corral, with its easily fenced Neck. Native vegetation still shows the changes brought about by grazing, which ended on the Island in 1975. From the main stem, branch roads go to Green River Overlook (and campground), Murphy Point (this road is rough; without a jeep you can stroll out 1.75 miles to a fine view looking west over Stillwater Canyon on the Green), and Upheaval Dome. Wander anywhere on the rims of the Island to find spectacular views. But Grand View Point is the climactic overlook.

Opposite: Backpack trips of up to two weeks are allowed by park permit.

Trails of Canyonlands National Park*

Island in the Sky District

Mesa Arch Trail: Starts at east side of Island in the Sky; ends at Mesa Arch; .5 mile round trip; .5 hour; 80-foot ascent; through piñon-juniper woodland to arch in sandstone; magnificent views of La Sal Mountains and below to fin known as The Washerwoman.

Whale Rock Trail: Starts at Upheaval Dome road; ends at Whale Rock; 1 mile round trip; .5 hour; 120-foot ascent; climb to top of sandstone butte with spectacular view of Upheaval Dome.

Upheaval Dome Trail: Starts at Upheaval Dome picnic area; ends at Upheaval Dome Rim; 1 mile round trip; .5 hour; 40-foot ascent; easy walk along sandstone rim of Upheaval Dome, with views into the center of the "crater."

Needles District

Chesler Park Trail: Starts at Elephant Hill or Squaw Flat Campground; ends at Chesler Park; 5 or 9 miles round trip; 4 hours; 500-foot ascent; Chesler Park is a great meadow dotted with islands of spires and enclosed by a circular wall formed by The Needles; Joint Trail, which starts at Chesler Canyon on the far side of Elephant Hill, passes through a deep slot between two fins.

Druid Arch Trail: Starts at Elephant Hill; ends at Druid Arch; 10 miles round trip; 8 hours; 640-foot ascent; winds through the buttes of The Needles and then follows the wash of Elephant Canyon to the 200-foot arch; fine views.

Confluence Overlook Trail: Starts at Big Spring Canyon Overlook; ends at Confluence Overlook; 10.2 miles round trip; 8 hours; 320-foot ascent; along jeep road into Big Spring Canyon, across fields and meadows, crossing Devil's Lane and Cyclone Canyon; .5 mile from end of road to rim of Colorado River's Cataract above confluence of Green and Colorado rivers; hot; carry water.

Colorado River Trail: Starts at Elephant Hill; ends at Colorado River at Lower Red Lake Canyon; 16 miles round trip; 2-4 days; 1,200-foot ascent; rough, difficult hike, partly on jeep roads; riverbank routes lead upriver to Confluence and downriver to rapids in Cataract Canyon, but this is not an established trail and depends on the water level; carry food and water.

Peekaboo Spring Trail: Starts at Squaw Flat Campground; ends at Peekaboo Spring; 10.8 miles round trip; 7 hours; 500-foot ascent; leads up Squaw Canyon, then crosses a pass and drops into Lost Canyon, crosses another pass and drops into Salt Creek at Peekaboo Spring; two ladders; very rough with much strenuous up-and-down hiking; carry water.

Squaw and Lost Canyons Trails: Starts at Squaw Flat Campground; ends at Lost Canyon; 5.2 miles round trip; 4 hours; 500-foot ascent; loop variation on the Peekaboo Spring Trail; leads into upper Squaw Canyon, crosses a pass into Lost Canyon, leads down Lost Canyon, and crosses back into Squaw Canyon; one ladder; fine taste of canyon floors and slickrock cliffs; extensive views.

Squaw and Big Spring Canyons Trail: Starts at Squaw Flat; ends at Big Spring Canyon; 7.5 miles round trip; 6 hours; 400-foot ascent; another loop, up most ot Squaw Canyon, across a strenuous pass into Big Spring Canyon; difficult slopes on both sides of the pass, but fine views; watch for potholes.

Angel Arch Trail: Starts at end of Salt Creek jeep road; ends at Angel Arch viewpoint; 1 mile round trip; .5 hour; 240-foot ascent; leads to the classic view of Angel Arch, with Molar Rock in foreground.

Maze District†

Horseshoe Canyon Trail (from east): Starts at end of Horseshoe Canyon jeep road; ends at Great Gallery; 3.5 miles round trip; 3 hours; 20-foot ascent; easy walk in canyon bottom with cottonwoods, to several panels of magnificent rock art; please do not touch fragile pictographs. It is also possible to reach trail from the west on a two-wheel drive road. Information available at park.

North Trail Canyon Trail: Starts at North Canyon Point turnoff on jeep road; ends at Maze Overlook; 28 miles round trip; 2 days; 1,450-foot ascent; hiker's access to The Maze; 6 miles in North Trail Canyon, then on jeep road; check with rangers for up-to-date information.

The Maze Trail: Starts at Maze Overlook; ends at Harvest Scene; 6 miles round trip; 5 hours; 640-foot ascent; drops off past the sandstone Nuts and Bolts balanced rocks, and down to the floor of The Maze; the Harvest Scene pictograph panel lies up the easternmost major canyon to the south (*not* south fork of Horse Canyon).

Golden Stairs Trail: Starts 1.5 miles from ranger station on Flint Trail jeep road; ends at Doll House; 22 miles round trip; 2 days; 800-foot ascent; along jeep road from mesa above The Fins, past the Standing Rocks to the rim of Cataract Canyon; hot.

Pete's Mesa Trail: Starts at Chimney Rock; ends at Pete's Mesa; 6 miles round trip; 5 hours; 100-foot ascent; follows narrow plateau between The Maze and Jasper Canyon; spectacular views.

Confluence Overlook Trail: Starts at Doll House; ends at Confluence Overlook; 13 miles round trip; 10 hours; 500-foot ascent; primitive trail on slickrock behind rim of Cataract Canyon to precipitous ledge immediately above confluence of Green and Colorado rivers.

Spanish Bottom Trail: Starts at Doll House; ends at Colorado River at Spanish Bottom; 2 miles round trip; 3.5 hours; 1,200-foot ascent; steep descent to river, with sweeping views to The Needles and along Cataract Canyon.

*An infinite variety of off-trail hiking routes exist. Some are well known, used by several parties each year, and may even be marked with rock cairns. Others have been hiked once or twice. Still others remain to be discovered. If you are interested in hiking unmarked routes off established trails, talk with park rangers and be certain that your party has the equipment and experience necessary to handle inevitable problems associated with "bushwacking," as well as potential emergencies.

†It is 65 miles from the turnoff on Utah 24 to the Maze District ranger station, and perhaps a few hours' hiking farther to the chosen trail head. It is a major commitment to hike in the Maze District, and you should not attempt it without plenty of water and a good topographical map. Dogs should not be taken into the Maze District.

See map on pages 102–103.

From Grand View the park falls away below, canyons and spires and rims leading to a horizon dominated at middle distance by the island mountains of the canyon country—the Abajos, the La Sals, and the Henrys. Directly below lies Monument Basin, sliced through the White Rim into the red Organ Rock Tongue of the Cutler, and packed with monoliths as high as 300 feet. Beyond, sunk deep in the labyrinth of rock, the Green and the Colorado join.

From the road, the trailless rim leads south for 1 mile to the final tip of Grand View Point, just across the gulf that separates the Island from its outlier, Junction Butte. Nowhere else can you so quickly grasp the park's formidable topography.

Mesa Arch Trail. On the east side of the Island a short trail (.5 mile round trip) leads to Mesa Arch. The trail winds through piñon and juniper woodland, blackbrush scrub, cryptogamic soil, and slickrock to an arch in the Navajo Sandstone that clings to the edge of the cliff. This "cliff-hanging" arch frames magnificent views eastward to the La Sal Mountains and below to the fin known as The Washerwoman.

This trail is a good place to learn to avoid cryptogams. Vibram soles

—or even the gentle footfalls of sandals—crush these black soil crusts of lichen, moss, algae, and fungi. They take decades to recover. Whenever you walk off trails in the Canyonlands, follow slickrock or sandy washes and small drainages.

Upheaval Dome Trails. Upheaval Dome is unique—a salt dome so abrupt that the eerie force of the buried Paradox is almost palpable. The dome is best seen from the air, but the .5-mile trail up Whale Rock gives a fair approximation of an aerial view. The central dome (or anticline) is surrounded by a ringlike recurved syncline. Eroded strata turned on end have left a Wingate cliff standing over the "crater" of soft, easily washed-away Chinle and Moenkopi. Great chunks of White Rim Sandstone lie jumbled in the center of the structure. A second short trail leads to the crater rim, on top of the Wingate.

Longer hikes are possible in the Upheaval area. Circle the dome in Syncline Valley and enter the crater through Upheaval Canyon—a 4-mile walk that leads 1,200 feet below the Wingate rim overlook. From

The Needles District is filled with spires and arches about 400 feet high.

here, head down Upheaval Canyon 3 miles to the Green River—the only water available on the hike—for a glimpse of Stillwater Canyon.

The White Rim. Midway between the top of the Island and the rivers lies the broad, arid ledge of the White Rim. An easy four-wheel-drive road circles below the Island for more than 100 miles through prime bighorn habitat. The White Crack provides a lively hiking route below the rim, and at Lathrop Canyon, jeeps can reach the Colorado. The White Rim road winds around Monument Basin, whose slickrock rim is great for ledge walking and pothole watching.

The Needles District

The Needles District is the most developed area of the park, with good reason. It is as rich in spires, arches, ruins, and side canyons as any place on the Colorado Plateau. Four-wheel-drive roads lead beyond the pavement, but considerable country still is reachable only on foot.

The entrance to the Needles area lies 14 miles north of Monticello on U.S. 191, and thence 38 miles on paved road down Indian Creek Canyon to Squaw Flat.

Squaw Flat is a broad grassy park surrounding Squaw Butte, in the center of the drainages that lead from Salt Creek to the Colorado. The paved road continues to Big Spring Canyon Overlook, passing by the Pothole Point Trail, a few minutes' walk on a Cedar Mesa Sandstone surface pocked with natural tanks of rain water, with superb views to The Needles and north to the Island.

The main dirt road reaches 3 miles from Squaw Flat Campground to the foot of Elephant Hill, where jeep roads pass over the 40 percent grade on into The Grabens and foot trails start to The Needles. A rough dirt (four-wheel-drive) road heads north to Colorado River Overlook. It crosses Salt Creek at Lower Jump—a high sandstone ledge that turns into a frothy red waterfall when the creek floods—and ends just above the deeply carved confluence of Salt Creek and the Colorado. Lastly, the road into upper Salt Creek starts near the Squaw Flat ranger station.

Salt Creek. Salt Creek and Horse Canyon, its largest tributary, drain the eastern half of The Needles district—in an intricate, extensive canyon system that has many arches and ruins. Four-wheel-drive vehicles can maneuver far up both canyons, mostly in the sandy washes. Salt Creek does not feel much like a road. At its undrivable extremes, the sandy track can be deep and dry, or wet enough to be saturated—quicksand.

Without a jeep, you must walk even the lower canyon. Either way, Angel Arch is 13 miles up Salt Creek from Cave Spring at the edge of

The Fremont pictographs called Thirteen Faces are found in Horse Canyon.

Squaw Flat; Fortress Arch is 8.5 miles up Horse Canyon. Cowboys used Cave Spring for years; the spring and cowboy line camp, under sheltering Cedar Mesa ledges, make a short historic walk. Watch for lazuli buntings and blue grosbeaks in tamarisk along the wash.

In Horse Canyon, fine Anasazi masonry survives at Tower and Keyhole ruins. The canyon contains three impressive arches—Gothic, Castle, and Fortress—and the powerful Thirteen Faces, unusual Fremont pictographs that line a cliff in somber dignity—perhaps a single shaman's painted "audience" for his chants.

Salt Creek itself passes Peekaboo Spring, where more pictographs speak in cryptic symbols. From Peekaboo Spring, trails lead through Lost and Squaw canyons back to Squaw Flat. Cottonwoods shelter the creek; they ease from green to gold in autumn, highlighting yellow hues in the banded Cedar Mesa cliffs. Side canyons hide rock art, ruins, blooming datura, wary lizards. And at the road's end lies Angel Arch.

Angel Arch is the symbol of Canyonlands, as Delicate Arch is that of Arches National Park. A .5-mile trail leads to its classic view with "Molar Rock" in the foreground. A scramble up to the base of the arch itself is crucial to comprehending its size.

Beyond a spur road where the drivable portion of Salt Creek ends is the upper Salt Creek hiking route, which reaches 12 miles from the end of the jeep road to the park boundary and the mesa that rims

An autumn storm over the Colorado River from Dead Horse Point.

its headwall. This walk—longest established hike in the district—leads through miles of empty, eventful wilderness, to arches, the remarkable pictograph of the All-American Man (a unique red, white, and blue Fremont shield figure), and the abandoned cabin of unsociable Claude Kirk, who lived for years in one of the canyon country's most isolated spots.

Lavender and Davis Canyons. The park protects the headwaters of Lavender and Davis canyons, which drain northeastward to Indian Creek. The canyons can be reached by jeep or on foot along their washes from the paved road east of the park. Both resemble Salt Creek in intricacy and rich resources, including many arches and ruins. Lavender Canyon is named for author David Lavender's Colorado ranching family. Lavender's *One Man's West* tells of his experiences as a cowboy in the days of Al Scorup's cattle empire in this place he describes as "wild, weird sandrock."

The Needles. To the west of Salt Creek are The Needles proper. Salt flowing in the Paradox created tensions that cracked this section of the Cedar Mesa in a checkerboard of joints. Water worked on the cracks to make The Needles a city of spires, with round bristling barricades surrounding grassy parks and tortuous canyons.

A network of trails extends into The Needles, with connections to Salt Creek, Squaw Flat, and The Grabens. Most popular are routes from Elephant Hill to Chesler Park (3 miles) and Druid Arch (5.4 miles one way), and the 1-mile slot of the Joint Trail, which provides access to Chesler Park from jeep roads in The Grabens. Needles ring the meadows of Chesler Park.

The trail to Druid Arch runs for several miles in Elephant Canyon, where the creek has cut a narrow channel beneath the Cedar Mesa into the Elephant Canyon Formation. This walk feels like a secret passage running beneath a great city; it remains soothingly shaded in early morning, while glare from scorching slickrock hovers just above the inner channel. Druid Arch is monumental—a towering dolmen.

The Grabens. Salt solution and flowage toward the Colorado has created its most dramatic effects just west of The Needles. The brittle sandstone, yanked along by moving salt, released stress along a series of very recent faults (starting perhaps 500,000 years ago). Blocks of the earth's crust that have dropped down between faults are called grabens, and The Grabens complex includes canyons 300 feet deep that vary in width from 7 feet to nearly 2,000 feet.

The dry valleys of The Grabens contain well-developed jeep roads, and one important hiking route extends 4 miles down Lower Red Lake Canyon to the Colorado River across from Spanish Bottom. Some hikers swim the river there to link up with the trail to the Doll House.

The Maze District

The journey to The Maze is still adventurous, and it will remain so; the National Park Service plans to manage this district to preserve its remote, primitive character. The Green and Colorado canyons isolate The Maze from other districts, and the roundabout approach is long. From Utah 24, 40 miles south of Green River, take a sandy track for 45 miles to Hans Flat ranger station on the summit of the Orange Cliffs.

The land gradually rises as you drive in across the treeless San Rafael Desert, past the dunes and pastures of Robber's Roost—little changed since Butch Cassidy made himself comfortable there. Kit foxes may loom up in headlights at night. Drifting sand may stop passenger cars. But traffic will not be a problem.

Three branch roads lead from the ranger station—one to the head of the Flint Trail (definitely the end of two-wheel drive), the second out to Cleopatra's Chair and Panorama Point (four-wheel drive), and the third jeep road north along The Spur, rounding the head of big, dry Millard Canyon, to Horseshoe Canyon's 2-mile trail.

Horseshoe Canyon. At Horseshoe, Barrier Creek has cut a beautiful curving Cedar Mesa canyon with smooth desert-varnished walls. Pictographs decorate these faces. Included among them is the 200-foot Great Gallery of ghost figures, which is unsurpassed by any other North American rock art. Archeologists as well as park visitors fall under the spell of these hollow-eyed, life-size figures. Scholars have yet to identify the painters of these Barrier Canyon-style figures—the Fremont or an even earlier culture. Telltale artifacts are so rare, we may never know.

Under the Ledge. Fourteen miles past Hans Flat, switchbacks of the Flint Trail jeep road plunge over the rim of the Orange Cliffs. After 3 slow miles, it meets the road that comes up 40 miles from Hite along the base of the Orange Cliffs. A back track along this road goes to the branch leading out past Ernie's Country and the Land of Standing Rocks toward the Doll House. The Standing Rocks rise as a series of remnant monuments of red Organ Rock; some are capped with White Rim Sandstone, and others are uncapped and doomed soon to disintegration: The Wall, Lizard Rock, The Plug, Standing Rock. From Chimney Rock, a 3-mile trail leads north to Pete's Mesa, in the center of the Maze canyon system.

Turn left at the foot of the Flint Trail, and you are headed for Maze Overlook. The road crosses Elaterite Basin—named for the petroleum resin that seeps from the White Rim—winds around the high, spiky Wingate tower of Elaterite Butte and along the rim of Horse Canyon, and finally ends at the brink of The Maze—some 80 miles from pavement and 170 miles by road from park headquarters in Moab, though just 34 linear miles for a raven or an eagle.

The Maze. The view down into The Maze makes the long, tantalizing drive worthwhile. Even for those who arrive by foot, walking the 14-mile North Trail Canyon, The Maze is the climax of the journey. Its canyons are not quite the labyrinth you might expect. In fact, a 2.5-mile trail starts at the overlook, passes through the White Rim pillars known as the Nuts and Bolts, and reaches into The Maze as far as the Harvest Scene, a phenomenal Barrier Canyon-style pictograph panel.

In this painting, eyeless beings gracefully offer up puffs of Indian rice grass. Rabbits run down their arms, while birds fly around their crowned heads. Hunchbacked attendants carry seed-beaters and sickles; their humpbacked profile may be an abstraction of conical burden baskets. Rice grass was a major resource for the Maze Anasazi and Fremont. In small hunting parties, they made seasonal trips to the canyons and uplands from home bases on farmable river bottom to search for wild game, wild grass to harvest, and jasper for spear points.

Some evidence exists of hunters and gatherers using Maze uplands prior to the Fremont and Anasazi, and Barrier Canyon rock art usually is associated with their grassland campsites.

The Doll House Area. The Cedar Mesa Sandstone walls all the inner canyons of The Maze—Jasper, Shot, Water, The Fins, and The Maze itself. In *Desert Solitaire*, Edward Abbey likens its banded spires to "melted...Neapolitan ice cream." The same formation stands in pinnacles above Cataract Canyon at the Doll House, and shelters little Surprise Valley perched on the brink of the river gorge.

Semideveloped trails circle through the mischievous spires of the Doll House. And a primitive route leads to a spectacular overlook of the confluence. Unmarked hiking routes traverse all these Cedar Mesa

The park's canyons are composed of sandstone, shale, siltstones, mudstones, limestones, salt, gypsum, and jasper.

canyons; hikers must pay attention to detail to avoid losing their way. Park rangers can suggest possible backpacking trips.

Lastly, a good trail leads from the Doll House down to Spanish Bottom on the Colorado, forming a link between bench lands and rivers.

The Rivers

Anyone who rides the white water of Cataract Canyon will understand the experience recorded by Fred Dellenbaugh, a member of Powell's 1871 expedition. When the party rowed out onto the Colorado at the confluence, Dellenbaugh wrote of feeling "at last on the back of the Dragon" itself.

The run down the Green from the town of Green River takes boaters through 120 miles of gliding canyon walls, through Labyrinth and Stillwater canyons, to the confluence. The Colorado runs for 47 miles from Potash to the confluence; starting at Moab adds 17 river miles. Some prefer these quiet reaches to the rapids of Cataract.

Nothing so merges one's being with the slowness and silence of the Canyonlands as floating with the lazy current, basking in the sun, surprising deer, beaver, and fox on the banks, and spotting Anasazi granaries mortared in cracks like wasp nests. Great blue herons flap heavily downstream from sand bar to sand bar, keeping a precise distance ahead until they tire of the disturbance and fly up to the rim of the inner canyon to let boaters pass—settling gracefully into stillness, a pose like a shrine or a lookout, waiting.

Both the Green and the Colorado rivers above the confluence meander in gentle grades—flat waters that are navigable by rafts, canoes, and power boats captained by amateurs. But below the confluence, the Colorado runs in formations whose gradient dips southward. The river steepens as it flows *with* the dip of the rocks, and bears almost straight through Cataract Canyon. Its average drop of 8 feet per mile exceeds that of the Grand Canyon.

To run Cataract requires skilled boatmen, professional equipment, and a permit from the park. At high water, the rapids above Lake Powell remain awesome. The biggest is The Big Drop, where the river drops 30 feet in 1 mile. When side creeks are flooding, the river turns to chocolate and red, roiling with debris and extra power. The red dust gives the water a unique smell that is not instantly recognizable. Even immersion in water cannot take away its character.

This flooding Canyonlands river has an aroma like its paradoxical nature. It smells like the land it creates and destroys, like red rock baking in the sun. Its red waters smell like dryness.

Opposite: Gnarled, shaggy bark of Utah juniper. In the distance, the Green River.

CAPITOL REEF

NATIONAL PARK

Sulphur Creek has several small waterfalls and the oldest exposed rock in the park.

CAPITOL REEF NATIONAL PARK
TORREY, UTAH 84775, TEL.: (801) 425-3791

Highlights: Capitol Gorge □ Cathedral Valley □ Fruita □ Water-pocket Fold □ Muley Twist Canyon □ Wingate Cliff □ Navajo Cliff Kayenta Cliff □ South Desert □ Thousand Lake Mountain □ Strike Valley Overlook □ Hartnet Desert

Access: From east or west, take Utah 24. From south and Bryce Canyon, take Utah 12. See map on pages 134–135.

Hours: Daily, year-round; Visitor Center, 8 A.M.–6:30 P.M., June to Labor Day, 4:30 P.M. thereafter. Closed Federal holidays, November to April.

Fees: Entrance, $3. Camping, $5/vehicle; group camping, $1/person.

Parking: At Visitor Center, picnic areas, scenic pullouts.

Gas, food: At Hanksville, Torrey, Bicknell, Loa.

Lodging: At Hanksville, Torrey, Bicknell, Loa.

Visitor Center: Off Utah 24; slide show and book sales.

Museum: Exhibits in Visitor Center.

Pets: Permitted on leash, except on trails and in backcountry.

Picnicking: At 3 sites.

Hiking: Designated trails in headquarters area; suggested routes in backcountry. Carry water.

Backpacking: With permit. Carry water.

Campgrounds: 3 sites; first-come basis; Fruita Campground, 70 sites, $5; Cedar Mesa primitive, 5 sites; Cathedral Valley primitive, 5 sites. No showers.

Tours: In summer. In English only.

Other activities: Evening programs daily during high season.

Facilities for disabled: For mobility impaired, access to Visitor Center, restrooms, part of Fremont River Trail. For hearing impaired, printed texts available. For visually impaired, some exhibits have touch access; cassettes available.

For additional information, see also Sites, Trails, and Trips on pages 148–160.

THERE IS NO MISTAKING CAPITOL REEF. ON ANY APproach to the park, its great cliffs loom in a line 100 miles long, cleaving south-central Utah in two. The park outlines these cliffs in a long, narrow 270,000-acre strip that runs from Thousand Lake Mountain almost to the Colorado River; the cliffs, in turn, outline a major feature of the earth's surface: the Waterpocket Fold. Here, the flat rock layers of the Colorado Plateau were uplifted unevenly, creating a giant stair-step. Overlying formations did not break, but drooped over the step in a great S-curved bend. Erosion has exposed the upswept layers in a barrier line of sandstone cliffs that pioneer travelers likened to an ocean "reef."

A single paved road crosses the Reef along the Fremont River canyon; gravel and dirt roads parallel either side of the Fold; and trails and hiking routes lead to potholes, natural arches and bridges, overlooks, and tortuous narrows. At the north end of the park, Cathedral Valley spreads below the Fold, its isolated temples rising above harsh desert flats. Irrigated orchards, the remnant of the old Mormon village of Fruita, surround park headquarters. This green oasis—in a vast sea of aridity—is as much a symbol of the park as are domes atop the Fold.

Away from the Fremont River and the few perennial creeks, piñon and juniper woodland and desert shrubs scatter across slickrock and

The Hamburger Rocks are an unusual result of water erosion.

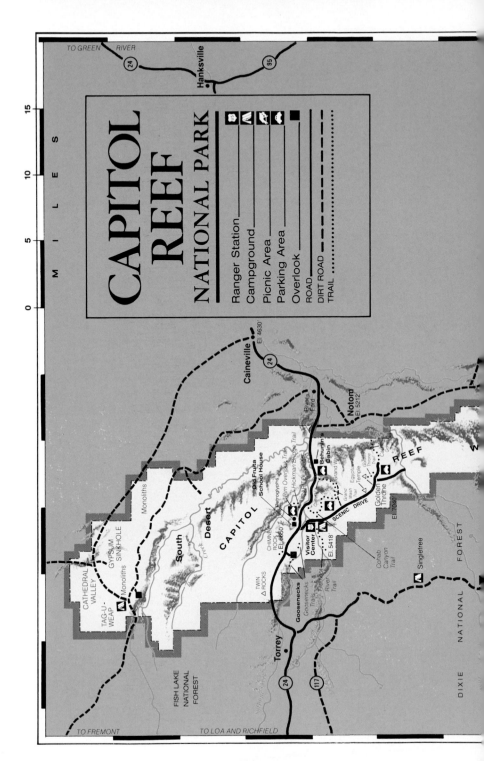

CAPITOL REEF NATIONAL PARK

Ranger Station
Campground
Picnic Area
Parking Area
Overlook

ROAD
DIRT ROAD
TRAIL

TO GREEN RIVER
Hanksville
24
95

MILES
0 5 10 15

Caineville
El. 4630'
24

Notom
El. 5212'

REEF

Monoliths

South Desert

CAPITOL

Old Fruita School House

Petroglyphs

Rim Overlook Trail

Hickman Bridge Trail

River Ford

Behunin's Cabin

Grand Wash

CHIMNEY ROCK El. 6600'

Visitor Center

El. 5418'

Pleasant Creek

TWIN ROCKS

Gooseneck
Goosenecks Trails

Fremont River Trail

SCENIC DRIVE

Egyptian Temple

Golden Throne

Golden Throne El. 7040'

Cohab Canyon Trail

CATHEDRAL VALLEY

GYPSUM SINKHOLE

TAG-U-WEAP

Monoliths

FISH LAKE NATIONAL FOREST

Torrey
24
117

Singletree

DIXIE NATIONAL FOREST

TO FREMONT
TO LOA AND RICHFIELD

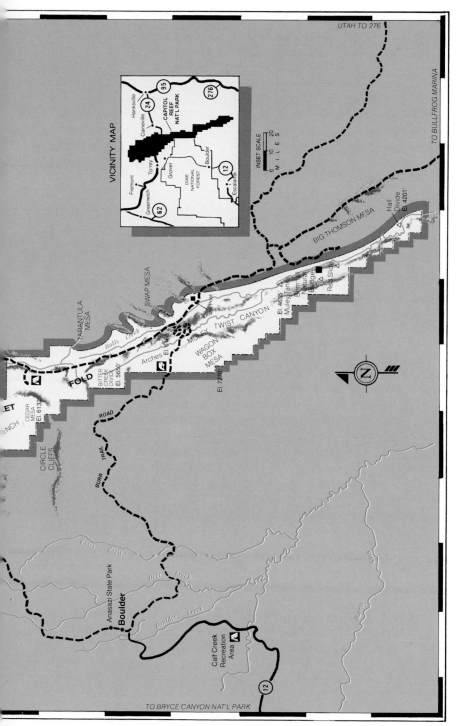

sand. Animals of the high desert live here in abundance, although the only vertebrates that risk the heat of daytime are ground squirrels, lizards, and birds. The rest of the life of Capitol Reef waits for cool nighttime, secreted by day in shade or burrows. It is this sense of hiding—of latent possibility—that gives Capitol Reef much of its appeal: the rocks hide the real life of the park; the blank wall of the Fold opens into side canyons lush with hanging gardens; the fiercely barren badlands give rise to delicate wildflowers; a sandy wash transforms into a raging river in flood. With a delight in surprise, Capitol Reef yields up endless wonders.

H   I   S   T   O   R   Y

The Waterpocket Fold is a paradox; it stands as an implacable barricade to travel, yet the few canyons that do pierce it funnel travelers across south-central Utah right into its heart. On either side of the passageways, the Fold runs on for miles, an inhospitable humpback of golden sandstone. The history of Capitol Reef, then, is the history of its canyons.

The Fremont: A River and a Culture

First to follow these drainages through the cliffs were members of a simple Desert Culture, the earliest people in the Southwest. Ten thousand years later, the Fremont people came to the rivers and creeks of Capitol Reef and dominated Utah for 500 years. They first were recognized and named as a result of research along the Fremont River at Capitol Reef in 1931.

Fremont farmers lived in pit-house "ranchettes" on hills above their fields, and they hunted and gathered intensively to supplement their crops. Their strain of maize was unique—extremely resistant to drought and climatic extremes, and able to flourish in a short growing season. The Fremont made no elegant stone houses, as did their Anasazi neighbors. But they left behind other evidence of their sophisticated culture: ornately decorated figurines, and on canyon walls remarkable paintings (pictographs) and carvings (petroglyphs) of magnetic spiritual power.

Human figures dominate the Fremont galleries—broad-shouldered beings resplendent in headdresses, necklaces, earrings, sashes, and shields. Animals, particularly bighorn sheep, surround them. It will never be known for certain just what the Fremont artists meant to communicate, but their messages are more than an undeciphered code—they are art.

The Fremont abandoned their farmsteads by A.D. 1300, when cli-

The members of the Wild Bunch who hid out in the park in the 1890s are identified by number in this photograph: 1, Robert LeRoy Parker (Butch Cassidy); 2, Harvey Logan; 3, Ben Kilpatrick; 4, Bill Carver; 5, Harry Longabaugh (Sundance Kid).

matic changes destroyed their crops, thus pushing them past the boundary of possibility in a land given to the impossible. Their destination remains a mystery, but Southern Paiutes newly arrived on the Colorado Plateau may have begun to compete with the Fremont for native plant harvests. Only the Southern Paiutes were living in the area when the first whites arrived several centuries later—a few families hunting through Capitol Reef in winter, summering at Fish Lake, and demonstrating an incredible ability to survive on slim resources.

Explorers Off the Beaten Track

Capitol Reef lay off the trappers' and traders' beaten trails, so there is no definite evidence of explorers having passed through the Fold before 1866. In that year, a troop of Mormon militia chased cattle-rustling Paiutes down the Fremont River. Five years later, two prospectors left the first signatures in the "pioneer register" on the walls of Capitol Gorge.

The first real *exploration* began when John Wesley Powell's men turned their attention this way in their great survey of the Colorado Plateau. In 1872, Almon H. Thompson, Powell's chief topographer, worked down from the Aquarius Plateau and crossed the Fold by way of Pleasant Creek. The Powell Survey also named the Fremont River for John Charles Frémont, who had struggled across its headwaters, which lie west of the park, in the winter of 1853.

The Mormon Frontier

As the Latter-Day Saint population burgeoned, Brigham Young sent his people in search of new land. By 1880, the Mormon frontier reached down the Fremont River to Capitol Reef. In the 1880s, pioneers moving into southeastern Utah left Escalante and navigated the Waterpocket Fold via the "road" through Muley Twist Canyon, which had been pioneered by Charles Hall, who operated a ferry at Hall's Crossing. In 1882, Elijah Cutler Behunin took the first wagon through Capitol Gorge; this spectacular narrows served as the main road across south-central Utah until 1962, when the paved Fremont River Highway was completed.

Fremont bottom land provided good grazing land and irrigable farmland, and the protected valleys at the base of the Fold were as mild as hothouses. At the junction of the Fremont River and Sulphur Creek, a few families established the village of Fruita. For the next eighty years, they sold peaches, cherries, apples, and apricots to settlers upriver and to travelers headed east from the High Plateaus. Besides selling produce, the little town supplied prospectors dashing for the San Juan River in the gold rush of the 1890s, cowboys trailing cattle down from the plateaus to winter range in the canyons, and Butch Cassidy and his Wild Bunch riding for their hideout at Robber's Roost. Later came moonshiners, anthropologists, tourists, and uranium prospectors. The last combed the Fold in the 1950s, widening many old trails to jeep roads, including the Burr Trail—the only road across the southern Fold.

Establishment of the Park

In the 1920s, local people led by Joseph Hickman and Ephraim Pectol began to press for the establishment of a national monument to promote tourism and to preserve the spectacular country. In 1937, their efforts were rewarded. The last residents of Fruita moved away in the 1960s, although their orchards remain. In 1971, the whole length of the Waterpocket Fold was added to the small original monument to create Capitol Reef National Park.

G   E   O   L   O   G   Y

Aerial view of Hall's Creek Narrows.

More than those of any other national park in the region except Grand Canyon, the boundaries of Capitol Reef follow the outline of its major geographic feature. A look at a relief map of the Colorado Plateau reveals a striking line of cliffs in south-central Utah. Running for about 100 miles, these cliffs trace the structure of the earth that Capitol Reef National Park preserves—the Waterpocket Fold.

The Waterpocket Fold: Creation

The Fold is a great step in the rocks of the plateau: a single, sideways, S-shaped bend that links flat-lying rocks at two levels. The Fold owes its existence to tremendous pressures that were generated in the West as the Rockies were formed some 70 million years ago. Over a span of 10 million years, regional uplift associated with this mountain building also raised the Colorado Plateau, but not without side effects. A wrinkle or three developed in the surface of the rising plateau in Utah, well west of the Rockies themselves.

One such blemish in the flat rock stack took the form of a sharp upsweep in more than a dozen layers, rolling up and over from east to west in the arching stone of the Waterpocket Fold. Layers below were uplifted at different rates, and the layers above gradually "drooped" over the step between the two buried blocks.

Almost all the rock formations that were contorted by the Fold date to the Mesozoic era (230 to 65 million years ago), the Age of Dinosaurs. Later sediments buried the Fold with flat-lying formations, but this even-keeled plain could not survive when regional uplift of the Colorado Plateau really hit its stride.

Uplift and Erosion: The Great Race

In the last 10 million years, the Colorado Plateau has been lifted 1 mile above its neighboring landscapes. As it rose—ever so slowly—the unavoidable forces of erosion whittled and whirred at it: rasping out canyons, whisking rock debris down rivers, slicing away whole formations from the land.

Uplift raised some chunks of the earth's crust higher than others;

just west of Capitol Reef lie the 11,000-foot-high plateaus of Boulder Mountain and Thousand Lake Mountain. Lava caps these high mesas; as ice-age glaciers on their summits melted, chunks of the plateaus' lava flows tumbled down the flooding rivers to come to rest at Capitol Reef as deposits of black lava boulders.

Younger rocks that were stripped from the Fold left the great flexure in the earth exposed to winter ice and summer storms, to the persistent power of flooding streams and sandstone-loosening seeps. Since soft rocks erode more quickly than hard ones, the tough sandstones of the Fold began to stand higher and higher above rapidly eroding shale valleys on either side. On the west, the steepest face of the Fold forms a barrier "reef" between Torrey and Pleasant Creek that gives the park its name. On the east, the Fold plunges into the earth in stone humpbacks that form what the Paiutes called a "Sleeping Rainbow."

A Vocabulary of Rocks

The rocks that warped in the Waterpocket Fold already were ancient— records of Permian rivers, Triassic mud flats, Jurassic deserts, and Cretaceous seas. Sandstones of the Glen Canyon Group make up the great cliffs of the Fold: Wingate, Kayenta, and Navajo. The Wingate face of the reef is unmistakable—fluted red walls that wind from Thousand Lake Mountain southward along the park's Scenic Drive, a palette for ever-changing light and shadow. Above inconspicuous Kayenta Formation ledges lie the domes and thrones of Navajo Sandstone—massive, cross-bedded, and dune-deposited like the Wingate, but creamy and golden in hue. The Navajo erodes grain by grain, unlike the Wingate, whose undercut blocks fall free to create vertical cliffs. Navajo domes crown the reef; one that resembles the United States Capitol gives the reef its name.

Above and below these cliff-formers, every formation has its distinctions. Moenkopi shales along the Scenic Drive support precariously balanced Shinarump Conglomerate boulders from the overlying Chinle Formation. Moenkopi slabs show ripple marks that were formed in tidal shallows and the fin marks of primitive amphibians that swam in early Triassic seas. The clays of the much younger multihued Morrison and gray Mancos east of the Fold erode in the intricate mazes of drainages that make for truly "bad" badlands.

And along the north end of the park, 500-foot cathedrals of soft Entrada Sandstone grace the dry valleys of South Desert and Cathedral Valley. These monoliths stand in broad flats that are completely different from any other park landscape.

Opposite: Splintered battlements of the 650-foot Castle make it a prominent landmark.

The word *canyon* may owe its origin to a medieval Spanish word for "street." Passages that wind through the Waterpocket Fold certainly fit this meaning; their rocky pavement is used by almost every creature seeking water, food, and migration routes. Along such streets are alcoves and cracks, burrows and crannies—"houses" in the cliffs.

Canyon Streets and Pothole Wells

Along the Fremont River "street," a permanent stream waters lush banks of cottonwood, willow, and tamarisk, irrigates historic orchards, and creates an oasis used by such diverse creatures as mule deer, yellow warblers, leopard frogs, and beaver. Elsewhere in the park, year-round moisture nourishes living communities along Pleasant Creek, Oak Creek, and Lower Hall's Creek.

The Fold owes its name to another water source: potholes that collect rain water in natural tanks, or "waterpockets." Potholes nourish a finely tuned community of organisms that are adapted to long dry spells. Adult toads wait out the time encased in a protective "bivouac sack" of mucus and burrowed deep beneath the dried mud crust. Gnat larvae can lose 92 percent of their body weight and still swarm into activity when water comes. Fairy and tadpole shrimp eggs stay viable for twenty-five years in pothole dust, waiting for rain with a patience that approaches that of the tough seeds of desert annual wildflowers.

Mature piñon pines often reach 200 years; some trees have been discovered to be between 800 and 1,000 years old.

Usually, they need not wait quite that long. Along most of its length, Capitol Reef gets a bit more than 7 inches of rain yearly. Summer thundershowers make August the wettest month. Winter brings about 15 inches of snow, which does not often take long to melt.

Plants on the Fold

At its north end, the Waterpocket Fold laps onto the flanks of Thousand Lake Mountain. There the park reaches an elevation of 8,800 feet and includes ponderosa pine forest and perhaps as many as 100 montane plant species found nowhere else in the park.

A cross section of the Fold nearly anywhere else along its length would map a standard sequence of plant communities. If one follows such a course across Upper Hall's Creek, south of Bitter Creek Divide, the real force behind the diverse life of Capitol Reef will be discovered: the variety of its rocks.

Start at the rim of Tarantula Mesa to the east. Its Mancos Shale is nutrient poor, its clays miserly about freeing water for uptake by plants. Only saltbush, shadscale, and galleta grass grow on the shales. Alluvium that once covered some of the Mancos supported an Indian rice grass and galleta grassland; but a century of grazing has weakened the native plants, and exotics such as cheatgrass and Russian thistle now flourish.

Just east of Notom Road, sage and rabbitbrush dominate on the Dakota Sandstone hogback (the Oyster Shell Reef, named for its phenomenally abundant fossil shells). To the west comes the Morrison, whose purple clays are nearly barren, but whose sandstones provide a fissure-ridden home for piñon pine and Utah juniper, along with a number of larger shrubs such as cliffrose and buffalo berry. Here also grow astragalus and prince's plume, which tolerate—and concentrate—poisonous selenium from the uranium ores of the Morrison. Prospectors sometimes use these plants to guide them to possible bodies of ore.

Summerville sands support grassland with scattered four-wing saltbush; deeper sand eroded from the Entrada is dominated by Mormon tea, with old-man sage and grasses. A wash cut in alluvium allows plants seasonal access to the water table; Fremont cottonwood, rabbitbrush, big sagebrush, greasewood, Gambel oak, and tamarisk flourish until they are uprooted by a powerful flash flood.

As the Carmel Formation rises onto the Reef, piñon and juniper woodland begins, and dominates through the breadth of the great slickrock bald of the Fold. Associated shrubs change with each succeeding formation: Navajo, Kayenta, Wingate. And in the center of the Fold, where Muley Twist Canyon cuts deeply into tilted rocks, shrubs that characterize open side canyons join the two conifers: single-leaf ash, squawbush, serviceberry, Apache plume, cliffrose, and Fremont barberry. The overpoweringly fragrant blossoms of the last two scent the breezes of side canyons with sweet perfume.

Beyond the Fold to the west lies another inhospitable layer of shale—the Chinle—and finally comes the ledgy Moenkopi, which at this 7,000-foot elevation supports piñon and juniper.

At the extreme southern end of the park, where Hall's Creek Gorge drops to 3,875 feet, blackbrush forms pure stands as far north as the Burr Trail. Hall's Creek side canyons have spectacularly diverse plant communities, particularly at seeps. Isolated from other pockets of moisture at each wet alcove, a miniature jungle grows, an elfin paradise of orchids, monkey flowers, columbines, and maidenhair fern.

Animal Voices

Through these environments wanders the wildlife of Capitol Reef. Some animals range widely, particularly predators and scavengers such as gopher snakes, bobcats, gray fox, ravens, golden eagles, and cougars.

Most Capitol Reef residents, however, prefer to remain in specific plant communities. Kangaroo rats and badgers burrow in sand under desert shrubs; piñon jays chorus from a piñon grove as they gather pine nuts; and canyon tree frogs stay close to potholes high on the Fold.

One mammal that is thoroughly tuned to the canyons is the ringtail. This slim, long-tailed relative of the raccoon hunts rodents at night from lairs in cliffs not far from water. Ringtails are remarkably agile, capable of chimneying between walls, ricocheting off cliffs, and performing handstands to reverse direction on a narrow ledge—all useful maneuvers when hunting wood rats through narrowing crevices.

The endangered Utah prairie dog has been reintroduced at the far northern end of Capitol Reef. Poisoning, hunting, and habitat destruction almost wiped out this sociable mammal, but with protected colonies such as the one in the park, its prospects are improving.

As we have chosen a future for the prairie dog, we must choose a future for Capitol Reef. Coal seams in Swap Mesa, directly across from viewpoints along the Burr Trail, would, if developed, put a huge strip mine right up against the park boundary. We can listen to coal-company executives and politicians, on the one hand, or to ecologists, archeologists, and hikers, on the other. But the most vital voices are the gilt-edged call of a canyon wren, the cackle of a yellow-breasted chat, and the dry rattle of a midget faded rattlesnake. Our most trustworthy guidance lies within the enigmatic silence of flood-scoured slickrock deep in the Waterpocket Fold.

The sego lily is the state flower of Utah. Its petals resemble a butterfly's wings, and the plant has a thick underground stem that looks like a bulb. Early Mormon pioneers cooked and ate the stems.

Top left: Long claws, sharp teeth, and a ferocious temper make the badger a formidable foe. Top center: Prairie dogs' deep burrows insulate them from heat and cold. Top right: The Steller's jay is the only jay west of the Rockies that is identifiable by its crest. Below: The mule deer's best defense is its remarkable speed.

SITES, TRAILS, AND TRIPS

First impressions and strongest memories? For most visitors it is the orchards of Capitol Reef whose image lingers. In this land of little water, the irrigated oasis of the old town of Fruita is a green treasure not soon forgotten—particularly if hand-picked tree-ripened apricots or peaches or apples sweetly cement the memory.

Little remains of the village: a house or two; lime kilns; in the campground, the old Pendleton barn built around 1905; and the Fruita schoolhouse, which dates to about 1896. As late as 1924, Fruita residents used the schoolhouse for dances, town meetings, elections, celebrations, and Sunday-school classes. But the population of Fruita schoolchildren began to dwindle, and 1941 saw the last class.

Fremont River Trails

Fremont River Trail. Surrounded by orchards, the campground is situated on the bank of the Fremont River at about 5,350 feet. Wander upstream through the fruit trees, and you will find yourself on the trail to the Fremont overlook. After an easy .5 mile, the trail climbs about 800 feet in .75 mile to a point high on Miner's Mountain. Views are expansive over Fruita and along the Reef.

Cohab Canyon Trail. Just across the road from the campground, a trail leads up .25 mile of switchbacks into Cohab Canyon. This delightful little canyon cut in Wingate cliffs forms an ideal introduction to slickrock in the Reef. Slots lead off into hidden grottoes; erosion detail is infinitely various. The canyon owes its name to legends that claim its use by Mormon polygamists (cohabitationists) hiding from federal marshals. Walk 1.75 miles more through the Reef to arrive at the river across the highway from the Hickman Bridge parking area.

Hickman Bridge Trail. The 1-mile walk to Hickman Bridge provides another fine sampling of park landscapes. Small canyons lead up to a massive 133-foot natural bridge that frames Capitol Dome and the distant Henry Mountains. Black lava boulders—glacial outwash from Boulder Mountain—perch on slickrock below the great Navajo domes. Rice-grass puffs vibrate in winds that carry the scent of piñon pitch and honeylike barberry blossoms.

Opposite: Sandstone rims, resembling reefs, are a characteristic formation in the park.

Trails of Capitol Reef National Park*

Fremont River Trail: Starts at campground; ends at Fremont Overlook on Miner's Mountain; 2.5 miles round trip; 1.5 hours; 770-foot ascent; first .5 mile very easy through orchards along river; then steep, strenuous climb to overlook of Fremont River canyon and Fruita valley below sheer cliffs of the Reef.

Grand Wash Trail: Starts at Grand Wash parking area; ends at Utah 24; 4.5 miles round trip; 3 hours; 100-foot ascent; mostly level along wash bottom; in the Narrows, walls rise 500 feet above 20-foot-wide canyon; usually hiked to Narrows.

Cassidy Arch Trail: Starts at Grand Wash parking area; ends at Cassidy Arch; 3.5 miles round trip; 3 hours; 900-foot ascent; steep climb from floor of Grand Wash to high cliffs, ending in sandstone slickrock above and behind the arch.

Frying Pan Trail: Starts at 1-mile mark on Cohab Canyon Trail; ends at 1-mile mark on Cassidy Arch Trail above Grand Wash; 3 miles one way; 1.5 hours; 600-foot ascent; usually hiked as connection between Cohab and Cassidy Arch trails; many ups and downs over slickrock and canyons; only maintained trail on the summit of the Reef.

Goosenecks Trail (east): Starts at Goosenecks Overlook; ends at Sulphur Creek Rim; .5 mile round trip; .5 hour; 30-foot ascent; views of Goosenecks of Sulphur Creek Canyon; panoramas of Waterpocket Fold and Henry Mountains; intricate erosion in Moenkopi Formation beside trail.

Goosenecks Trail (west): Starts at Goosenecks Overlook; ends at Sulphur Creek Rim; .2 mile round trip; .25 hour; 20-foot ascent; views of Goosenecks of Sulphur Creek Canyon; panoramas of Waterpocket Fold and Henry Mountains; intricate erosion in Moenkopi Formation beside trail.

Chimney Rock Trail: Starts and ends at Utah 24; 3.5 miles round trip; 2.5 hours; 540-foot ascent; strenuous climb up switchbacks and moderate hike on upper loop; views of Chimney Rock from below and above and panoramas of surrounding area.

Hickman Bridge Trail: Starts at Utah 24; ends at Hickman Bridge; 2 miles round trip; 1.5 hours; 380-foot ascent; nature trail through small canyon and under 133-foot Hickman Natural Bridge; Indian ruins and fine views of huge sandstone domes; self-guiding.

Rim Overlook Trail: Starts at Hickman Bridge parking area; ends at Rim Overlook; 4.5 miles round trip; 4 hours; 1,100-foot ascent; strenuous climb to top of cliffs with spectacular views over orchards of old Fruita to the face of the Waterpocket Fold.

Cohab Canyon Trail: Starts at Campground; ends at Utah 24; 3.5 miles; 3 hours; 400-foot ascent; steep climb for first .25 mile, then moderate; leads to hidden canyon above campground; short side trails to overlooks; details of erosion and small side canyons and grottoes.

Capitol Gorge Trail: Starts at Capitol Gorge parking area; ends at The Tanks; 2 miles round trip; 1.5 hours; 25-foot ascent; similar trail to Grand Wash plus prehistoric Indian petroglyphs. Pioneer Register, and waterpockets; hikers may continue through the Fold.

Golden Throne Trail: Starts at Capitol Gorge parking area; ends at Golden Throne; 4 miles round trip; 4 hours; 1,100-foot ascent; steep climb to top of cliffs and a lofty flat at the base of Golden Throne; panoramas.

*An infinite variety of off-trail hiking routes exist. Some are well-known, used by several parties each year, and may even be marked with rock cairns. Others have been hiked once or twice. Still others remain to be discovered. If you are interested in hiking unmarked routes off established trails, talk with park rangers and be certain that your party has the equipment and experience necessary to handle inevitable problems associated with "bushwacking," as well as potential emergencies.

See map on pages 134–135.

Spring Canyon, and the spring it is named for, are approached by Chimney Rock Trail.

Rim Overlook Trail. A branch off the Hickman Bridge Trail at about .25 mile winds up another 2 miles to reach the point of one of the big Wingate buttresses above Fruita: Rim Overlook.

West Entrance Trails

As you follow Utah 24 from Torrey, the Reef skirts your view on the left, growing ever higher, ever closer, until you drive down the hill from Panorama Point to the Visitor Center, headed straight for The Castle and the face of the Reef.

Goosenecks Trail. Panorama Point is a fine spot from which to view the Waterpocket Fold running both north and south, with the Henry Mountains in the background. Even better is the view from nearby Goosenecks Overlook, where the twisting course of 500-foot-deep Sulphur Creek Canyon makes a fine foreground along a short stroll. Enter the canyon of Sulphur Creek just west of Goosenecks Overlook, and walk in the stream for perhaps 4 miles to the Visitor Center. Along the way, you will skirt small waterfalls and get a look at the oldest exposed rock in the park, the elegant Kaibab Limestone (the layer that caps Grand Canyon) flooring the stream, with even a bit of the underlying Cutler showing through.

Chimney Rock Trail. Chimney Rock, an imposing pinnacle of Moenkopi capped by a block of Shinarump, dominates this drive from the west. A rather strenuous trail climbs for more than 500 feet to a high ridge that overlooks Chimney Rock, with views along the Reef. This loop trail runs 3.5 miles, and also provides access to the sheer Wingate cliffs in Chimney Rock Canyon, leading into the Fold toward Spring Canyon.
Spring Canyon is the longest canyon in the Waterpocket Fold. It begins on Thousand Lake Mountain, at more than 8,000 feet, and runs straightforwardly to the Fremont River, some 15 miles away. The drainage receives its name from a large ponded spring located upcanyon from where Chimney Rock Canyon joins it. Below, it is dry, and runs between 600-foot-high Navajo walls. The 9-mile walk from Chimney Rock to the river is a good introduction to off-trail canyon walking in the Reef.

Scenic Drive Trails

For 8 miles southward from the Visitor Center, the gravel Scenic Drive parallels Capitol Reef on the west. Spurs extend into Grand Wash and

Opposite: A capstone of Shinarump Conglomerate helps Chimney Rock resist erosion.

Capitol Gorge. This area encompasses the old national monument and is still the most heavily visited area of the park.

Grand Wash Trail. Just 2 miles past the campground is Grand Wash, over a divide called Danish Hill, which affords one of the classic views over Fruita to the face of the Reef. The Grand Wash road reaches 1.2

miles into the Fold, where an easy trail continues 2.2 miles farther to the Fremont River.

Grand Wash, long a route for cattle drives through the Reef, is one of only five corridors that pierce the Reef without ending in impassable

Driving cattle through the Waterpocket Fold to winter range outside the park.

headwalls. Its Navajo Sandstone narrows rise 500 feet from the 20-foot-wide canyon floor. Wildflowers (evening primrose, puccoon, asters, mustards) race to set seed in the floor of the wash before a flash flood sweeps through to pluck them loose. Few larger plants survive, for several times each summer the aftermath of a sudden thundershower wipes the narrows clean.

Trails and hiking routes climb from Grand Wash up side canyons and onto the summit of the Reef. Both Shinob and Bear canyons deserve exploration, and the latter leads to Fern's Nipple over a broken off-trail route. (Talk to a park ranger about hiking Bear Canyon.)

Cassidy Arch Trail. Winding up the north wall of Grand Wash, the Cassidy Arch Trail climbs 1,000 feet in 1.75 miles, through the Wingate and Kayenta to Navajo slickrock, in which the arch is cut. Piñon and juniper grow in sandstone cracks along the trail, each striking a unique pose.

Cassidy Arch is named for Butch Cassidy, the outlaw who grew up in Circleville (west of the park). Cassidy traveled through Capitol Reef many times, and remained friendly with local ranchers throughout his daring career. The arch is difficult to see from below; only the hike shows its real character.

Frying Pan Trail. The Frying Pan Trail begins .5 mile back toward Grand Wash from the arch and leads northward for 3 miles along the crest of the Reef to Cohab Canyon. It is the only maintained route on the summit of the Fold. The trail is a bit strenuous, with climbs totaling 800 feet, but easy to follow. It runs mostly in the Kayenta, but hikers will be tempted to wander west to the Wingate rim overlooking the Scenic Drive and east to the great domes and fins of Navajo. Wander freely— the most magical secrets of the Reef lie in its most secluded places.

From this spot, the Scenic Drive heads southward from Grand Wash over Slickrock Divide, a good spot to check the broken slabs of red Moenkopi for ripple marks left by sun-dappled waves washing over the tidal flats of Triassic seas. The Shinarump Member of the Chinle caps Moenkopi towers in the Egyptian Temple, farther on. The scattered distribution of the Shinarump testifies to its deposition by winding river channels.

Capitol Gorge Trail. Five miles from Grand Wash, the road plunges into Capitol Gorge, Cutler Behunin's pioneer road through the Reef. It is difficult enough to picture wagons clearing this route, but even more unlikely is the vision of the gorge as the main state highway through south-central Utah, as it was for eighty years. Beyond the 2-mile scenic road, Capitol Gorge again is a trail, just as it was for thousands of years.

In its first mile, the Capitol Gorge Trail leads through a bigger canyon than Grand Wash, with the extra attractions of Fremont petroglyphs, a register of pioneer signatures, and a set of waterpockets in a side canyon, whose upper tanks are frequently full in the summer rainy season.

Golden Throne Trail. Navajo towers stud the Reef in this section, and the Golden Throne is one of the most dominating. Its distinctive golden Navajo Sandstone has a thin cap of red Carmel. The trail up from Capitol Gorge climbs 1,100 feet from the parking area to a flat just below the throne; beyond lie little-visited broken heights along the Reef, which are accessible to backpackers along off-trail routes.

The road that goes south from the entrance to Capitol Gorge is an access route to the Sleeping Rainbow Ranch and Pleasant Creek hiking. Eph Hanks's pioneer Floral Ranch stood at Pleasant Creek. But since 1939 it has been known as the Sleeping Rainbow Ranch, long a commercial guest ranch but now part of the park. The hike down Pleasant Creek is pleasant indeed: a permanent stream, fine petroglyphs, and great Navajo domes for 3 miles in the Reef, then another 3 miles of open-country walking to Notom.

North of the Fold

Beyond the Fold to the north lie three broad, dry valleys that are protected by the park: Cathedral Valley, South Desert, and The Hartnet Desert. This is empty, little-known country. A complex of low mesas, volcanic intrusions, and great cathedrals of Entrada Sandstone is surrounded by a huge expanse of what most would judge to be wasteland: purple bentonite hills in the Morrison Formation, and the other-worldly gray badlands of the Mancos Shale. Roads reach Cathedral Valley from three directions: from the top of Thousand Lake Mountain, dropping down into the desert just north of where the Fold plunges from underneath the plateau, full-blown and headed south; along the rim of South Desert from an easy ford of the Fremont River about 11 miles east of the Visitor Center on Utah 24; and from Caineville, through the Mancos moonscape to lower Cathedral Valley.

These huge valleys, often treeless and sometimes even shrubless, are wide open to the sun. Most visitors do little hiking, although short rambles around the temples and buttes are essential to begin to feel their size. South Desert is a good place for horses. And to hikers who seek a pure desert experience, these flats offer solitude, silence, aridity, eeriness, and stark beauty.

Golden Navajo Sandstone crowned by reddish Carmel make up the Golden Throne.

The Entrada of these valleys is soft-layered sandstone that bears little resemblance to the massive cliff-forming Entrada Members at Arches National Park. Its soft ledges erode easily; but hard, white Curtis caps give cathedrals an edge on survival that allows them to remain for a time after the surrounding mass of sandstone has washed away.

The flanks of Thousand Lake Mountain drain through the heights of the Fold to South Desert. Several drainages make rewarding walks, but isolation from trail heads and many miles without water make them challenging. Deep Creek and Water Canyon are spectacular examples of these cross-country wilderness routes.

The East Side of the Fold

The Capitol Reef Scenic Drive gives a good first look at the Waterpocket Fold. The Fremont River Highway leads through its breadth. But to grasp its incredible scale, only the drive down its east side suffices.

For 75 miles south of the Fremont, the Fold divides Utah in two. Its cliffs yawn back toward the High Plateau horizon; then farther south they shield the Escalante canyons. The good dirt Notom Road reaches far south along the Fold, eventually veering off to Bullfrog Basin on Lake Powell. The Burr Trail road cuts up and over the Fold from Upper Hall's Creek. Lower Hall's Creek, perhaps the most exquisite place in the park, can be reached only on foot.

This long escarpment breaks naturally into sections. To the west between the Fremont River and Notom (about 4 miles) rise the already familiar high points of the Reef—dominated by the Golden Throne. From Pleasant Creek to Oak Creek (about 10 miles), four washes (Burro, Cottonwood, Fivemile, and Sheets) head in the Fold and drain outward to where the road crosses them. Hikers can enter each from the road; all have high cliffs, pockets of life, alcoves, narrows, and tantalizing glimpses of color gleaming off desert varnish. Sheets Wash actually pierces the Fold in a 1,000-foot canyon, and can be hiked.

Oak Creek runs perennially and irrigates fields at Sandy Ranch. From there to Bitter Creek Divide (about 11 miles), the road leaves the open country and enters a gradually narrowing passage between high Tarantula Mesa on the east and the Fold on the west. A simple campground (tables, toilet, no water) at Cedar Mesa forms the trail head for the 4-mile round-trip walk to Red Canyon, an enormous box canyon.

The Bitter Creek Divide area is a good one for flowers. Hood phlox makes cushions of white-blossomed green under junipers; Indian paintbrush puts out its outrageous crimsons and orange-reds; sego lilies wave delicately in white, yellow, and even lavender clusters. Cliffrose wafts its charms downwind: the fragrance of its nectar is the perfume of the canyons.

Hall's Creek begins at this divide, and flows southward for almost 40 miles to Lake Powell. It slices through soft formations at the base of the Fold, creating the "strike valley" that is controlled by the parallel layers, which here are tilted their steepest at 70°. Eight miles below the Divide, the Burr Trail heads west, zigzagging steeply up the only place where a road climbs *over* the Fold.

Views from the Burr Trail are phenomenal; although the Henry Mountains are not within Capitol Reef National Park, they dominate all views eastward along its entire length. Here they are close—just beyond the massive tops of the Mancos mesas, Tarantula and Swap. Just at the top of the Burr Trail, before the road leaves Capitol Reef for the Circle Cliffs and the town of Boulder, a wash crosses right through the heart of the Fold.

This wash, Muley Twist Canyon, is an anomaly. Like Spring Canyon to the north, it runs *in* the Fold rather than through it. The cracked Kayenta, turned almost on end, gave the canyon its start. But now it plunges between high Wingate and Navajo cliffs as well.

North of the Burr Trail is Upper Muley Twist Canyon, with its fluted little narrows, numerous arches, and superb panorama of the Fold from an overlook 3 miles up (its approach is the only section of the canyon that is open to vehicles). Beyond, the canyon leads through balds and ledges for 5 miles, where a return route climbs to the summit of the Fold for easy slickrock walking and sweeping views in every direction.

Lower Muley Twist Canyon runs 12 miles southward from the Burr Trail to Hall's Creek. This is the route taken by 1880s pioneers headed from Escalante to Hall's Crossing on the Colorado. The canyon owes its name to these early travelers, who claimed that the narrows were so tight that their mules had to twist to get through. A route leads out from Lower Muley Twist about 4 miles down, up and over the Fold to The Post. Those who hike the entire canyon return to The Post through the greasewood of dry and open Upper Hall's Creek.

The Post—once a cowboy camp—lies 2.5 miles below the Burr Trail road. From The Post the road swings eastward, never to return to the Hall's Creek Gorge. The Post is hikers' last chance to enter Hall's Creek easily. Hall's lower canyon is worth weeks of their time; from The Post down to the lake, side canyons that drain the great Navajo whaleback of its flood waters turn up about every mile. Each has its own hidden potholes, springs, desert-varnished walls, traces of pioneer roads. Near The Post are Surprise and Headquarters canyons. Not far south are Cottonwood, Willow, and Muley tanks.

This is Capitol Reef's climax, and, fittingly, it is wild, rugged, and difficult to reach. The road toward Bullfrog swings back one last time to an overlook high above Hall's Creek Gorge, and a maintained trail heads down this cliff to Brimhall Double Bridge—an impressive span seen from the viewpoint. To the south lies Hall's Creek Narrows, where the creek has sliced back into the Fold, carving a huge canyon in the Navajo Sandstone. Seek the advice of rangers if you want to hike this most remote section of the park. Distances are great, water is sparse, and the heat in summer is intense.

But it is the intensity of the experiences that draws us. Books only whet appetites for the real thing. No matter how fine the photograph or how clever the writing, they cannot match a single juniper for vividness. The *distinctness* of scaly leaves and rough-barked limbs—as opposed to generalizations about ecology; the stubborn craziness of balanced rocks, their powerful unlikelihood—as opposed to dense geologic history: this is the *reality* of Capitol Reef.

This is why we protect the park. This is why we come here.

Opposite: The Henry Mountains, at about 10,000 feet, flank the park's eastern boundary.

CARLSBAD
CAVERNS
NATIONAL PARK

Stalagmites build upward from cave floors in spires composed of calcified water drops.

CARLSBAD CAVERNS NATIONAL PARK
3225 NATIONAL PARKS HIGHWAY
CARLSBAD, NEW MEXICO 88220, TEL.: (505) 785-2232

Highlights: New Cave □ Walnut Canyon □ Rattlesnake Canyon The Big Room □ Iceberg Rock □ Green Lake Room □ King's Palace □ Queen's Chamber □ Papoose Room

Access: From Carlsbad, 27 miles south on U.S. 62/180 and New Mexico 7. See map on pages 166–167.

Hours: Daily, year-round, except Christmas. No overnight stopping in park.

Fees: Carlsbad Cavern, adults $4, children (6–15) $2, under 6 free. New Cave, adults $5, under 16 $3. Golden Age, Golden Access passes, 50 percent discount.

Parking: At Visitor Center.

Gas, food: In Whites City and Carlsbad. Food available in park.

Lodging: In Whites City and Carlsbad.

Visitor Center: In summer, 8 A.M.–8 P.M.; all other seasons; 8:00 A.M.–5:30 P.M. Exhibits and talks; nursery care for infants.

Museum: Exhibits in Visitor Center.

Gift shop: In Visitor Center.

Pets: Permitted on leash in some areas; kennel available. Some trails suitable for horses; no rentals; bring own feed and water. Holding pen available. Register in Visitor Center.

Picnicking: At Rattlesnake Springs and near Visitor Center.

Hiking: Permitted. Carry water.

Backpacking: Permitted west of Visitor Center, permit required. Must be .25 mile from road and out of sight to camp, and must carry water.

Campgrounds: None in park. Private campground at park entrance.

Tours: Self-guided tours in Carlsbad Cavern during summer and weekends during winter; ranger-guided tours in New Cave (reservation required). Guided trips through main corridor and scenic rooms on weekdays during portions of winter season.

Other activities: Nature walks, evening bat flight program in summer.

Facilities for disabled: Access to Visitor Center, restaurant, part of Cavern.

For additional information, see also Sites, Trails, and Trips on pages 178–182.

THE BROAD DESERTS OF WESTERN TEXAS AND SOUTHeastern New Mexico strike the car-borne visitor as an ocean that may take days to cross. The judgment is right, albeit a little late in geologic terms, for the land was formed from sediments of a great sea. Like landfall, the horizon is broken in places by mountains, each a geologic event in itself. One group, the Guadalupe Mountains and the Capitan reef formation, which stretches southward from present-day Carlsbad, New Mexico, was a huge reef complex. Today, it is one of the greatest fossil reefs on earth, and carved into it is Carlsbad Cavern, an interior window into a strange and fascinating world.

Slaughter Canyon and the rugged desert country above Carlsbad Caverns.

165

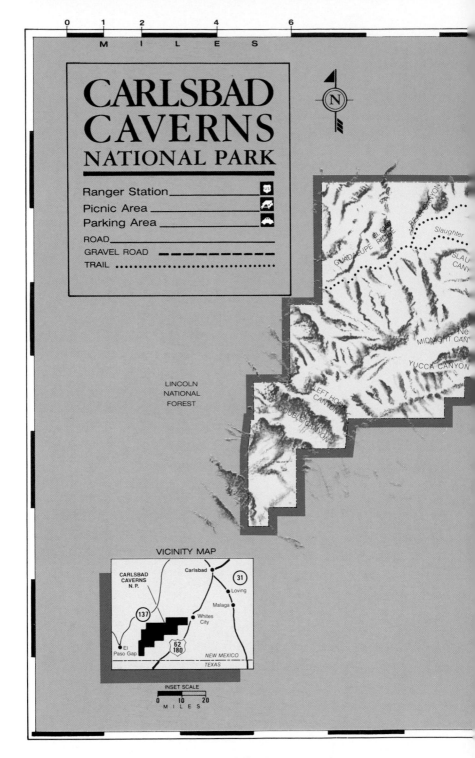

CARLSBAD CAVERNS
NATIONAL PARK

Ranger Station _____ ⬛US
Picnic Area _____
Parking Area _____

ROAD _____
GRAVEL ROAD – – – – – – – –
TRAIL ••••••••••••••••••••••

N

BEAR CANYON
GUADALUPE RIDGE
El 6368 RIDGE
Slaughter
SLAU CANY
Ne
MIDNIGHT CAN
YUCCA CANYON
LEFT HORSE CANYON
DOUBLE CANYON

LINCOLN
NATIONAL
FOREST

VICINITY MAP

CARLSBAD
CAVERNS
N. P.
Carlsbad
31
Loving
Malaga
137
Whites
City
62
180
El
Paso Gap
NEW MEXICO
TEXAS

INSET SCALE
0   10   20
M I L E S

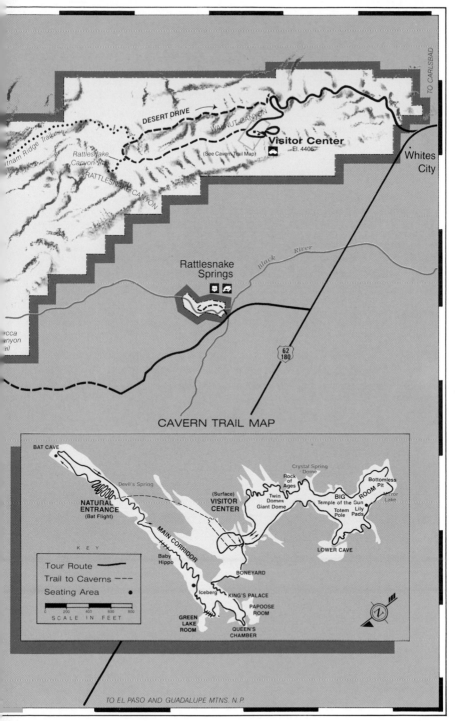

TO CARLSBAD

DESERT DRIVE

WALNUT CANYON

Visitor Center
El. 4406'

(See Cavern Trail Map)

Whites City

Putnam Ridge Trail

Rattlesnake Canyon Trail

RATTLESNAKE CANYON

Rattlesnake Springs

Black River

Yucca Canyon Trail

62 180

CAVERN TRAIL MAP

BAT CAVE

Devil's Spring

NATURAL ENTRANCE
(Bat Flight)

(Surface)
VISITOR CENTER

Crystal Spring Dome

Rock of Ages

Twin Domes
Giant Dome

Temple of the Sun

BIG ROOM

Bottomless Pit

Mirror Lake

Totem Pole

Lily Pads

LOWER CAVE

MAIN CORRIDOR

K E Y

Baby Hippo

BONEYARD

Tour Route
Trail to Caverns
Seating Area

Iceberg

KING'S PALACE

PAPOOSE ROOM

0 200 400 600 800
SCALE IN FEET

GREEN LAKE ROOM

QUEEN'S CHAMBER

N

TO EL PASO AND GUADALUPE MTNS. N.P.

Discovery

There is some evidence that Native Americans lived around Carlsbad Cavern, but little is known of their identity or of what they did here. Mescal-roasting pits are nearby, one just a few feet from the cavern entrance, and pictographs are on the entrance wall; moccasins, debris, and even skeletons reportedly were found during the early explorations of the caverns, but records were not carefully maintained and most of that original information is lost, if indeed it was accurate at all. Since they did not have modern exploration equipment, the Indians probably could not have entered the main part of the cave, so it seems safe to assume that their ramblings were kept to the outside, which, all things considered, probably was a safe distance. Here was a cave that they could not enter, yet one from which each evening there came a whirlwind of millions of bats that spiraled upward for hours.

It was this bat flight that led modern explorers to the cave. As with most things, the precise "first" is lost in vagueness occasionally tinged with controversy. In one story, while a father and his son were seeking a lost calf, they saw and heard the black cloud of bats swooshing from the cave entrance. In another—this one recorded rather than legend—a cowboy named Jim White discovered the caverns. In any case, by the 1890s, folks living in Carlsbad knew about the bats. And they took advantage of what the bats left behind.

Mining

What the bats left in "Bat Cave" was an enormous deposit of guano. The dry, powdery accumulation of centuries of bat dung beneath a roosting area was and still is one of the richest natural fertilizers known. California was just then developing its citrus industry, so it was not long before mining claims were filed and operations were begun. None of this was particularly startling, since other caves in the area—there are over seventy just in Carlsbad Caverns National Park—were being mined for guano. Nor was the operation itself unusual; a shaft was punched directly into the "Bat Room" and men and equipment were lowered in buckets. In a 20-year span, more than 100,000 tons of guano were removed.

Exploration

There was nothing on the surface to suggest that this one cave was any different from any other, until Jim White, cowboy turned guano miner, began to explore it during his off-hours. Today, with electric lights, paved trails, and foreknowledge, it is difficult to recapture the awe of those early explorers as they crawled and climbed and saw hints of what captivates present-day visitors. Their torches and later inefficient, smoky kerosene lanterns were Aladdin's lamps that lit up a new world. White led the way—he spent twenty years exploring, building trails, and escorting visitors—but professionals soon followed.

The guano business began to fade as transportation costs rose, but a thriving tourist industry, crude at first, became increasingly successful. Visitors rode down in the old guano mining buckets, and, with some difficulty, clambered through the cave. Today's approximately 800,000 visitors must remind themselves that the easy paths are actually the result of careful engineering and construction. The cavern was not designed for humans!

Establishment of the Park

The fame of the huge cavern spread. On October 25, 1923, President Calvin Coolidge designated it a national monument. Shortly thereafter, the National Geographic Society published an extensive article in its magazine (January 1924), and the fame of the cavern spread even more. In 1930, Carlsbad Caverns became a national park.

Early tourists descend into the caverns in guano buckets.

Reconstructing an ancient landscape from clues—most of them tiny, uncoded, and constantly churned by subsequent geological events—is not easy. A few have done it for the joy of the puzzle, and some, more recently, because of oil potential. Each investigator has uncovered a small piece of the earth's history.

The entrance to the cave was once a vertical drop of over 30 feet. Now a paved path bypasses the drop-off and descends steeply past the massive bedded rocks that loom like a large forehead over the entrance. Except for one other small, inaccessible crevice, this is the only natural entrance to the cave known today, but there may have been other openings that have since been sealed. Pleistocene animal bones have been found in areas that animals would have difficulty reaching by today's routes.

The Reef

Two hundred million years ago, the mountains out of which Carlsbad Cavern was hollowed were a reef. It was not the coral reef familiar from South Sea pictures, but a kind of reef that has no exact parallel in the world today. This reef was not at the surface, near the shore, but formed at the lip of the shelf, where the long downslope from the shore seaward broke and dropped sharply toward the depths. Here, in some places at depths of as much as 600 feet, the reef formed.

Huge numbers of tiny plants and animals lived on, in, and around one another. Some contributed their shells or skeletons to the material that would eventually become the structure of the reef. Lime was precipitated from the sea water, forming limestone that in some places has much more cement than material cemented together. Sediment washing in from the land slowly piled behind this barrier and grew on itself until it reached nearly to the surface of the water, and in some places above it.

The rock found at the cave entrance is part of the Tansill Formation. A small chip examined under a microscope would reveal the remains of tiny algae called *Dasycladaceae*. Today *Dasycladaceae* live only in very shallow, warm seas, and almost certainly they did so when this reef was formed. Other microscopic animals whose fossils are found here, the crinoids, for example, were constructed of tiny barrel-like segments attached end to end to form "stems." When the animals died, these segments easily came apart and scattered, yet here complete fossils can be found; the water must have been still. This area was the lagoon behind the reef. A line of stalactites on the cave wall marks the

The China Wall in New Cave, which is a lateral cave surveyed as 1.25 miles long.

spot where the back-reef sediments meet the reef itself.

On the open side are fossils of creatures that need well-agitated, aerated water, provided by the currents and waves of the open sea meeting the reef. Typically for reefs, this outer face was steep. Pieces broke off and fell, forming a talus slope, or pile of debris against the face of the reef, which combined with sediment that was washing over as well. It appears that this consolidated debris sloped down to the depths at an angle of perhaps 30°. Today visitors walk on this talus, which is well exposed near the Bottomless Pit in the Big Room.

The depth of the sea was considerable. (Look eastward at the desert below the reef to get the idea.) There was little deep circulation and little or no oxygen at the bottom. Organic matter that filtered down from above did not decay but began the long and still only partly understood process that leads to oil.

Cave Formation

It took eons, but as the climate changed, sediments washing down from surrounding highlands actually filled the sea as it slowly evaporated. The region became a broad plain, with the reef buried at one edge of it. Animals and plants spread across the plain; it seemed permanent.

Just a few million years ago, during the late Cretaceous period, the area was uplifted. Sometime during the process, strains cracked the great reef. Now ground water worked along the cracks. The water had absorbed carbon dioxide from the air and from organic material near the surface to become an extremely dilute carbonic acid that dissolved and carried away the reef rock. The cracks became corridors and even rooms. Although the cave seems random at first visit, it does have a certain pattern born of its geologic past. The fractures were roughly at right angles to each other, and the modern corridors and rooms are at that angle. This is obvious at the place called the Top of the Cross in the Big Room. Vertically the cave seems to have three main tiers, at 200 feet, 750 feet, and 830 feet below ground level, which suggests that the water stayed at these levels for long periods of time. Patches of what the cave was like at first are exposed at the Boneyard. It resembled a giant limestone sponge, shot through with solution pockets. As the water receded, some of the spongelike rock collapsed, creating larger chambers.

Cave Decoration

Once the cave was above the water, air entered and the "decoration phase" began. Indeed, it continues today. The features that visitors wander among, the fantasy-inducing stalactites and curtains and dams and flowstone, are still being formed by the action of dripping water. Drops of water, each carrying a tiny load of dissolved limestone, work slowly through the rock. When a drop reaches the air—the void in the cave—the pressure on the drop is reduced, and in a reaction that can be duplicated in the laboratory, carbon dioxide is released into the air and

Opposite: The white-hooded Klansman, one of the most famous Carlsbad attractions.

the tiny load of limestone is deposited at that spot. This explains why those stalactites are in a line where the back-reef sediments meet the main reef. The water was working its way along that joint, and it left the line of stalactites where it reached the void of the cave.

The process is slow; the ages involved in the geological time charts are beyond comprehension. At Carlsbad, although the cave decoration takes place during a much lesser time period, one's sense is stretched to comprehend it by the visible evidence of an eon of occasional drops slowly materializing and disappearing in the dark. One hundred million such reactions may build a small stalagmite, but some formations are huge; the Giant Dome is over 60 feet high.

The forms of decorations vary widely, depending on conditions when the limestone precipitated. A stalactite hanging from the ceiling has had an overhead supply of calcite-laden water drops. If enough drops fall and splash on the floor, a stalagmite will begin to build upward. It will be wider than the stalactite because of the water's splash. A stalactite and its stalagmite may meet to form a column.

Some forms are tiny. For reasons that are not yet understood, calcite sometimes precipitates in a beautiful crystalline form, aragonite. Epsonite needles are even more delicate. Perhaps most remarkable of all the forms are helictites, tiny stalks that may grow down or up or sideways. Their water passages are so tiny that the water droplets are affected by forces other than gravity, and the particular crystals involved have random ways of stacking. A helictite can look like a snake dancer or a corkscrew.

There are draperies that can be small or large; the Whale's Mouth is a spectacular collection. Some pools of water in the cave contain formations that look like stone water lilies. Other small pools have small, rare spheres at the bottom called "cave pearls."

The large areas of "popcorn" in the cave tell something else about the cave's history, but researchers are not yet quite sure what. If some geologists are correct in supposing that popcorn is a carbonate precipitated out of water, these extensive deposits indicate that there were repeated floodings of the cave, some for geologic periods of time. These hypothesized refloodings are held responsible, too, for the large gypsum deposits in the cave. In places the trail cuts through these massive deposits, and spectacular vertical tubes remain where dripping water has cut away the soft gypsum. Other scientists are troubled by the "precipitated during reflooding" explanation, though. There is a huge amount of gypsum, and its placement is not easy to explain in terms of precipitation. And the popcorn *may* be the result of a process that happened in the air, not under water. Research goes on.

The Landscape

The shape of the land within the park has created wide variations in temperature, sunlight, soil, and moisture, all of which, in turn, are responsible for life forms in just as wide a variety. On the flatlands near the base of the Guadalupe Mountains are creosote bush and desert shrubs. In the canyons, where there is more moisture, black walnut, oak, desert willow, and hackberry flourish. Canyon walls and ridge tops are covered with agave, yucca, sotol, ocotillo, and desert grasses. On the higher elevations are juniper, Texas madrone, and pine. More than 600 plant species have been identified.

Wildlife

Carlsbad Caverns National Park, although most famous for its tremendous cavern, has within its confines an abundance of mammals, desert reptiles, and birds. Ground squirrels, raccoons, skunks, kit foxes, jack rabbits, and gophers move through the brush, often at night (as do most desert animals). There are snakes, but visitors rarely see them, for they are both secretive and usually nocturnal. Lizards abound, fascinating small children from other parts of the country where these reptiles may not be common. More than 200 species of birds have been identified in the park; perhaps most spectacular are the turkey vulture and the occasional golden eagle. Mule deer are plentiful; visitors should be careful when driving park roads at dawn and dusk. Appearing less often are bobcats, coyotes, badgers, even mountain lions. While each of these animals goes about seeking a living in the scrub vegetation on the surface, it is a certain small mammal that lives in the cave that visitors ask about most often.

Bats

Besides the fantasyland of the cavern, one of the chief attractions of Carlsbad Caverns National Park is the nightly bat flight. Each evening, starting at sundown and continuing for about an hour, the cave's entire population of bats (except for babies, which remain clinging to the ceiling) comes swirling out in what appears to be a black whirlwind. Formerly the population was several million, but it has declined, apparently as a result of pesticides that the bats ingest with their nightly feast of insects. It is now estimated to be about 300,000—still enough to consume perhaps three tons of insects nightly!

Bats use a remarkable location-finding device that is comparable to

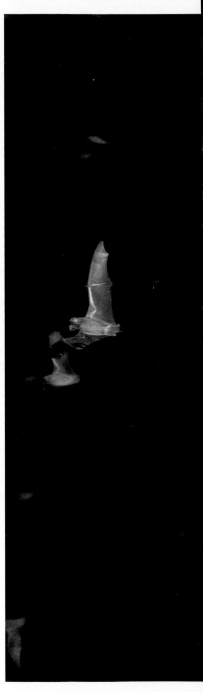

Top: A Mexican freetail bat, about four inches long. Above: Fossilized bat. Right: Bats in flight.

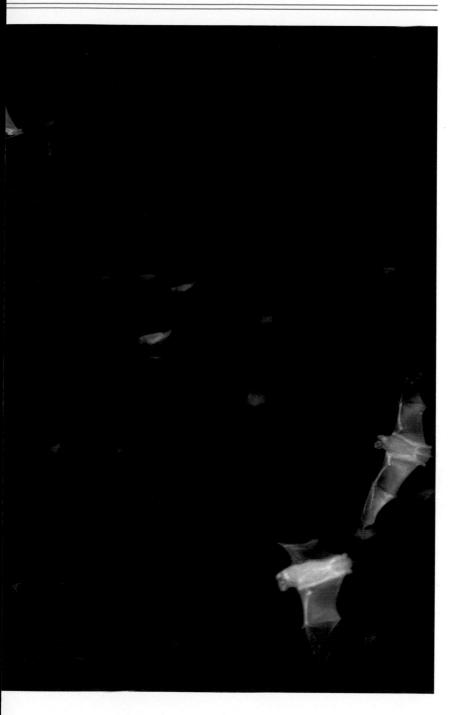

the sonar used by submarines, but much more precise. While flying, bats emit a very high sound and actually detect flying insects by their echo. The bats at Carlsbad spend the night ranging the area and, about dawn, reenter the cave with spectacular dives from several hundred feet up. Every evening throughout the summer (the bats migrate to Mexico for the winter), visitors can enjoy a ranger-conducted program at the entrance to the cave that culminates in the bat flight.

SITES, TRAILS, AND TRIPS

Carlsbad Cavern

There are two ways to enter Carlsbad Cavern. Both are equally fascinating, one for man's engineering ability, and the other for nature's eerie charm. For those who choose to take an easy, convenient trip, elevators in the Visitor Center descend to the Big Room, 750 feet below. The full tour begins at the "natural" entrance and winds its way down for 1¾ miles to the Big Room. Both tours return to the Visitor Center by way of the elevators.

The natural entrance was the one first discovered and the one from which the bats take their nightly flight. The "complete" tour enters there, passes the huge side chamber in which the bats congregate during the day, and then descends sharply into the cavern to the Big Room. The first .5 mile or so of the path is devoid of the familiar stalactites and stalagmites that are usually associated with caverns. Carlsbad's fantasyland becomes evident a little farther along, however, as the trail levels off at about 830 feet beneath the surface and enters the Scenic Rooms. Visitors must circumnavigate, so to speak, the great Iceberg Rock, a gigantic chunk of rock that many eons ago crashed through the network of caves then being formed; much of the descending trail follows the path of the fall of the Iceberg.

In the cavern proper, stalactites are abundant—virtually an inverted forest of them—and on the floor are the strange, stone toadstools that geologists say came from minerals in waters now long gone. Passing through the Green Lake Room, the King's Palace, the Queen's Chamber, and the Papoose Room, and by a number of remarkable formations, the trail leads to the elevators and to those who selected the easy way down. Visitors can have a quick lunch before entering one of the most incredible sites of all.

The Big Room. The Big Room cannot be seen all at once; indeed, on first entering, spectators will find this huge chamber deceptively small.

Upper left: Aragonite crystals. Upper right: Blue stalactites. Bottom: New Cave, which was not discovered until 1937.

Trails of Carlsbad Caverns National Park

Carlsbad Cavern Trail: Starts at natural entrance; ends at Big Room; 3 miles; 3 hours; 830-foot descent; descent through three levels of cave; limestone features, including stalactites, stalagmites, and helictites; evening bat flight.

Rattlesnake Canyon Trail*: Starts at Walnut Canyon loop road; ends at mouth of Rattlesnake Canyon; 1.5 miles one way; 2 hours; 1,000-foot descent; rugged, rocky hike into desert backcountry; desert vegetation.

Putnam Ridge Trail*: Starts at Walnut Canyon loop road; ends at Putnam Cabin; 10 miles one way, 8–10 hours; 2,000-foot ascent; gradual climb to highest point in park through heart of wilderness area; most of hike is along top of ridge.

Slaughter Canyon Trail*: Starts at Putnam Ridge Trail; ends at New Cave parking area; 4.5 miles one way; 6 hours; 2,000-foot descent; rugged trail passes below the entrance to New Cave, which is 500 feet up the side of the canyon.

Yucca Canyon Trail*: Starts at Slaughter Canyon Trail; ends at Yucca Canyon; 2 miles one way; 3 hours; 1,000-foot ascent; climbs to the top of an escarpment.

*Backcountry trails are primitive and undeveloped and should be hiked after planning and with care.

See map on pages 166–167.

Above: An unusual stalactite formation in Carlsbad Cavern.
Opposite: A narrow ridge separates North Double Canyon from South Double Canyon. Double Cave runs through this ridge and has an entrance in each canyon.

Once the immensity takes hold of the imagination, however, a six-story-tall stalagmite—alongside which one may be standing—is dwarfed by its surroundings. The Big Room could house fourteen football fields; in one corner could sit the nation's Capitol, dome and all. Awesome hardly begins a description.

The cavern temperature stays at 56° F year-round. Although this temperature may seem comfortable at first, after several hours below, 56° becomes chilly. A sweater or jacket is recommended. And for the walk from the natural entrance, shoes with good traction soles are recommended.

New Cave

The Guadalupe Mountains are laced with caves, and each, in its own way, is just as exciting as Carlsbad. All the caves that are within the national park boundaries are protected and restricted, however, and for very good reason. Many are still unexplored, still to yield their treasures, and are just as dangerous as was Carlsbad when it was first discovered. Most are closed to the public, but a few can be entered with a special permit.

New Cave is 23 miles from the park Visitor Center; the last few miles of road are gravel. There is a hike of about .5 mile rising 500 feet, which makes it seem a lot longer. Access is only with a pre-arranged tour led by a park ranger.

Above Ground

Walnut Canyon Loop Drive. A 9.5-mile, one-way, gravel road leads away from the Visitor Center parking lot into Walnut Canyon and eventually loops around to the main entrance road. This is a pleasant, 45-minute drive into desert-canyon country.

Desert Nature Walk. A .5-mile nature walk that begins at the Visitor Center presents a pleasant diversion for visitors who are waiting for the evening bat-flight program. Desert plants and flowers are identified.

Backcountry Hiking. Most people visit Carlsbad to see the cavern and not the general terrain. There are old ranch trails, however, and desert hiking is permitted; but these trails are not marked, as are those in other parks. This land is much like that at Guadalupe Mountains National Park, and with proper preparation, maps, and advice from park rangers, hikers can make some exciting excursions into the desert wilderness.

Opposite: Stone draperies, 60 feet high, form a false wall in the Sequoia Room.

GRAND
CANYON
NATIONAL PARK

GRAND CANYON NATIONAL PARK, BOX 129
GRAND CANYON, ARIZONA 86023
TEL.: (602) 638-7888

Highlights: South Rim □ North Rim □ Inner Gorge □ Tusayan Ruins and Museum □ Yavapai Point □ Hopi Point □ Yaki Point Bright Angel Point □ Walhalla Overlook □ Hermits Rest □ Tuweep □ Cape Royal

Access: For South Rim, from Tusayan (airport), 7 miles via Arizona 64. From Flagstaff, 89 miles via Arizona 64 and I-40. From Williams, 59 miles via Arizona 64. For North Rim, from Jacob Lake, 45 miles via Arizona 67. From Kanab, Utah, 81 miles via Arizona 67. See map on pages 188–189.

Hours: South Rim, daily, 24 hours, year-round. North Rim, daily, 24 hours, May to October.

Fees: Entrance, $5/vehicle; camping, $6.

Parking: Ample at public-use points.

Gas, food: Throughout park, and at nearby towns.

Lodging: In park: cabins, motel units, and hotels. Write well in advance.

Visitor Center: In Grand Canyon Village. Exhibit area, auditorium, bookstore, information desk. Talks and slide program.

Museums: Yavapai Geology Museum and Tusayan Archeological Museum.

Gift shop: General store in Mather Center and at other areas.

Pets: Permitted on leash, but not on trails. Kennel available on South Rim only. Horseback riding permitted; rentals available with guided tour on both rims; private stock needs permit.

Picnicking: At designated areas.

Hiking: Permitted. Carry water.

Backpacking: Permits needed and must be obtained well in advance. Water sources intermittent; check with backcountry reservations office near Mather campground and on North Rim.

Campgrounds: North Rim, 82 sites, first-come basis. South Rim, Desert View and Mather, first-come basis except in summer, when reservations necessary. Trailer Village, full hookups and bath facilities. Showers available.

Tours: On South Rim throughout the year; on North Rim in summer. In English. Private guides available for backcountry tours.

Other activities: Mule trips; river tours; sightseeing flights.

Facilities for disabled: At many public-use points. When making reservations, please specify needs. Special brochure available.

For additional information, see also Sites, Trails, and Trips on pages 205–216 and the maps on pages 188–189 and 214–215.

THE GRAND CANYON IS A LAND OF DAZZLING EXtremes that encompasses four life zones, ranging from arid desert to moist coniferous forest. In winter, when the North Rim is blanketed by 140 inches of snow, the weather inside the canyon is mild. Over millions of years, the great Colorado River, which bisects the canyon, has performed one of the most stupendous feats of erosion in geological history. Aided by the uplift of the land and by other geological factors, the river has cut down thousands of feet through sheer rock to form, in John Van Dyke's words, "Nature's most colossal piece of stage-setting." Many different rock strata lie exposed, varying in age and composition from the metamorphic Vishnu Schist of the Inner Gorge to the sedimentary layers of the Kaibab and Toroweap formations. Making a home along the sheer face of the canyon are almost 90 species of mammals and 287 species of birds, ranging in size from shrews and hummingbirds to mountain lions and turkey vultures.

The buttes and temples of the North Rim as seen from Maricopa Point.

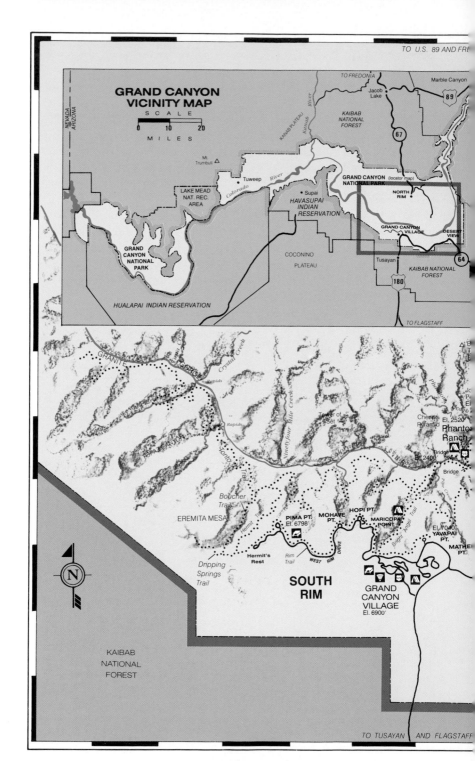

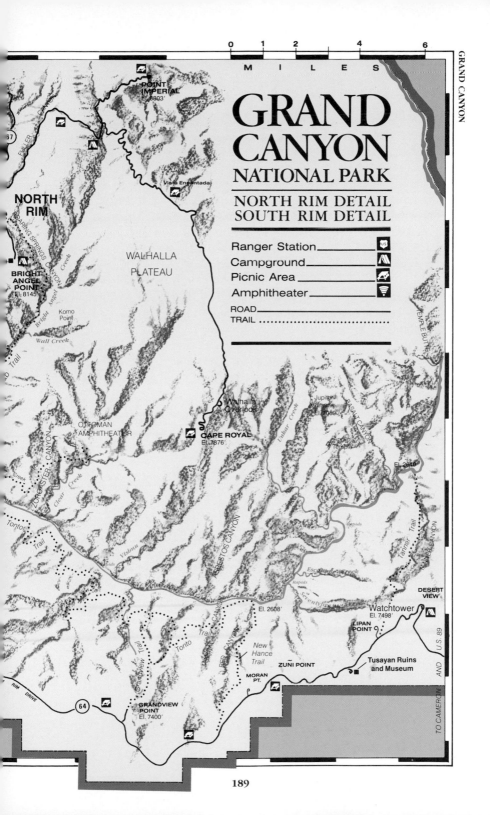

GRAND CANYON NATIONAL PARK

NORTH RIM DETAIL
SOUTH RIM DETAIL

Ranger Station	🇺🇸
Campground	🏕
Picnic Area	🏞
Amphitheater	📢

ROAD

TRAIL

NORTH
RIM

WALHALLA
PLATEAU

POINT
IMPERIAL
El. 8803'

Vista Encantada

BRIGHT
ANGEL
POINT
El. 8145'

Komo
Point

Wall Creek

Walhalla
Overlook

OTTOMAN
AMPHITHEATER

CAPE ROYAL
El. 7876'

Jupiter
Temple
El. 7089'

BASALT CANYON

Apollo
Temple

El. 2810'
Rapids

ZOROASTER CANYON

Clear Creek

Tonto
Trail

Rapids

Vishnu

Rapids

ASBESTOS CANYON

Tanner Trail

Escalante Creek

Rapids

Seventyfive Mile

El. 2608'

DESERT
VIEW

Watchtower
El. 7498'

LIPAN
POINT

Grandview Trail

Tonto
Trail

RED CANYON

New
Hance
Trail

ZUNI POINT

Tusayan Ruins
and Museum

MORAN
PT.

RIM   DRIVE

64

GRANDVIEW
POINT
El. 7400'

TO CAMERON   AND   U.S. 89

189

First Inhabitants

In 1933, archeologists discovered a number of split-twig figurines—apparently representations of animals—inside caves within the Grand Canyon. These figurines were to alter archeologists' chronology of the human habitation of the canyon, pushing the known dates back to at least 2,000 years before Christ. These first inhabitants probably were hunters and gatherers from the deserts to the west; scholars do not know how long they stayed in the canyon, or why they left.

Prior to the discovery of the figurines, the earliest known inhabitants of the canyon were thought to have been the Anasazi, who entered the region around A.D. 500, during the Basketmaker phase of their culture. In addition to hunting, they cultivated corn and squash. By A.D. 1000, their culture had evolved to include the manufacture of pottery, the use of intensive cultivation methods, and the construction of pueblo dwellings.

The Cohonina, originally from what is now west-central Arizona, settled on the South Rim of the canyon around A.D. 700. Their material culture was strikingly similar to that of the Anasazi, although their social and religious life probably was very different.

Theodore Roosevelt designated the Grand Canyon a national monument in 1908.

Around 1150, due to prolonged drought, the Grand Canyon was abandoned by both the Anasazi and the Cohonina. About 150 years later, the Cerbat migrated to the South Rim from the deserts of the lower Colorado River. These hunters and gatherers (who also practiced agriculture) lived in rock shelters and brush wickiups on the Coconino Plateau and in the tributary canyons. The Cerbat were the direct ancestors of the Hualapai and the Havasupai, two tribes that still live in the western reaches of the canyon.

Also around 1300, ancestors of the present-day Southern Paiute settled in the heavily forested regions of the North Rim and its tributary canyons. They moved into old Anasazi ruins, mingling their artifacts with those already there and giving archeologists more material over which to puzzle.

Spanish Exploration

The Cardenas expedition of 1540 brought white explorers to the canyon for the first time. The Spaniards spent three days looking for a path down to the Colorado River before finally giving up.

Two hundred years later, another Spaniard passed through the region. In 1776, while the American colonists on the eastern shore of the continent were struggling for independence, a Franciscan padre named Francisco Tomás Garcés traveled alone from the lower Colorado River Valley into the country of the Havasupai at the western end of the canyon. After spending time with the natives, he traveled to the Hopi villages, where he was coldly rebuffed in his effort to spread the Word of God. Undeterred, Father Garcés returned to the Havasupai, who welcomed him with six days of feasting.

In the same year, two other Franciscan fathers, Francisco Atanasia Domínguez and Sylvestre Vélez de Escalante, started out from Santa Fe to find an overland route between New Mexico and California. They traveled a difficult path north through the Rocky Mountains and west into present-day Utah before turning south and crossing the Colorado River in Glen Canyon and circling back to Santa Fe. Although they did not actually see the canyon, Domínguez and Escalante helped to pioneer a route across the northern section of the region that later explorers and settlers would follow.

American Exploration

The first Americans to see the Grand Canyon were the intrepid mountain men—the fur trappers and traders whose wanderlust opened up many areas of the West. In 1826, a character named James Ohio Pattie may have passed through the region. Unlike most mountain men, Pattie was literate, and he kept a journal, which makes gloomy mention of the "horrid mountains" he encountered at Grand Canyon.

It was the mid-nineteenth century before news of the discovery traveled to the rest of the world. By the terms of the Treaty of Guadalupe Hidalgo of 1848, following the Mexican War, the future states of New Mexico, Arizona, and California became United States territories. During the 1850s, the federal government sent surveying parties led by military officers to map the new terrain, specifically to locate routes for future railroads. The most interesting of these expeditions, as far as the Grand Canyon is concerned, was led by Lieutenant Joseph Ives. In 1857, Ives and his party chugged up the Colorado River in a sternwheeler called *Explorer*. At Black Canyon, near the spot where the Hoover Dam now stands, the *Explorer* struck a sunken rock, and Ives had to abandon the damaged steamer. The party continued overland, into the depths of the "Big Cañon." While Ives admired the beauty of the place, he was pessimistic about its usefulness. "The region is, of course, altogether valueless," he said in his report. "Ours has been the first, and will doubtless be the last, party of whites to visit this profitless locality."

Prospectors and Tourists

After the explorers came the prospectors, in a pattern that characterized much of the development of the West. In the 1870s and 1880s, sizable deposits of lead, zinc, copper, and asbestos were found in the canyon, and enterprising miners staked out claims down in the depths. The difficulties of extracting the ore and transporting it to the rim were the main reasons that mining at the Grand Canyon was never very successful. By the early 1900s, most mines had been abandoned. The discovery of uranium at Orphan Mine near Powell Memorial Point in the 1950s stimulated new activity. In 1987, the claim at Orphan Mine will revert to the National Park Service.

Around the turn of the century, the sensibility of many Americans toward their natural heritage began to change. They began to realize that there was a dimension to the land other than the economic one. Artists like Thomas Moran and writers like Clarence Dutton and John Van Dyke depicted the Grand Canyon in terms that had far more to do with aesthetics than with utility.

In response to this shift in attitude, a whole new industry evolved. In the 1890s, the Bright Angel Trail was completed, enabling tourists to walk or ride down to the spacious mantle of the Tonto Plateau. J. W. Thurber's stagecoach route between Flagstaff and the South Rim was made obsolete when the Santa Fe Railroad constructed a spur from

Conservationists John Muir and John Burroughs (fourth and sixth in line) descend by mule into the canyon.

Williams in 1901. Old miners soon came to see great potential in this new source of gold, and they build accommodations like Bass Camp and the Grand View Hotel. The Age of Tourism had begun.

A settlement of sorts, later to be known as Grand Canyon Village, sprang up on the South Rim. The El Tovar Hotel was built in 1905, followed by the Hopi House, Babbitt's General Store, and Verkamp's Curios. The North Kaibab Trail was carved from the North Rim in 1903, enabling hikers to reach Rust's Camp, the forerunner of Phantom Ranch, deep in the Inner Gorge.

With the construction of Bright Angel Lodge in 1935 and the completion of a road system along the South Rim at about the same time, tourism increased dramatically. Grand Canyon Lodge, an imposing limestone structure, was built on the North Rim in 1928. Down below, at the mouth of Bright Angel Creek, Phantom Ranch, the hostel designed by Mary Jane Colter, was built in 1922.

The Colorado River and Its Runners

The identity of the first explorer to float the length of the Grand Canyon by boat has long been debated. James White possibly may have done so in 1867, two years before the expedition of John Wesley Powell. White kept no record of his ordeal, and his memory of it was hazy at best. Be that as it may, Major Powell's famous expedition of 1869 was one of the most important of the century. Powell's expedition, supplemented by a second trip through the canyon in 1871, filled in one of the last remaining blank spots on the map of the continental United States.

Madmen and hardy fools followed in the wake of Powell. In 1889, an ill-fated party led by Robert Brewster Stanton shoved off on an expedition to determine the feasibility of constructing a railroad along the bottom of the canyon. The trip was badly organized, and the expedition party lacked equipment; as a result, three men drowned. Other float trips followed, capped by the 1911 voyage of Ellsworth and Emery Kolb, two photographer brothers who had a studio perched on the lip of the South Rim. On their float, the Kolbs made the first film of the Grand Canyon—a flickering, sepia-tinted feature of the Inner Gorge and its ferocious rapids.

With the completion of Glen Canyon Dam upstream from Lees Ferry in 1965, some 2,000 people were known to have made the journey between the granite walls. By 1972, more than 16,000 claimed the adventure, and the Colorado River was in danger of becoming overcrowded. In response, the National Park Service laid down stringent regulations to control the number of boaters.

But the river is in danger from other quarters as well. The construc-

Sunrise after a storm over Isis Temple.

tion of Glen Canyon Dam altered the Colorado's ancient pattern of flooding and subsidence. Instead of scouring the inner walls of the canyon every spring with its annual convulsion, the river is now regulated by the dam. The Colorado is thus unable to rebuild its own eroded beaches and to cleanse the debris that washes down from tributary sources.

Establishment of the Park

In 1903, during a trip to the Grand Canyon, President Theodore Roosevelt made a speech in which he referred to the canyon as "the most impressive piece of scenery I have ever looked at." An ardent outdoorsman, Roosevelt was an early and vociferous champion of a national policy of conservation. By 1908, part of the Grand Canyon already had been declared a game preserve and a national forest. In that year, taking advantage of his powers under the Antiquities Act of 1906, Roosevelt designated the Grand Canyon a national monument. Shortly after Arizona became a state in 1912, the more complicated process of transforming the monument into a park began in earnest. Woodrow Wilson declared the Grand Canyon a national park on February 26, 1919. An act, signed into law by President Ford in 1975, almost doubled the size of the park. The new boundaries include all of the interior of the canyon, with the exception of various Indian Reservations, from the Paria River near Lees Ferry to the Grand Wash Cliffs at the western end.

A rainshower in the depths of Havasu Canyon, just outside the park.

G E O L O G Y

Vishnu Schist.

The rocks in the Grand Canyon illustrate 2 billion years of the earth's development, or nearly half of its total history. Nowhere else in the world can one look so deep into the earth's crust and so far back into the planet's evolution. "Geology is an anthology of stories," says geologist Michael Collier, "the best in the world." And the geological layers of the canyon can be read like the pages of a book.

Metamorphic and Sedimentary Rock

The canyon is primarily composed of metamorphic and sedimentary rocks. The Inner Gorge, sections of which are visible from the South Rim, contains some of the oldest exposed rock surfaces in the world. The Vishnu Schist, as this rock is called, is all that remains of a once giant mountain range that existed about 2 billion years ago during the late Precambrian era. The vertical seams of dull rose quartz in the walls of the Inner Gorge were formed by molten material from the interior of the earth that penetrated into the base of the mountain range and forced its way into cracks in the rock before cooling and hardening. Gradually, the mountains were worn down by erosion, and the great sedimentary deposits that compose the rest of the canyon were laid down on the eroded roots millions of years later.

At various times during the Precambrian era (2 billion to 600 million years ago), wide, shallow seas covered most of northern Arizona. Shell-bearing animals had not yet evolved, and the most common rock types laid down during this period were sandstone and shale. A few limestone layers were deposited by algae, which grew abundantly in these seas. About 1 billion years ago, the land in the Grand Canyon region rose above sea level, tilting northeastward as it rose. The layers that are exposed at the top of the Inner Gorge were originally deposited horizontally; but as a result of the uplift, they now lie at a 10° to 12° angle.

This era of uplift was followed by an interval of erosion that lasted for perhaps 400 to 500 million years. Erosion was so severe that all traces of several earlier sedimentary deposits were obliterated. These missing deposits are known as unconformities. Other types of unconformities were created when the Grand Canyon was above sea level and no sediments were laid down and, as a result, no rocks were formed.

Vast seas again flooded the Grand Canyon region during the Paleozoic era, which began about 600 million years ago. The deposits they laid down as they receded were subjected to some erosion before being inundated by new seas. Unlike the earlier seas, those of the Paleozoic era were populated by a hard-shelled animal similar to the modern oyster, clam, and coral. The remains of these animals now form enormous limestone layers in the Muav and Redwall formations. This cyclical

The Grand Canyon, with the Colorado River more than 3,000 feet below.

pattern of deposition and erosion continued until about 70 million years ago, resulting in an accumulation of sandstone, limestone, and shale layers that amount to more than 3,000 feet.

In the Permian period, which began some 270 million years ago, the Grand Canyon region remained arid. Formations such as the Coconino Sandstone were created by desert conditions. Sand, blown by stiff winds, stacked up in shifting dunes covering thousands of square miles. The layers left by these dunes are easy to recognize by their buff color and their distinctive herringbone pattern, which geologists call dune cross-bedding.

The desert period was followed by one of warm, shallow seas that resulted in the Toroweap and Kaibab layers, the latter being the uppermost stratum of the canyon. Fossils of brachiopods and mollusks, as well as fossils of sponges and sharks' teeth, are found in these layers, indicating abundant marine life.

Little evidence remains of yet another chapter in the unfolding story of the Grand Canyon. During the Mesozoic era, which began 230 million years ago, additional layers of sediment, 8,000 feet thick in places, were deposited. Wind and rain took their toll, and only two remnants remain: Cedar Mountain, near Desert View and the eastern boundary of the park; and Red Butte, about 15 miles south of Grand Canyon Village.

The Cenozoic era, which began some 70 million years ago, was the last great formative period of the canyon's history. During this era, the region remained above sea level. The dominant geological process was a combination of widespread erosion and sustained volcanic activity. The San Francisco Peaks, 70 miles to the southeast, were created, and thousands of feet of rock deposited during the preceding Mesozoic era were stripped away. Later in this period, the Colorado River began to cut down in earnest through the rock layers to the Inner Gorge. The spectacular buttes that stand out in the canyon like lonely sentinels are a byproduct of the action of the river. The buttes, which are made up of once-continuous strata that stretched from rim to rim, are identifiable by the small caps or tips that rise from their flat tops. Over the years, various explorers and surveyors have given them exotic names such as Vishnu and Wotans Throne.

The Colorado River

The formation of the Grand Canyon is intimately related to the complex development of the Colorado River system, which extends its tentacles—a far-flung array of tributaries—throughout the Southwest. The headwaters lie far away from the Grand Canyon, in southwestern

Wyoming, western Colorado, and northwestern New Mexico. The tributary rivers—the Gunnison, the Green, the Yampa, the Upper Colorado, the San Juan, and the Little Colorado—merge into the Colorado River before it enters the Inner Gorge of the Grand Canyon; they drain much of the southern and central Rocky Mountains.

Geologists are divided in their opinions of how and to what extent the Colorado River influenced the creation of the Grand Canyon. There are several theories, the most popular of which is the "stream-piracy" theory. The South Rim of the canyon stands at 7,000 feet, the North Rim at approximately 8,200. Why did the river cut through some of the highest country in the region? Why did it not seek the line of least resistance and go around the area?

The "stream-piracy" theory suggests that more than 5 million years ago, the Colorado flowed southward into Marble Canyon (just upriver from the Grand Canyon) and then southeastward through the channel of the present-day Little Colorado River, into a huge lake. At some time less than 5 million years ago, a small drainage flowing westward through the Grand Canyon eroded its way upstream until it intercepted the canyon of the Little Colorado. The interception resulted in the "capture" of the waters of what was then the main channel of the Colorado. A new channel to the west opened up, and instead of flowing southeastward, the river began to flow in the directions (west and north) the Little Colorado and the main Colorado flow today. This relatively sudden change in direction was to have a profound effect on the rock formations in the area, resulting in the cutting of the Grand Canyon to its present depth. According to this theory, the rapid erosion of the Grand Canyon was largely completed 1 to 2 million years after the shift in direction of the currents of the Colorado and Little Colorado.

During the past 6 million years, volcanic activity has also helped to shape the Grand Canyon. Much of this activity was contemporaneous with the cutting of the canyon by the river. Evidences of the tumult are still visible, especially in the Toroweap Plateau at the western end of the canyon. Great lava deposits cascaded over the area, temporarily damming up the Colorado River. Vulcan's Forge, located at river mile 177.9, marks the remains of a volcano that erupted through the present riverbed.

The formation of the Grand Canyon is an ongoing process; the region still may be rising, and the Colorado River, despite having been dammed at Glen Canyon, is still eroding its bed. Heavy rainfall followed by flash floods in the tributary canyons tumble vast quantities of debris into the main channel, and this debris in turn is pulverized by the action of the current, which continues to deepen the canyon.

Kaibab squirrel.

Within the Grand Canyon are located many ecological systems, as well as four of the seven major temperate zones of the North American continent. The difference in elevation—from 2,400 feet above sea level at the bottom of the canyon to 12,670 feet at the top of Mount Humphreys in the San Francisco peaks—is responsible for the wide variation. As the crow flies, only 90 horizontal miles separate those points, but at the Grand Canyon, distance is vertical. A 1,000-foot increase in elevation up the canyon walls is equivalent to a 300-mile move northward across flat country. As a result, the contrast in vegetation and animal life between the lowest and the highest points in the park is like that between Sonora, Mexico, and British Columbia!

Inner Gorge

The life zone at the bottom of the canyon is designated Lower Sonoran. In summer, the weather is steamy, and the temperature is 20° warmer on the average than that at the South Rim. Less than 10 inches of rain falls annually, and the vegetation is sparse. Willows and cottonwoods grow along watercourses like Bright Angel Creek and around seeps that form natural springs. Warblers, grosbeaks, and vireos make use of the leafy cover these trees provide. Hummingbirds flit among the shrubs searching for nectar. Under the murky surface of the Colorado River, the native fish that once flourished have nearly been annihilated as a result of the frigid change in water temperature created by Glen Canyon Dam. Squawfish, chub, and razorback sucker have been replaced by carp and rainbow trout.

Along the riparian corridor and on the Tonto Plateau are found different varieties of cactus, agave, and yucca. Lower Sonoran forms like mesquite, ocotillo, and creosote bush are also present. The black-throated sparrow, a popular desert bird, lives here. Blackbrush, found at similar elevations of the Mojave Desert, is a common shrub.

As in most arid environments, the mammals have adopted a nocturnal way of life. Western pipistrelle bats search the air at night for insects. The spotted skunk steals forth in the moonlight to look for deermice. At midday, when the heat is suffocating, chuckwallas and other lizards retreat to shadowy crevices. Located at this level, too, is the Grand Canyon rattlesnake. Over the millennia, this species has developed a protective adaptation—its salmon-colored skin blends in with the pink rocks.

Among larger animals, mule deer dip their delicate tongues into the cold river. Bighorn sheep move nimbly along the narrow ledges of the Inner Gorge. Colin Fletcher, in his book *The Man Who Walked Through Time*, tells of seeing beaver and wild burros. The burros, descendants of those used by miners to haul out ore from the canyon, are a controversial newcomer to the wildlife of the canyon. They feed on grasses that normally provide forage for the mule deer and the bighorn sheep. During the past decades, their numbers have increased. Recently, a few burros were rounded up and removed from the park.

South Rim

From the South Rim, the ground slants southward onto the broad slope of the Coconino Plateau, carrying most of the scant rain water and much of the soil with it. Due to the light rainfall—approximately 16 inches a year—trees do not grow very tall on the South Rim. Their abbreviated height has caused them to be termed a "pygmy forest." The ponderosa pine, which grows back from the rim, may reach 100 feet, but this is unusual. Common trees like the piñon pine and the Utah juniper are no more than 20 to 30 feet tall.

Wildflowers grow in abundance on the South Rim. Cliffrose—a gnarled, shaggy evergreen with creamy, aromatic blossoms—is everywhere. Fernbush, another member of the rose family, flowers in August and September, which is late considering the warm climate. Three varieties of pentstemon are found in the park. The most prevalent on the South Rim is the Eaton pentstemon. Down in the canyon it flowers in April; on the South Rim, in June and July. Eight species of thistle are present, including the carmine thistle, which blooms from May to October.

Smaller animals that make the South Rim their home are the porcupine, the striped skunk, and the Abert, or tassel-eared, squirrel. Cliff chipmunks and rock squirrels scamper fearlessly along the rim.

Opposite: The prickly growth of spines covering the hedgehog cactus prevents animals from eating the soft pulp underneath.

Turkey vultures wheel in wide circles looking for carrion. Ravens with glossy black wings glide over the canyon, making peculiar croaking sounds. Violet-green swallows zoom overhead. In the trees and shrubs along the rim are chickadees, nuthatches, scrub jays, and Steller's jays.

North Rim Developed Area

The North Rim is more than 1,000 feet higher than the South Rim, and ecologically it is a much different place. The South Rim belongs to the Upper Sonoran and Transition life zones, the North Rim to the Canadian. The average annual rainfall on the North Rim is 28 inches, compared with half that on the South Rim; the North Rim receives around 140 inches of snow a year, compared with only 61 inches on its counterpart. The North Rim's higher elevation and additional moisture support two distinct coniferous forests—the spruce–fir–aspen and the yellow and ponderosa pines. The piñon pine and Utah juniper "pygmy forest" grows far below the rim, along the steep slopes of the canyon. Masses of warm air that rise out of the depths feed these growths. In the late summer months, the warm air, cooling as it rises, forms dark thunderheads that keep the North Rim liberally doused with rain.

Back from the canyon, the landscape of the North Rim is characterized by pristine forests and flowing meadows. Although the growing season is shorter than that of the South Rim, the variety of wildflowers is greater. Pink phlox blooms in early spring. Goldenrod, sunflowers, and mountain dandelions add a splash of color to the green meadows. Asters bloom in late summer, after many other flowers have wilted.

The soil on the North Rim is richer and deeper than that on the South Rim, and it supports a diverse group of burrowing animals such as voles, weasels, and pocket gophers. The lush meadows provide a perfect habitat for them; above their tunnels they beat innumerable tiny paths through the high grass, out of reach of predatory birds.

Shrews, skunks, wood rats, deermice, and horned toads add to the list of small animal life. Among the larger creatures are mule deer, coyote, porcupine, and an occasional mountain lion. Birds include wild turkeys, flickers, great horned owls, and red-tailed hawks.

Perhaps the most distinctive animal on the North Rim is the Kaibab squirrel. A large squirrel, with tasseled ears and a bushy white tail, it is closely related to the Abert squirrel, which lives on the South Rim. The different coloration of the two squirrels evolved through speciation. As it cut down through the rock layers, the Colorado River gradually widened the gap between the rims. The squirrels, unable to cross the barrier, were isolated in different habitats and eventually developed different characteristics.

SITES, TRAILS, AND TRIPS

White-water rafting.

There are three kinds of trails in Grand Canyon National Park, classified according to use and condition—main trails, secondary trails, and routes. Secondary trails are not maintained and require some route-finding ability. They are infrequently patrolled by the National Park Service. Routes are difficult to follow, and for part of the way they may no longer even exist. To hike them safely, experience on Grand Canyon main and secondary trails is necessary.

All trails require twice as much time to hike up as to hike down. If it takes 5 hours to hike down a particular trail to the river, it will take at least 10 hours to hike back up to the rim.

South Rim Sites

The canyon from the South Rim presents an awesome spectacle. It is from this side that most tourists enjoy their first view. There are a number of points on the rim that offer superb vistas. Within Grand Canyon Village, three points—Grandeur, Yavapai, and Mather—provide excellent overlooks. Shuttle buses follow West Rim Drive to Hermits Rest, 8 miles from the village. The route follows the lip of the canyon and passes through or near all the major overlooks—Pima, the Abyss, Mohave, Hopi, Powell, and Maricopa. These points are excellent locations from which to photograph sunsets; they also offer fine views of the Colorado River far below.

At Grand Canyon Village are located several interesting old buildings. *Hopi House* was designed by Mary Jane Colter and constructed in 1905. The "house" is modeled after the Hopi Indian pueblo of Old Oraibi. The *El Tovar Hotel* was completed the same year, and offers the most luxurious accommodation on the South Rim. *Bright Angel Lodge*, also designed by Mary Jane Colter, was built in 1935. Among its many interesting features is a fireplace that was constructed out of all the types of rock in the Grand Canyon placed in proper chronological sequence. *Lookout Studio* was designed by Colter and built in 1914. Assembled out of rough-cut limestone, the studio blends with the rim and is hardly visible from the Bright Angel Trail, which winds below.

Overleaf: Watchtower at Desert View, designed by Mary Jane Coulter and built in 1933.

From Grand Canyon Village to the eastern entrance of the park is 25 miles. Along the way are Yaki, Grandview, Moran, and Lipan points. Desert View is the easternmost overlook, and it offers an excellent view of Marble Canyon and the Painted Desert. At Desert View is the famous Watchtower, designed by Mary Jane Colter and constructed in 1933.

South Rim Trails

Bright Angel Trail. For hikers, strollers, and loiterers, Bright Angel Trail is the main thoroughfare, a wide and well-marked trail that snakes down into the canyon in a series of tight switchbacks to the Tonto Plateau. This is also the trail that the famous Grand Canyon mules use for day trips or overnight treks to Phantom Ranch. The mule rides are fun, but very popular; it is best to make reservations early. Children must be over twelve years of age, and everyone, regardless of age, must have a tolerance for heights: although surefooted, the mules skirt perilously close to the edge of the trail.

The trail slants through the Kaibab, Coconino, and Supai formations, offering clear and graphic views of their colors and textures. At the bottom of the Redwall Formation, the trail levels out at Indian Gardens, and branches off in two directions. One branch leads to the rim of the Tonto Plateau, and offers a dramatic overview of the Inner Gorge. The other follows Garden Creek until it dips down into Pipe Creek, and then veers away from the creek and drops into the Inner Gorge via a series of switchbacks known as the Devil's Corkscrew. Just before reaching the Colorado River, the trail branches east 1.7 miles to the Silver Suspension Bridge, which leads to Phantom Ranch and Bright Angel Campground.

It is 9.5 miles from the canyon rim to Bright Angel Campground. The descent is 4,400 feet and takes about 5 hours to hike down and 10 to hike back up.

South Kaibab Trail. The South Kaibab Trail was completed in 1928 and is part of a cross-canyon route that links the two rims. The trail, though well tended, is quite steep. No water is available along the way.

The trail descends quickly to Cedar Ridge, 1.5 miles below the rim. Since South Kaibab Trail follows ridge lines instead of side canyons, the view along the trail, unlike the view from Bright Angel Trail, is unobstructed for practically the entire distance to the river.

The descent from Cedar Ridge takes the hiker past O'Neill Butte and down through the Redwall Formation. At the Tipoff, the trail drops into the Inner Gorge to the Kaibab Suspension Bridge, which spans the Colorado River. This bridge was constructed in the 1920s. The thick cables that help support it were carried down intact on the brawny shoulders of forty-two Havasupai Indians. On the other side of the bridge are Phantom Ranch and Bright Angel Campground.

The South Kaibab Trail begins near Yaki Point just off East Rim Drive. From the rim to the Colorado River is 6.4 miles, and the trail takes approximately 4 hours to hike down and 8 hours to hike back up.

Secondary Trails

On the South Rim there are several interesting secondary trails: Boucher, Hermit, Tonto, Grandview, New Hance, and Tanner.

Boucher Trail. The Boucher Trail is very difficult and requires some route-finding ability. Access to it is by way of the Dripping Springs branch of the Hermit Trail. The trail crosses the drainage above Dripping Springs, winds around the base of Eremita Mesa, then plunges down a series of switchbacks through the Coconino Formation. A broad shelf of the Supai Formation is then traversed, followed by a difficult section of loose rock and steep grades that lead over White Butte Saddle. From the Redwall Formation, the trail descends to the Tonto Plateau, where it links up with the Tonto Trail.

Both Boucher Trail and Boucher Creek, which are just beyond the junction with the Tonto Trail, are named after Louis Boucher, a French-Canadian prospector. The remains of his cabin can be seen on the east side of the creek, just south of where the trail enters the creekbed.

Hermit Trail. The Hermit Trail begins near Hermits Rest, the limestone curio shop and snack shop that was designed by Mary Jane Colter and constructed in 1914. The trail head is located at the end of West Rim Drive. The trail drops down through the Supai Formation to Santa Maria Spring. The path leading away from the spring passes through an area of rock slides to the Redwall Formation, which is negotiated by a series of switchbacks known as the Cathedral Stairs. The Hermit Trail then intersects the Tonto Trail and proceeds west to Hermit Camp and Hermit Creek. The Colorado River can be reached from this point by hiking 1.5 miles down Hermit Creek. The distance from the rim to the Colorado River is 8.5 miles and takes approximately 7 hours to hike down and 14 hours up.

Tonto Trail. The Tonto Trail, the main east–west route through the interior of the canyon, follows the Tonto Plateau for 72 miles. The trail

Overleaf: A canyon vista viewed from the El Tovar Hotel on the South Rim.

is seldom hiked in its entirety but is used to complete routes between various trails that lead into the canyon from the South Rim. For example, it links up with the Bright Angel Trail and the South Kaibab Trail, as well as with several secondary trails. The trail passes through desert terrain and is often difficult to follow in the western portion of the canyon.

Grandview Trail. The Grandview Trail goes as far as Horseshoe Mesa, a distance of 3 miles from the rim. After descending the north side of Grandview Point, the trail crosses a narrow saddle between Hance Canyon and Grapevine Canyon and continues down through the Coconino and Hermit formations. From there it eases out onto Horseshoe Mesa, on top of the Redwall. From the western prong of the mesa, the trail drops onto the Tonto Plateau, where it links up with the Tonto Trail.

New Hance Trail. The head of the New Hance Trail is located on East Rim Drive, about 1 mile south of the Moran Point turnoff. There are washouts in many places along the trail, so route-finding ability is a necessity. The trail zigzags down a shallow drainage to the base of the Coconino Formation. From there, it picks up a drainage that leads down the east side of the Coronado Butte to the top of the Redwall Formation. The descent off the rim of the Redwall is difficult to find; a large heap of stones indicates the proper trail. Once through the Redwall, the main trail is obscured by a maze of wild-burro trails, and to locate it requires a keen sense of direction. After the trail crosses a major drainage from the southeast below Moran Point, it heads down toward the bed of Red Canyon. By following this creekbed, you reach the Colorado River. Total hiking time, down and up, is 24 hours.

Tanner Trail. The Tanner Trail is located at the east end of the canyon; its head is about 100 yards from Lipan Point on the east side of the road. The trail descends quickly to the base of Escalante and Cardenas buttes, around which it contours until it reaches a break in the Redwall Formation. From there, it leads down through Tanner Canyon to the Colorado River.

The route was once known as Horsethief Trail. Horses stolen in Utah were driven down from the North Rim to a low-water ford near the Tanner Trail. From there, the horses were driven out to the South Rim and sold to unsuspecting ranchers.

Total hiking time, down and up, is approximately 27 hours. There is no water along the way. Hikers are urged to avoid this trail in the summer, as it can be blazing hot.

North Rim Sites

Standing on the North Rim, looking over the Grand Canyon, is an exhilarating experience. On a clear day, the San Francisco Peaks near Flagstaff, 70 miles distant, are visible. The South Rim and the Inner Gorge seem far away. There is much about the North Rim that enforces a sense of isolation. The rim is 1,000 feet higher than its counterpart. The river, tucked out of sight, is twice the distance from the North Rim than it is from the South Rim. North of the river, the rate of erosion is greater because the precipitation that falls there drains to the south of the canyon. The precipitation that falls on the South Rim also drains to the south, away from the canyon, and thus the erosive effect is minimized.

Fewer people visit the North Rim than visit the South Rim. The North Rim is located on the lip of the "Arizona Strip," an isolated section in the northwestern part of the state that abuts against the Utah boundary. Access to the North Rim by road is circuitous.

There are four main overlooks at the North Rim. From east to west they are Point Imperial, Cape Royal, Bright Angel Point, and Point Sublime.

The 72-mile Tonto Trail is the main east-west trail through the canyon's interior.

Trails of Grand Canyon National Park*

South Rim Trails

Rim Trail: Starts at Hermits Rest; ends at Yavapai Point; 18 miles round trip; 10 hours; safe, easy spectacular hike along the edge of the South Rim for those who wish to view the canyon without hiking into it; passes through or near all the major overlooks along West Rim Drive.

Bright Angel Trail: Starts at South Rim; ends at Bright Angel Campground; 19 miles round trip; 12 hours (not recommended for day trip); 4,400-foot ascent; wide, well-marked main thoroughfare (same trail used by mules); series of tight switchbacks to Tonto Plateau; trail splits at Indian Gardens, one branch leads to rim of Tonto Plateau for view of Inner Gorge, other follows Garden Creek to Pipe Creek, then into Inner Gorge to Colorado River.

South Kaibab Trail: Starts at Yaki Point off East Rim Drive; ends at Bright Angel Campground; 12.8 miles round trip; 12 hours (not recommended for day trip); part of cross-canyon route linking rims; unobstructed views almost entire distance; at Tipoff, drops into Inner Gorge to suspension bridge and on to Phantom Ranch.

Hermit Trail†: Starts at Hermits Rest off West Rim Drive; ends at Colorado River; 17 miles round trip; 12 hours (not recommended for day trip); drops down through Supai Formation to Santa Maria Spring, from there to junction with Tonto Trail and on to Hermit Camp.

Grandview Trail: Starts at Grandview Point; ends at Horseshoe Mesa; 6 miles round trip; 6 hours; at western end of Horseshoe Mesa, drops onto Tonto Plateau; carry water.

Tonto Trail: Starts at Garnet Canyon; ends at Red Canyon; 72 miles one way; main east-west route through interior of canyon; desert terrain with little shade.

Tanner Trail†: Starts east of Lipan Point on East Rim Drive; ends at Colorado River at Tanner Rapids; 16 miles round trip; 12 hours (not recommended for day trip); indistinct in places; low rock cairns mark difficult sections; little shade.

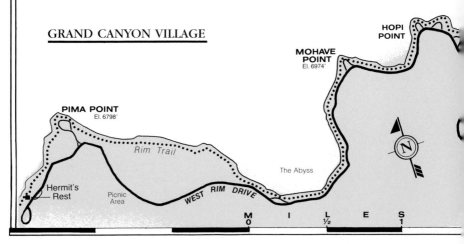

GRAND CANYON VILLAGE

HOPI POINT

MOHAVE POINT
El. 6974'

PIMA POINT
El. 6798'

Rim Trail

The Abyss

Hermit's Rest

Picnic Area

WEST RIM DRIVE

M I L E S
0   ½   1

Boucher Trail†: Starts at Dripping Springs Trail (via Hermit Trail); ends at Boucher Creek; 22 miles round trip (from head of Hermit Trail); 14-16 hours (not recommended for day trip); one of the more difficult trails; route-finding ability required; 1 mile beyond Columbus Point, descends through Hermit and Supai formations; start of descent poorly marked by rock cairns, which must be located before proceeding down.

New Hance Trail†: Starts west of Moran Point turnoff on East Rim Drive; ends at Colorado River at Hance Rapids; 16 miles round trip; 12 hours (not recommended for day trip); difficult, indistinct in spots, rocky, and very steep; doubles around corners and plunges abruptly; some bad rockslides.

North Rim Trails
North Kaibab Trail: Starts at North Rim; ends at Bright Angel Campground; 28 miles round trip; 36 hours; 5,840-foot ascent; descends sharply first 4.7 miles; Phantom Ranch is 14.1 miles from trial head; open only between mid-May and mid-November.

Clear Creek Trail: Starts at Phantom Ranch; ends at Clear Creek; 18 miles round trip; 10 hours (not recommended for day trip); runs along Tonto Plateau; branches off from North Kaibab Trail, switchbacks up talus slope, and ascends back to plateau; trout fishing in creek with license.

*Use permits, which are available at the backcountry office, are required for all overnight trips into the canyon. An infinite variety of off-trail hiking routes exist. Some are well known, used by several parties each year, and may even be marked with rock cairns. Others have been hiked once or twice. Still others remain to be discovered. If you are interested in hiking unmarked routes off established trails, talk with park rangers and be certain that your party has the equipment and experience necessary to handle inevitable problems associated with "bushwhacking," as well as potential emergencies.

†Do not attempt these trails unless you have tested your hiking ability on the Bright Angel or South Kaibab trails.

See map on pages 188-189.

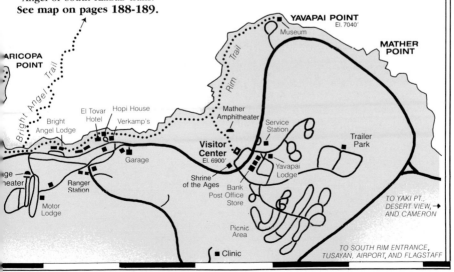

North Rim Trails

North Kaibab. The North Kaibab Trail originally was used by Indians and prospectors. François Matthes, a topographer working with the U.S. Geological Survey, improved the route for modern use in 1902. The path was so steep, Matthes reported, that his supply burros "fairly slid down on their haunches." When the first tourist camp was established at the mouth of Bright Angel Creek in 1903, the trail was further improved.

Because heavy snows blanket the North Rim, the North Kaibab Trail is open only between mid-May and mid-November. For the first 4.7 miles, the route descends at a precipitous angle through sheer Redwall Formation, offering spectacular views of the canyon. At the junction of Roaring Springs Canyon and Bright Angel Creek, there are several good swimming holes. From the junction, the trail then drops down to Cottonwood Campground, located 6.8 miles from the rim. Bright Angel Campground and Phantom Ranch are 7.3 miles beyond Cottonwood Campground. This portion of the trail is not as steep as the first miles; the trail winds over several high bridges that span creeks and chasms.

The total distance from the rim down to the river—14 miles—can be hiked in about 12 hours. It takes 24 hours to return to the rim, or 36 hours down and up.

Clear Creek Trail. In 1933, the Civilian Conservation Corps built this 8.7-mile trail from Phantom Ranch along the Tonto Plateau to Clear Creek. The trail branches off from the North Kaibab just before Phantom Ranch. It zigzags 1,000 feet up to the rim of the Inner Gorge and onto the Tonto Plateau. The trail remains on the plateau even after Clear Creek is sighted and contours along the drainage for some distance before descending to the Clear Creek streambed. The water in the creek is cold; when the Colorado River becomes muddy, trout swim up Clear Creek and other side streams.

From Clear Creek, it is 7 more miles to Cheyava Falls. *Cheyava* is the Hopi Indian word for "intermittent." At most times of the year, the fall is a mere trickle; in the spring, when snow melts off the North Rim, it swells to a major waterfall.

Opposite: Havasu Falls, in the western part of the canyon, is perhaps the most magical oasis in the Southwest.

GUADALUPE
MOUNTAINS
NATIONAL PARK

*El Capitan, at 8,078 feet, anchors the southern end of the park
and is one of the Southwest's most famous peaks.*

GUADALUPE MOUNTAINS NATIONAL PARK
STAR RTE. 1, BOX 480
CARLSBAD, NEW MEXICO 88220, TEL.: (915) 828-3251

Highlights: Smith Spring □ Frijole □ McKittrick Canyon □ Devils Hall □ Guadalupe Peak □ The Bowl □ El Capitan □ Williams Ranch □ The Pinery □ Dog Canyon

Access: From Carlsbad, 55 miles southwest on U.S. 62/180. From El Paso, 110 miles east on U.S. 62/180. See map on pages 222–223.

Hours: Daily, year-round, brief closures in winter due to storms. Visitor Center, 8 A.M.–4:30 P.M., later in summer.

Fees: $4/site.

Parking: At each public-use point.

Gas, food: In Pine Springs, Nickel Creek, Whites City, Carlsbad, and El Paso.

Lodging: In Whites City, Carlsbad, Van Horn, and El Paso.

Visitor Center: Frijole Visitor Center, on U.S. 62/180, offers exhibits, information; maps for sale. Pine Springs, McKittrick Canyon Visitor Center, 4 miles from U.S. 62/180.

Museum: Exhibits in Visitor Center.

Pets: Permitted on leash in campgrounds, not on trails or in public buildings. Horseback riding permitted on designated trails; no rentals; no overnight camping with horses; call in advance.

Picnicking: At Pine Springs Campground, McKittrick Canyon, and Dog Canyon.

Hiking: On 80 miles of trails; water at trail heads only, so carry it.

Backpacking: Permitted with permit. Camp only at 10 designated backcountry campsites. Carry water.

Campgrounds: 24 tent sites, 29 trailer sites, 2 group sites. No hookups or showers.

Tours: Nature walks, campfire programs in summer.

Facilities for disabled: McKittrick Canyon Visitor Center and 1 campsite at Pine Springs Campground.

For additional information, see also Sites, Trails, and Trips on pages 234–244.

GUADALUPE MOUNTAINS NATIONAL PARK IS A STUDY in contrasts. What was once a reef awash on the edge of the sea is now a mountain range baking in the desert sun. Yet in a few hours' climb, a hiker can leave the desert behind and, almost miraculously, enter a cool forest that seems as though it should be hundreds of miles north. There are other contrasts and extremes: hidden places where water transforms the desert into a leafy, bird-filled oasis; hot summer days with comfortable evenings and, at high elevations, cool nights; harsh winters with fierce winds that whip through canyons and passes and threaten the existence of man and his vehicle!

Clouds lift after a heavy rainstorm in McKittrick Canyon.

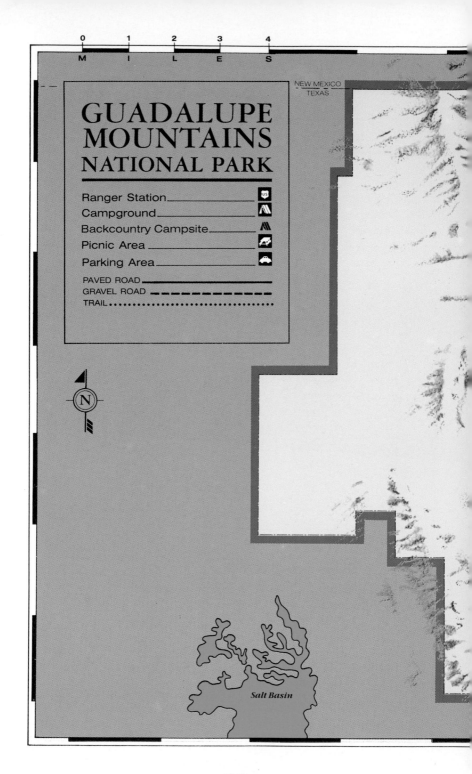

GUADALUPE MOUNTAINS NATIONAL PARK

NEW MEXICO
TEXAS

Ranger Station	🛈
Campground	🏕
Backcountry Campsite	🏕
Picnic Area	🖼
Parking Area	🚗

PAVED ROAD
GRAVEL ROAD — — — — —
TRAIL • • • • • • • • • • • • • • • • •

N

Salt Basin

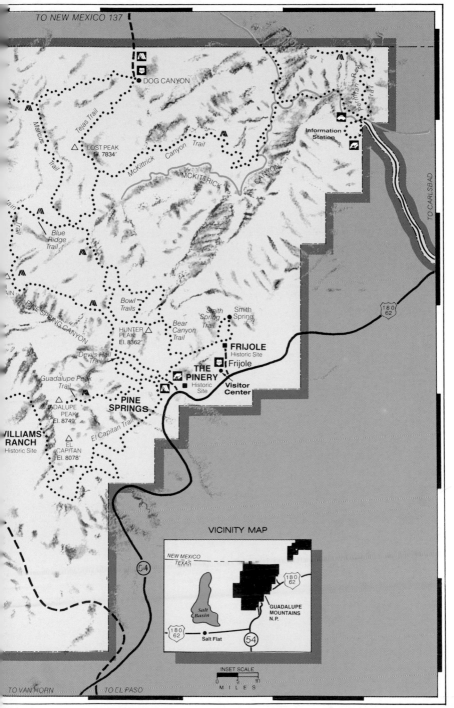

TO NEW MEXICO 137

DOG CANYON

Tejas Trail

Marcus Trail

LOST PEAK
El. 7834'

McKittrick Canyon Trail

MCKITTRICK CANYON

Information Station

Pe_____ Trail

TO CARLSBAD

Blue Ridge Trail

PINE SPRING CANYON

Bowl Trails

HUNTER PEAK
El. 8362'

Smith Spring Trail

Smith Spring

Bear Canyon Trail

Devils Hall Trail

FRIJOLE
Historic Site

Frijole

Guadalupe Peak Trail

THE PINERY
Historic Site

Visitor Center

PINE SPRINGS

180 62

GUADALUPE PEAK
El. 8749'

WILLIAMS RANCH
Historic Site

EL CAPITAN
El. 8078'

El Capitan Trail

VICINITY MAP

NEW MEXICO
TEXAS

54

Salt Basin

180 62

Salt Flat

54

GUADALUPE MOUNTAINS N.P.

180 62

INSET SCALE
0   5   10
M I L E S

TO VAN HORN

TO EL PASO

Native Americans

When humans first saw the skyline of the Guadalupe Mountains, it probably looked pretty much as it does now; El Capitan was just as awesome. But in human terms that was long ago, perhaps 10,000 years. The mountain was similar, but the flora and fauna were different. People who lived and hunted in these mountains saw and knew the taste of mammoth, of four-horned antelope, of camel—all extinct now. The early hunters left enough signs of life that we know they were here, but not much more. Undoubtedly they sought shelter in the mountains' many caves, and were familiar with the streams and canyons. But until the desert gives up some of its secrets, these early people will remain ghostlike.

Not so the Apache! Occupying the Guadalupes when Europeans arrived, the Apache played a major role in the history of the Southwest and perhaps an even greater role in southwestern literature. They deserve the recognition, if only for having been so successful in wresting a living, and a culture, from the desert. The Apache appear to have come from the north, and even without the horse (which came later, from the Spanish) they ranged far, following seasons and food sources. Their houses were temporary brush *jacales* and occasionally a tepee-like leather tent, suitable for people who moved often. The Apache traded with the more sedentary Pueblo farmers to the northwest near the Rio Grande, from whom they no doubt learned about the Spaniards, a new people who came from the south in the 1500s bringing such miracles as the horse and the gun. But few Spaniards got this far from the river. The Guadalupe Mountains remained the domain of the Apache.

The Road West

Because of faraway events, the Guadalupes passed into American control in 1848. Few people yet knew they existed, but the young country was spilling west. Texas miners in the California gold rush may have passed the range in 1849, and certainly army expeditions did in the next few years. The young country was exploring its new land, especially seeking a way to connect its east and west coasts. The Guadalupes seemed to lie in the path of progress.

Faced with the urgent need for rapid and reliable mail service to the burgeoning west coast, the United States Congress in 1857 gave a profitable contract to John Butterfield; overnight the famous Butter-

A way station on the Butterfield Overland Mail Line, around 1875.

field Overland Mail Line was born. The route stretched from St. Louis to San Francisco, and under the terms of the contract the company was granted 320 acres for each way station. One was built in the Guadalupes; its stone walls are still visible near the Pine Spring Campground—the same spring that supplied water to the station. Exhausted horses were replaced by new teams here, while motion-dazed passengers bolted a meal of venison pie, coffee, and the inevitable baked beans.

The cross-country stage became history and then legend in just a few years. More Americans arrived, looking for minerals or establishing ranches. The Apache saw what was happening and resisted, but the new culture was a powerful one. Devastating encounters between the Apache and the army occurred within the borders of the present park. At Manzanita Spring, near the park Visitor Center, on December 30, 1869, the army drove the Indians from an encampment and destroyed the winter's cache of food and supplies. The tactic was effective, and slowly the Indians were pressured and weakened. For a while the Apache kept up a guerrilla effort—Geronimo often rode the Guadalupes, and so did Victorio—but the newcomers prevailed. The Apache today, famed for their skill as cattlemen, live on a reservation to the northwest in the Sacramento mountains.

Establishment of the Park

After the Civil War and the Indian wars, ranching came to the Guadalupes. The area was desert, and times were hard. Few imagined the boom that was to come to the area east of the mountains—the Permian Basin oil field. The mountain range was crucial to an understanding of the geologic history of the oil-bearing basin, so many of the people who were involved in the new industry began working in the Guadalupe region. One geologist who knew and came to love the area was Wallace Pratt. During an immensely successful career in oil exploration, he bought huge tracts of land in the Guadalupes, including beautiful McKittrick Canyon. There he built a house, which still can be seen by hikers in the park. Due largely to Wallace Pratt's efforts and donations of land as a start, as well as the influence of Judge J. C. Hunter, the other large landowner, in the 1960s a movement was organized to have this unique area set aside as a park. Congress passed the bill in 1966, and the Guadalupe Mountains became a national park in 1972.

G E O L O G Y

The Resurrection of a Reef

Guadalupe Mountains National Park encompasses the southern, highest part of the 50-mile-long Guadalupe Mountain Range. Rising gradually from the broken plains around Carlsbad, New Mexico, the long, narrow block has spectacular drop-offs on both the east and west sides. At the southern end, it abruptly drops back to the desert; El Capitan, the last, massive promontory, is one of the famous peaks of the Southwest.

It is a curious coincidence that erosion has revealed the mountain in this particular way, for it resembles to some degree the form in which it was created about 250 million years ago. Then part of it was a largely submerged sea wall, bordering an arm of a shallow Permian ocean. Today it is a wall thrown across the Texas desert, and travel routes must skirt it at one end or the other.

The Rocks Form

The Guadalupe Range is a study in the rocks that form where a shelf meets the sea, and is especially famous for its exposure of a section of an ancient reef. *Reef* is the correct word, and is used by geologists; but the ancient reef was not a barrier reef like those around South Sea atolls.

The area to the south and east of the present-day town of Carlsbad

Boulders and pool in upper McKittrick Canyon.

was a basin of the trilobed Permian ocean; today it is called the Delaware Basin. (The Midland Basin to the east and the Marfa Basin to the west are the remains of the other lobes.) The Glass, Delaware, and Apache mountain ranges are other exposures of the rocks that surrounded the basin, although they are not as geologically clear as the Guadalupes. Oil-well borings have traced underground sections of the formation in a circle 400 miles around!

According to current geological thinking, an imaginary Permian explorer who was traveling from dry land to open ocean would first have encountered a restricted lagoon that was slowly filling with erosional debris from the land. Next, separating the lagoon from the ocean, was an area of tidal flats, in some places tens of miles wide, that sloped down to the sea. Finally, deep underwater, the shelf ended in a lip, and the bottom dropped toward the ocean depths. It was along this underwater "edge" that the reef formed. Much of it was the remains of tiny organisms, mostly algae. Some donated the limy part of their own bodies, while others secreted lime that cemented the sediment together. In addition, a remarkable amount of lime precipitated from the water and thus further contributed to the growing reef. In some places, the amount of precipitated lime greatly exceeded the amount of organic material.

The Permian reef has no known counterpart among the "active" reefs in the world. South Sea reefs are made up largely of coral and calcareous algae; the Permian reef was composed of sponges and calcareous algae. South Sea reefs are themselves "walls" between the open ocean and lagoons; in Permian times, the highest point was the tidal flat, which was shoreward from the reef. The reef itself was submerged; if the Permian explorer had had a Permian boat, he could have sailed right over it! Finally, coral reefs are derived mostly from living creatures. While the ancient reef was partially composed of organic remains, it was largely formed of precipitated limestone. The origin of other parts of the Permian reef still puzzle geologists.

The Time Between

Even seas are only temporary. Eventually the sources of the sea became blocked, and the process of evaporation began. It was remarkably rapid in geologic terms, perhaps as short as a few million or only 1 million years. As water evaporated into the drying air, it left behind salts and minerals that became the great gypsum beds that underlie the surface, while in some places special circumstances produced the potash deposits that are so valuable as a source of fertilizer. With successive geologic ages came slow burial in sediments that became massive. For 200 million years (compared with the perhaps 50 million years that the sea existed), the whole complex lay buried. Weight and heat did their slow work. The sediments in the tidal flats and in the lagoon became rock adjoining the reef rock. In some places petroleum formed, as it had ages earlier in layers beneath even these. No hint of the buried complex appeared at the surface, where strange creatures evolved, dominated for a while, and then disappeared. The weight of the overlying sediments was enormous, and even though the reef was basically intact, a 100-mile-wide limestone bracelet in a gypsum setting deep in the earth, it cracked. The cracks formed a pattern that would be identifiable millions of years later.

Reemergence

The land lifted again. In the complex, slow churning that changes the earth's surface, the whole region was uplifted. Uplift led to more erosion, as water rushed faster to the sea. Layer after layer of the overburden was stripped away. The removal was rapid in geologic terms, beginning a "mere" 10 or 12 million years ago. Had there been a film, run now at fast speed, it would show the reef emerging, its limestone resisting the erosion that quickly took away the softer surrounding gypsum.

Limestone is not immune to erosion, though; it is soluble. Slightly acidic water seeping in along the cracks that had developed when the reef was underground slowly carried away tiny amounts of the lime. As a result, the Guadalupe Mountains are laced with caves. Many are known, and certainly hundreds more are unknown, for a cave does not have to have an opening to the surface. One cave may be the most famous in the world—Carlsbad Caverns, a major hollowing of the reef that is now a national park about 40 miles north of Guadalupe Mountains National Park.

Geological processes did not occur just to get to where we are now; the earth is always en route to something else. Today the ancient fossil reef is a mountain range in a desert, clothed in desert garb. But each flash flood and each rockfall, even a tiny one, reduces it some small amount. It is a great mountain range, and a great display of the earth's history.

N A T U R A L   H I S T O R Y

Water! In the Guadalupe Mountains it is water that determines where life will be and what form it will take. The winds that blow across western Texas carry little water, but they do carry some. The mountains cause the winds to rise and cool, dropping their moisture. Thus the top, including the fine basin known as "the Bowl," gets more than 20 inches of precipitation a year, compared with half that amount down in the surrounding desert. But the water does not stay at the top, where there is no natural permanent surface water. It sinks into the porous limestone and eventually comes out in springs at the base of the mountains. Life flourishes around each of these springs, and from the road it can be seen as a band of green along watercourses.

The park has three distinct life zones: the desert, the wet places, and the forest at the top.

The Desert

In the desert is the least water and the most evaporation, and a glance at the creosote bush points up these conditions. If these stingy bushes seem rather evenly spaced across the desert floor, there is good reason;

Clockwise, from top: Texas horned lizard. Columbine. Maple leaves, McKittrick Canyon. Great horned owl.

each has staked out its own territory, just as far out as its roots can reach the precious little moisture that falls. And that is where the next one survives, and so on. The plant's small, leathery leaves impede evaporation and thus help hoard what water the plant gathers.

Cactuses are here in prickly profusion; these highly specialized desert plants have all but forsaken leaves, modifying some into spines and performing photosynthesis in the green stem. The cholla produces spectacular waxy, purple flowers in June. It is a bad cactus to bump into, since the outer segments are only loosely attached. The plant self-prunes, dropping those segments during droughts.

A spectacular show is put on by the agave, or century plant (locally sometimes called Spanish bayonet). It looks like the yuccas, though fatter. The plant does not flower for years, but stores energy in the fat leaves. Each leaf has a needle-like point that can puncture a tire, and has a chemical that gives even a small prick to the skin an odd, chilling effect. Then after fifteen years or so, the plant suddenly sends out a stalk, actually growing several inches a day. It reaches higher than a one-story building and produces great bunches of pale blossoms that are spectacular, especially in the moonlight.

The animals of the desert are specially equipped for dryness too. The adaptation seems to reach an extreme in the various rodents that *never* drink water. They need it, of course, so they manufacture it chemically from seeds in their diet.

Wildlife have habits to protect against the heat. Most desert mammals are nocturnal. Deer are common in the park, and can be seen virtually every dusk coming out to browse. Coyotes are heard then too, but primarily in the early, early morning. Skunks and badgers make their way at night, almost never seen by visitors. The night is busy, but the day is largely left to the lizards and the insects.

The Wet Places

Smith Spring is a wonder, a Japanese garden tucked away in the desert. It is one of the wet places, where water is the magic ingredient in transforming the desert into an oasis of green.

The plants change in such places. Even as you enter you can see it, smell it, and feel it; there are ponderosa pine, walnuts, maples and oaks. McKittrick Canyon is justly famous for its autumn foliage, which is unusual in this part of the country. And there are Texas madrones, trees that most people have never seen before visiting Guadalupe. The distinctive red tree looks as though it were bursting out and growing *over* its own bark, inside out. Insects and, of course, birds abound. There are wrens, tanagers, and sparrows. The seldom-seen desert reptiles are not in the wet places, but garter snakes and newts are.

These are very special areas, properly hidden behind a curtain of grapevine. Perhaps they are appreciated because they almost always appear at the end of a hot desert hike—quite unexpected and most welcome!

The Forest at the Top

That the springs are beautiful is at least predictable, as water in the desert is almost always beautiful. But the forest at the top is unexpected. The long block of the Guadalupes is avalanche-steep on the sides but flat on top—at least in comparison to the sides. Actually the top has considerable relief, cut primarily by South McKittrick Canyon. A special place is "the Bowl," a large, heavily timbered, basinlike area that is quite invisible from below. The dense forest in the Bowl seems to belong somewhere else; Douglas fir, limber pine, and ponderosa pine make the hiker feel hundreds of miles north. Many of the plants and animals here—including elk (reintroduced after extinction by hunting), bear, even mountain lion, and birds, such as mountain chickadee, nuthatch, and warbler—are at the southern limit of their ranges.

This is a relict forest. A few tens of thousands of years ago, ice sheets covered much of North America. They did not reach the Guadalupe region, but their effect did. A great coniferous forest extended this far south and perhaps even a little farther. But when the ice sheets retreated, the forest could not take the warming, drying climate, and junipers and other plants that are now common in the area took over. But the conditions changed by *altitude*, not just by distance from the receding ice sheets, much as water rises in a tub in which a child has made an irregular pile of stones. At first a nonswimming insect might have the run of the pile, but as the water rises, high places gradually become islands. If trapped on one, our nonswimming insect would find itself stranded, perhaps able to continue but only in isolation, far from others of its sort. The great forest has long since retreated far northward, but here on the Guadalupes is an island left behind, a relict forest.

Of course, the life-zone divisions are not clear cut, though sometimes they appear to be. Along the trails that rise rapidly up a cliff face, the change at the rim from desert to the relict forest is astonishing. But along a natural pathway up, such as McKittrick Canyon, there are all possible combinations of trees, shrubs, and animals, some of them quite unlikely. The Guadalupe Mountains, by the circumstances of their creation and location, provide a bewildering array of conditions for life, and life has moved in accordingly.

There are two kinds of hiking experiences in the Guadalupes: on roads that go around the base of the mountains and occasionally poke in a short way, and in the deserts and desert mountains. Hiking is especially rewarding, and in walks of just of just a few hours, visitors will find the quiet and natural beauty of Guadalupe National Park.

Guadalupe Pass. U.S. 62/180 passes the foot of El Capitan in Guadalupe Pass, the break between the Guadalupe Range and the Delaware Mountains to the south. The Mescalero Apache knew and used this pass. Forty-niners heading for the California gold fields traveled through it, and the famous Butterfield Overland Mail Line stagecoaches struggled over it. After a hundred years of improvements, the road has become a comfortable paved highway, but El Capitan probably looks much as it did when the going was tough.

Williams Ranch. A four-wheel-drive road on the west side of the range leads to the old Williams Ranch. Interested persons may get a map and the gate key at the Visitor Center. The road is rough, and the abandoned ranch house strikes most visitors as a lonely place—perhaps as desolate as any they will see on their whole vacation. Yet people did homestead here, and grass grew. Bone Spring, free-flowing pools of water that soon disappear into the ground, is about 1 mile behind the ranch house. A hiking trail (El Capitan Trail) goes from the Pine Spring Campground to the Williams Ranch; but it is long, and overnight camping is recommended.

Low Hikes into the Backcountry

Smith Spring Trail. About .5 mile behind the Visitor Center on an old dirt road is a shaded ranch complex, with a small main house and some outbuildings. The spring that supplies it is called Frijole Spring, named after the beans that were the staple for the early ranchers. It was not luxurious, but it was, and is, beautiful. It is now a ranger station.

The trail to Smith Spring is an easy one. It goes gently uphill through waist-high scrub brush, and hikers think they can see the whole mountainside and wonder where the spring could be hidden. Then in less than 1 mile, the trail crosses a gentle shoulder, heads up a canyon, and suddenly comes upon the spring. It is green here, with small pools, as exquisite as a Japanese garden. The trees are walls and a roof that keep the desert out. There are dragonflies and birds, and large animals come to drink at dawn and dusk. This is fragile land, and the hiker should stay on the trail, but the trail itself is in the heart of the oasis.

Coming back down, the trail passes Manzanita Spring. This quiet spot—another watering place; one may even see elk—has not always been so peaceful. It was here that the cavalry surprised an Apache rancheria and in a brief battle destroyed their winter supplies.

The Smith Spring Trail is about 2 miles round trip, ideal for a visitor with limited time. It gives a small taste of the desert and shows the miracle of water, all in less than 2 hours.

Heavily timbered, the Bowl receives more than 20 inches of precipitation a year.

Trails of Guadalupe Mountains National Park*

Guadalupe Peak Trail: Starts at Pine Spring Campground; ends at Guadalupe Peak; 9 miles round trip; 6 hours; 3,000-foot ascent; leads to highest point in Texas (8,749 feet); magnificent views of surrounding peaks; 5,000-foot drop to the salt flats to the west.

Devil's Hall Trail: Starts and ends at Pine Spring Campground; 5 miles round trip; 4 hours; walk along wash floor between narrow canyon walls of clearly stratified sedimentary rock; no climbing.

Tejas Trail: Starts at Pine Spring Campground; ends at Dog Canyon Campground; 11.7 miles one way; 8-10 hours; 2,000-foot ascent; main route to the high country intersects Bush Mountain, Marcus, and McKittrick Canyon trails; excellent views of all the Guadalupe peaks; one highlight is view from 7,830-foot Lost Peak; good view of Bowl and the reef structure as it slopes downward to the northeast.

Bear Canyon Trail: Starts at Pine Spring Campground; ends at Bowl trails; 3.4 miles one way; 3-4 hours; 2,000-foot ascent; alternate route to the high country (used more often for returning from high country); connects with Bowl trails; steeper and more rugged than Tejas Trail.

Bowl trails: Start at Tejas Trail; end at Bear Canyon Trail; three short, connecting trails in the Bowl; one has spur to Hunter Peak; another passes through the thick fir and pine forest of Bowl, with its variety of mammals, birds, and reptiles.

Bush Mountain Trail: Starts at Tejas Trail (3.7 miles up from Pine Spring Campground); ends at Dog Canyon Campground; 11.4 miles one way; 8-10 hours; 3,000-foot ascent; passes Bush Mountain, second highest peak in Texas (8,676 feet) and Cox Tank, an earthen dam; excellent views to Cutoff Mountain.

Blue Ridge Trail: Starts at Bush Mountain Trail; ends at Tejas Trail; short connecting trail.

Marcus Trail: Starts at Blue Ridge Trail; ends at Bush Mountain Trail; 3.8 miles one way; 2 hours; 1,800-foot ascent; historic abandoned jeep trail into the high country; gradual climb into heavily forested area.

McKittrick Canyon Trail: Starts at McKittrick Canyon parking area; ends at Tejas Trail; 9.6 miles one way (most one-way hikes start at Dog Canyon and end at McKittrick Canyon); 8-10 hours; 2,380-foot ascent; arduous climb, but spectacular views; follows floor of McKittrick Canyon for 4 miles, then climbs steeply out; walk into canyon and back is excellent 1-day introduction.

Smith Spring Trail: Starts and ends at Frijole Ranch House; 2 miles round trip; 1.5 hours; 500-foot ascent; gentle climb up hill from historic site to oasis overlooking desert; best introduction to terrain of park.

Permian Reef Geology Trails: Starts at McKittrick Canyon information station; ends at north park boundary; 4.9 miles one way; 8 hours; 2,000-foot ascent; leads up north wall of canyon through ponderosa pine forest; close look at major formations of the Permian reef.

El Capitan Trail: Starts at Pine Spring campground; ends at Williams Ranch; 9.8 miles one way; 16 hours; gently rolling hike, skirting base of El Capitan (8,078 feet) and under the west cliffs of Guadalupe Peak; spectacular views of salt flats.

*The Guadalupe Mountains National Park trails are interconnected; a "hiker's guide" and trail map are essential.

See map on pages 222–223.

Smith Spring, north of Frijole near the eastern boundary of the park, is an oasis in the desert.

Devil's Hall Trail. Starting at Pine Spring Campground, the Devil's Hall Trail leads along a wash in the canyon. More strenuous paths branch off to climb the canyon walls on either side, but the main trail continues on the canyon floor. In just over 2 miles, with very little rise, the canyon walls close in dramatically, thus the name "Devil's Hall." Pools of water are often found; the rock formations are clear, and fossils abound.

El Capitan Trail. The El Capitan Trail begins at the Pine Spring Campground and leads off to the west around El Capitan and Guadalupe Peak, passing directly beneath the sheer cliffs of both. This is a long trail, but it is one that offers a taste of the desert and spectacular cliffs.

Hikes into the High Country

The following hikes lead into the high country with considerable climb, and they are all strenuous. The Guadalupes rise abruptly; so do the trails. Hikers must be in reasonably good physical condition, wear sturdy shoes, and carry plenty of water.

Guadalupe Peak Trail. The Guadalupe Mountains emerge from the broken country around Carlsbad, 50 miles north in New Mexico, and slope upward to reach 8,749 feet at Guadalupe Peak, the highest point in Texas.

Leaving from the Pine Spring Campground, the Guadalupe Peak Trail begins to climb abruptly and seems never to stop. It is only a little more than 4 miles to the peak, but the climb is 3,000 feet. On the way up, there are views back over the plains to the east—great reasons to stop and rest. Walking up is like walking north. Scrub brush gives way to a few ponderosa and then a pine forest. About .5 mile before the top is a side trail that leads a few hundred yards to a campground with fine views, but no water. Finally the trail breaks out of the forest and climbs onto the rocky, windy peak itself. The view—or rather the 360° panorama—is spectacular. To the east are the plains, broken by isolated mountain ranges blue-gray in the distance. To the south is the famous massif of El Capitan, which looks quite different when viewed from *above*. To the west and far below are the salt flats, scene and cause of the bloody El Paso Salt War of 1877. To the north are the jumbled peaks and ridges of the Guadalupe Range, stretching toward Carlsbad.

Do not treat lightning casually at the peak. Afternoon thundershowers are common and spectacular to watch as they build and move, but hikers should leave if they get even close. The peak is struck often.

Tejas Trail. The Tejas Trail is the hiker's main route into the high country, and, like those that branch off here and there along the way, it is spectacular. It begins at the Pine Spring Campground and climbs the north canyon wall in a rapid rise that soon reveals incredible views of the canyon and the plains to the east.

It is 11.7 miles on to the Dog Canyon Campground, where the Tejas Trail ends. Along the way it intersects first with the east end of the Bush Mountain Trail, the Bowl trails to the east, the Marcus Trail to the north, and the west terminal of the McKittrick Canyon Trail. About 3 miles from Dog Canyon, the Tejas Trail passes Lost Peak, one of the more impressive landmarks in the park. The view from this 7,830-foot mountain is worth the climb, or, as one park booklet understates, it is "especially noteworthy."

The dramatic change in the "personality" of the Guadalupe terrain along this trail cannot be overstated. The climb up from Pine Spring Campground is rather steep in comparison to the gentle up-and-down rolling of the trails in the high country, and the environment is just as different—from hot, dry desert to thick, green forest.

Bush Mountain Trail. The rugged Bush Mountain Trail begins about 2.5 miles up the Tejas Trail—already in the high country—and branches off to the west along a ridge toward Bush Mountain, the second highest peak in Texas (8,676 feet). Later it passes the Cox Tank, an earthen dam that supplied the early-twentieth-century goat ranching operation with water, crosses the Marcus Trail, and then drops down into Dog Canyon, where it again meets and ends with the Tejas Trail.

Blue Ridge Trail. This is a short connecting trail between the Bush Mountain and Tejas trails.

Marcus Trail. This is an old jeep road that leads into the park from the north and rises into the high country to join the Tejas Trail.

McKittrick Canyon Trail. A good introduction to the Guadalupes is the walk into McKittrick Canyon, long famous for its beauty. In 1912, a young oil geologist, Wallace Pratt, made the then-rough trip in to see it and realized that besides being spectacular, the canyon was a slice through an ancient reef that would give geologists an "inside look" at what had been largely theoretical. (Along the road to the trail head are the remains of some concrete tables, "The Arm-waving Spot." A fine cross section of the reef is visible just there, and Pratt's employees

Overleaf: Gypsum dunes, remnants of an evaporated sea, produce potash, a source of fertilizer.

noticed that the place "just naturally seemed to make geologists want to wave their arms around!")

There is an information station at the trail-head parking lot, but it may not be manned. A trail brochure is available there. Almost immediately, the trail enters the canyon. It stays on the canyon floor, is shaded, and has much to delight the eye. The trees are maples and oaks, stark contrast to the desert just "outside." In autumn, the colors can be breathtaking. The stream runs year-round, but there is a geological oddity in the canyon. Dissolved limestone in the water coming off the old reef is deposited on the streambed as travertine, which cements the rocks together and seals the streambed. Breaks are common, however, and there are sections where the stream runs *under* the streambed, which then appears to be dry.

About 2.75 miles in is Pratt Cabin, the home that geologist Wallace Pratt built of selected native stone. Water and restrooms are found here in summer. Just beyond, the canyon forks. There is no trail up North McKittrick, which becomes more beautiful, with pools (even trout),

small waterfalls, and even some Douglas fir. This is a rather dramatic case of an isolated life zone.

About 1 mile beyond Pratt Lodge is "the Grotto," replete with dripping water, ferns, and cave formations. Here the trail begins to climb out of the canyon on a very steep grade. This is a good place for the day hiker to turn around, or perhaps to climb another .5 mile to Turtle Rock, with its spectacular views. The trail continues up into the high country, but that is a more formidable hike that requires planning.

The total hike—from the parking lot, past Pratt Cabin and the Grotto to Turtle Rock, and out again—is about 10 miles; but there are so many glens and special places that the hike deserves a whole day.

Bear Canyon Trail. Years ago, rancher J. C. Hunter (for whom Hunter Peak is named) wanted to provide for animals he had introduced into the high country. His men built a pump station far below at upper Pine

A half-moon rises behind a sotol, a yuccalike plant commonly found in the park. Its young flowers were eaten by Indians and the leaf fibers were used for rope.

Spring and laid a pipeline to the top. The pumping system has long been abandoned, but the pipeline can still be seen along the trail.

This is an alternative trail to the high country, but it is used more often for returning rather than climbing; the route is more strenuous than the Tejas Trail. It rises more than 2,000 feet in less than 2 miles.

Bowl Trails. There are three short trails in and around the oasis called the Bowl. One connects the Tejas Trail with the head of Bear Canyon Trail, and passes by a spur to Hunter Peak on the east edge of the ridge. (Hunter Peak offers an exciting view of Pine Canyon and the eastern plains on one side and the Bowl on the other.) About halfway along this trail, a path leads down into the thick fir and pine forest of the Bowl and joins another Bowl trail that connects the Bear Canyon and Tejas trails.

Permian Reef Geology Trail. This special trail is for those who are interested in the geology of the Guadalupes. The Permian Reef Geology Trail takes the explorer through a ponderosa pine forest along a canyon wall where the features of the reef are revealed—clear exposures of layered rock that was formed about 280 to 230 million years ago.

Overnight Hikes

Many of the Guadalupe trails into the high country are long and arduous and require more than just a few hours or a day to appreciate; there are campsites on all the major trails. Permits are required for overnight hikes and can be obtained at the main Visitor Center and at the ranger station at Dog Canyon. Both day hikers and overnight hikers must sign trail-head registers before departing; these registers are checked regularly. The Guadalupe backcountry is rugged and can be dangerous for the inexperienced. There are regulations for the hikers' protection and also for the preservation of the park and its flora and fauna.

El Capitan. To have entered into legend, to have a train and even a rousing march named after it, a rock must be dramatic—and El Capitan is. It is the last towering monolith at the southern end of the Guadalupes, where they abruptly break off and drop back down to the desert. It seems almost a mountain by itself. At 8,078 feet, El Capitan is not the highest point of the range; Guadalupe Peak (8,749 feet), just behind it, is. But from many points, "El Cap" blocks the higher peak from view, and it is El Capitan that has become the symbol of the Guadalupes.

Opposite: McKittrick Canyon's autumnal colors are unique in the Southwest.

MESA VERDE
NATIONAL PARK

---

*Cliff Palace, with its many rooms and towers, is the largest
and perhaps the most beautiful ruin at Mesa Verde.*

MESA VERDE NATIONAL PARK, COLORADO 81330
TEL.: (303) 529-4465

Highlights: Cliff Palace ◻ Balcony House ◻ Spruce Tree Ruin Long House Ruin ◻ Weatherill Mesa ◻ Ruins Road Drive ◻ Step House

Access: From Cortez, take U.S. 160 east to entrance. From Mancos, take U.S. 160 west to entrance. See map on pages 250–251.

Fees: Entrance, $5/vehicle; $2/person on bus. Camping, $6/unit, 50% less with Golden Age or Golden Access pass. Group fee, $1.00/person, minimum $10/site.

Parking: At Far View, Morefield; and Chapin Mesa.

Gas, food: In park from mid-May to mid-October. Off season, in Cortez and Mancos.

Lodging: In park from mid-May to mid-October. Off season, in Cortez and Mancos.

Visitor Center: Open only during summer at Far View.

Museum: Open year-round in headquarters area.

Gift shops: From mid-May to mid-October at Far View, Spruce Tree Terrace, and Morefield Campground.

Pets: Permitted on leash, except on trails or in public buildings.

Picnicking: In museum area, Ruins Road, Weatherill Mesa, and Morefield Campground.

Hiking: Restricted to 5 trails only; 2 require permit.

Campground: Morefield Campground, open May 1 to October 31, both tents and trailers. No reservations, no wood gathering. Showers available.

Tours: During summer months, all ruins open and 2 ruins have guided tours. In fall, winter, spring, 1 or 2 ruins open for guided tour, weather permitting.

Other activities: Bicycling. Rentals available.

Facilities for disabled: At Far View and Chapin Mesa, some campgrounds.

For additional information, see also Sites, Trails, and Trips on pages 264–272 and the map on page 269.

M

ESA VERDE NATIONAL PARK LIES BETWEEN CORTEZ and Durango in southwestern Colorado. A 21-mile drive from its entrance leads to the finest collection of prehistoric cliff dwellings preserved in the United States. The dwellings, occupied by the Anasazi Indians until A.D. 1300, are so rich in history and beauty that in 1978 the United Nations declared Mesa Verde a World Heritage Site.

Numerous vista points overlook an unbroken panorama of the Four Corners states. The park lies between the 14,000-foot peaks of the San Juan Mountains in Colorado and the Navajo Reservation in Arizona. The park is home to Rocky Mountain mule deer and a variety of other game animals. Occasionally cougar, bear, and bighorn sheep are sighted. More than 160 species of birds have been observed in the park, nesting among the Douglas fir of the northern slopes, the piñon and juniper of the mesa tops, and the sagebrush of the canyon bottoms.

Park elevations range from 5,000 to 8,500 feet above sea level. The mesa is a great block of Cretaceous sedimentary rock, mostly shale and sandstone, that was deposited 90 million years ago and has been tipped gently to the south.

H   I   S   T   O   R   Y

The cliff dwellings of Mesa Verde have been empty since the last years of the thirteenth century. The inhabitants, a people called the Anasazi, who lived not just at Mesa Verde, but throughout the Four Corners

John Wetherill, whose family rediscovered Mesa Verde, at Cliff Palace in 1891.

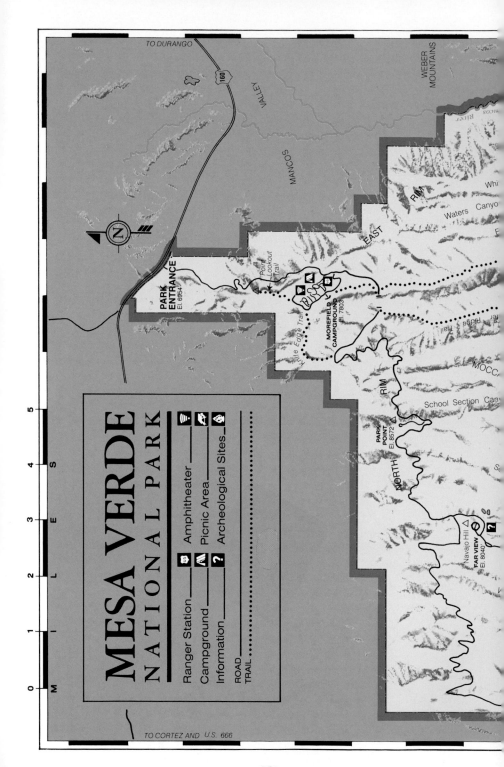

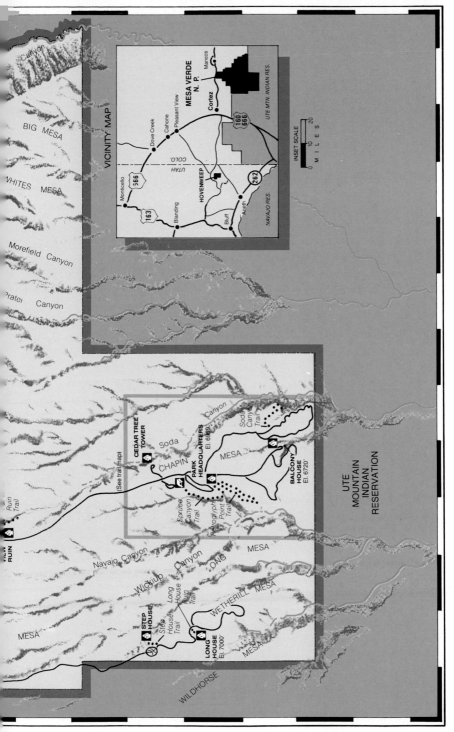

VICINITY MAP

MESA VERDE N. P.

Mancos

Cortez

UTE MTN. INDIAN RES.

Pleasant View

Cahone

Dove Creek

Monticello

566

HOVENWEEP

UTAH
COLO.

160
666

262

163

Blanding

Bluff

Aneth

NAVAJO RES.

INSET SCALE

0   10   20

M I L E S

BIG MESA

WHITES MESA

Morefield Canyon

Prater Canyon

Canyon

CEDAR TREE TOWER

Soda Canyon

CHAPIN

PARK HEADQUARTERS
El. 6969'

MESA

BALCONY HOUSE
El. 6720'

Soda Canyon Trail

Spruce Canyon Trail

Petroglyph Point Trail

(See trail map)

Ruin Trail

RUIN

Navajo Canyon

Wickiup Canyon

LONG

MESA

WETHERILL MESA

Long House Ruin Trail

STEP HOUSE

Step House Trail

LONG HOUSE
El. 7000'

MESA

WILDHORSE

UTE MOUNTAIN
INDIAN
RESERVATION

region, walked away from the home that had been theirs for 700 years, leaving no sign of turmoil, fanfare, or regret. They simply left. And the entire Four Corners region lay silent, seemingly empty for 500 years.

The Anasazi

Who were the people who lived in the cliffs? The Navajo Indians, who live south and west of Mesa Verde, call them Anasazi—"Ancient Ones" or "Enemy Ancestors." Navajos of historic time have hesitated to tread amidst the unquiet spirits among the cliff dwellings.

The comings and goings of a people are difficult to trace. Twelve thousand years ago, hunters and gatherers stalked deer and elk, and gathered piñon nuts and prickly pear, across the region that is Mesa Verde. Four thousand years ago, an event occurred that would alter southwestern life at least as much as the invention of the steam engine altered European civilization. Corn was introduced, probably from Mexico or Central America. At first people would merely drop kernels in favorable places and return months later to see if anything had grown. But slowly these people learned to tend their plants and cultivate their land. Perhaps by the year A.D. 500, they could be called an agricultural people, relying for their subsistence more on the seeds they sowed, which by then included beans and squash, than on the animals they hunted or the nuts and fruit they gathered.

The Anasazi evolution to agriculturalism probably occurred well south of Mesa Verde. It was not until A.D. 550 that the Anasazi arrived there. The Green Mesa, covered with juniper and piñon, offered plentiful firewood, and there were seeps and springs along the cliff edges. The people stayed.

These people, the Basketmaker Anasazi, built permanent pit houses, singly or in small clusters. With wood or stone they dug out a pit 10 to 15 feet across and 3 feet deep. The roof and walls, which were supported by four corner posts, were made of mud-covered juniper and piñon branches. Attached to one side of the pit house was an antechamber used for storage. Entrance was by ladder through a hole in the roof of the main room.

The Basketmaker people, secure in their Mesa Verde home, began to experiment. Finely woven baskets of yucca fiber and rabbitbrush had been used for storing seeds, carrying water, and even cooking; but pottery, once introduced, was gradually developed into the traditional black-on-white ware typical of Mesa Verde. The atlatl (a spear-throwing device) and the throwing stick were replaced by the more accurate bow and arrow. Turkeys were domesticated.

Around A.D. 750, the Anasazi underwent social changes that are per-

Opposite: A reconstructed Basketmaker pit house on Wetherill Mesa.

haps best reflected in their architecture. The isolated pit house of the Basketmakers evolved toward the many-roomed pueblo. People lived in villages, no longer as single families. Located above ground, living quarters faced a central ceremonial room called the kiva, which was built below ground. The kiva served as a social gathering place or as a religious center. Archeologists, twelve centuries later, used these changes in building methods to mark the end of the Basketmaker period and the beginning of the Pueblo period.

Changes in Anasazi social order are further underscored by the development of trade with neighbors to the south and by the communal water projects undertaken near Far View Ruin and south of Morfield Campground. Many hands were needed for the construction of Mummy Lake Reservoir near Far View, and the mile-long catchment channel that fed it. Work was begun around A.D. 950 and continued as long as the Pueblo Anasazi occupied the mesa top. Success may have swollen their numbers, and the subsequent crowding forced them to farm land that previously had been considered too poor to cultivate. Many small check dams were built at this time to catch silt and to hold water that would otherwise have been wasted.

The Classic Pueblo period, the culminating chapter of the Anasazi story at Mesa Verde, began around A.D. 1100. Mesa-top villages were consolidated into larger communities. A good example is Far View Ruin, which is surrounded by sixteen satellite villages within a half mile. Archeologists have observed but not explained this concentration of population at Mesa Verde. Perhaps there was a need for defense. External walls of these pueblos were built without doors. Kivas were drawn into courtyards within the pueblos. Towers were built more often, frequently connected by tunnels to a nearby kiva.

The Anasazi art of masonry reached its zenith with the construction of these mesa-top cities. Stones were worked into rectangular blocks; their surfaces were distinctively pecked or dimpled. These and other refinements provided the strength needed to build to a height of three or four stories. But they also satisfied aesthetic yearnings. The Anasazi of Mesa Verde, at the height of their success as farmers and traders, had earned time for the arts.

Almost all the great cliff dwellings of Mesa Verde —Cliff Palace, Spruce Tree House, Long House—were built and occupied only during the thirteenth century. These fortress cities grew out of the walls of the mesa, made of the same rock. Though hastily built, the dwellings are a graceful presence that complements the cliffs.

What triggered the move? We may never know. Certainly the cliff dwellings were more defensible. Had the Anasazi acquired real or imagi-

The 1,700-foot-high volcanic plug Shiprock, south of the park.

nary enemies? No increase in burial sites, which would suggest fighting, has been found, and the mummies and skeletons that have been found usually indicate death by natural causes. Firewood, harvested continually for six centuries, was surely growing scarce. Perhaps the caves required less heating. Water sources may have dried up. Intensive agriculture, coupled with droughts such as that from 1090 to 1101, may have forced the people to seek and protect springs along the rim of the mesa and in the back of the caves in which they built their new homes.

And having built the cliff dwellings, the Anasazi simply disappeared before the year 1300. They left mugs, pots full of corn, bows and arrows, and jewelry scattered about their homes with a casualness that implied their intention to return later in the day. Archeologists believe that they migrated to the upper reaches of the Rio Grande and the Zuñi villages in New Mexico, and to the Hopi mesas in Arizona.

A severe drought, recorded in the shrunken rings of trees, struck the Mesa Verde region from 1276 until at least 1299. But these people had survived worse droughts. Sudden disease or warfare would be evident in an increase of burials, but no such increase has been found. The mesa top, cultivated more and more intensively for seven centuries, may have grown too alkaline—too nutrient-poor—to be farmed any longer. Perhaps... Archeologists, if pressed, hypothesize that a combination of any or all of these or even more puzzling factors may have led to the mysterious evacuation of Mesa Verde.

The Spanish

Sylvestre Vélez de Escalante and Francisco Atanasia Domínguez, two Franciscan priests, stumbled across the foot of the La Plata Mountains and down into the Mancos Valley in August 1776, while looking for a route from Santa Fe to the missions of California. They were the first Europeans to see much of the parts of Colorado, Utah, Arizona, and New Mexico now called the Colorado Plateau. Certainly, they were the first to see the great green highland lying to the west of the Mancos; years later it was to be named Mesa Verde. Although they discovered none of the ruins of the mesa, they did find the ruin complex near Dolores, Colorado, that bears Escalante's name.

The Spaniards who followed Escalante and Domínguez, and the occasional nineteenth-century geologist who surveyed the great Colorado Plateau, just missed, perhaps by several miles, the treasures known only to a few Native Americans.

The First Settlers and Discovery

The Ute Indians occupied western Colorado when the early explorers and trappers moved through. For the most part, the Utes were not threatened by these transient men. But in the 1870s, silver was discovered in the nearby San Juan Mountains, and people flocked to the Colorado Territory to seek their fortunes. Among them was Benjamin Wetherill, a Quaker from Missouri who was down on his luck. His story was that of most—he found little, if any, silver. So he staked out some land and, in 1879, took up cattle ranching in the Mancos Valley. The Utes were slowly pushed back onto a fraction of the land they once had roamed. But, unknown to Wetherill and his neighbors, the Indians held the real treasure—Mesa Verde and the ruins of a civilization long since vanished.

In 1874, members of the Hayden Geological and Geographical Survey, who were sporadically exploring the Mancos River at the foot of Mesa Verde, had discovered dwellings in the canyon walls. William Henry Jackson found Two Story House; a year later, W. H. Holmes discovered Sixteen Window House. In some, they found corncobs and bits of pottery. Their curiosity was piqued: Who were the people who had lived in the cliffs?

Pottery made by the Anasazi, who lived at Mesa Verde between A.D. 550 and 1300.

Richard, Wetherill's eldest son, learned from a Ute of a large stone house that was located up one of Mesa Verde's side canyons. The Utes considered it sacred and, like the Navajos, never visited it. Richard's curiosity grew unbearable when the Indian refused to tell him how to find the dwelling.

In 1887, another of the sons stumbled across what he described as a vast cave filled with an entire city of ruins—towers and multistoried buildings reaching beyond sight. The hour was late, however, and he had to continue on his way. Once again, discovery had slipped by.

Cliff Palace, Spruce Tree House, Square Tower House—these ruins had remained undisturbed for 600 years. But on December 18, 1888, Richard Wetherill and his brother-in-law, Charlie Mason, while tracking stray cattle on Chapin Mesa during a heavy snowstorm, walked to the edge of Cliff Canyon. Through the swirl of blinding snow, they spotted the ruin now called Cliff Palace. Lashing logs together in a makeshift ladder, they scrambled down the sheer face of the cliff and across to the ruins and stepped into the past.

The Wetherills—generous perhaps to a fault—wanted all the world to know of their discovery. They guided reporters, tourists, and pot hunters through the ruins, and unlucky was the visitor who left without a souvenir. They sold pottery, baskets, sandals, axes, and arrowheads —all from Mesa Verde. But the Wetherills also worked with Baron Gustaf Nordenskiold, who, in 1891, conducted the first systematic archeological survey of the ruins of the Mesa Verde. As the significance of the ruins came to be appreciated, a new ethic of preservation slowly emerged. The Wetherills ceased selling artifacts to tourists in 1895; from then on they contracted only with privately funded research expeditions for the excavation of intact collections. By good fortune, the great majority of the treasures they found ultimately ended up in the collections of four major institutions. Such were the painful beginnings of the science of archeology in southwestern Colorado.

Establishment of the Park

In 1891, and again in 1894, the Colorado General Assembly called on the United States Congress to preserve Mesa Verde as a national park; a sense of national heritage was evolving to replace the blunter instincts of free enterprise. In 1901, the Colorado Cliff Dwelling Association managed to persuade the Ute Indians and the United States Congress to give it control of Mesa Verde; in return, the Utes were to receive an annual sum of $300 from the Congress. On June 29, 1906, President Theodore Roosevelt signed a bill granting Mesa Verde the full status of a national park, and what was left of a civilization long past was preserved.

A pair of old crutches, thought to have been used by an Anasazi.

G E O L O G Y

To see this expanse of almost empty land is to grasp at intangibles. How old are these rocks? How were they placed here? How were they sculpted into their present form? Wallace Stegner, writing about the Colorado Plateau, once said, "This is country that leads one to think in terms of geologic time, which if I am not mistaken is about the same as thinking in religious terms." Certainly the Navajos would agree. According to them, Shiprock, to the south, is Tse-bi-ta-i, the winged rock that brought their ancestors to this land. Sleeping Ute Mountain, just west of the park, is a Ute god, asleep on his back.

The geology of Mesa Verde, taken one step at a time, is really quite simple. Some 90 million years ago—before the Colorado Plateau or the Rocky Mountains had been lifted far above sea level—this land was under water. As the sea floor subsided, 2,000 feet of mud and sand were deposited. Upon hardening, this mud became the Mancos Shale.

Above the Mancos lies the sand and shale of the Mesa Verde Group. Within the park, this is composed of three distinct layers. The lowest layer is the Point Lookout Sandstone, which forms the lower of two prominent cliffs visible in canyon walls throughout the park. As the sea that deposited the Mancos Shale retreated to the northeast, sandy beaches were continuously deposited along the shoreline. Eventually, 250 feet of sand accumulated.

As the sea withdrew, the land became a swamp, crossed by river flood plains. Trees lived and died, and in time were compressed into coal. Along with sand and silt, they became part of the Menefee Formation, a 400-foot layer of rock named for a pioneer family of the Mancos Valley. Coal within the Menefee is found in two zones near the top and bottom of the formation. Many outcrops of coal have burned naturally when ignited by lightning or forest fires. Modern men have mined the coal in the recent past, but the Anasazi apparently left well enough alone and did not use the coal as fuel.

The sea returned once again following deposition of the Menefee. The swamps were flooded, and rivers carried into the area the sand and clay that compose the 400-foot-thick Cliff House Sandstone—the third and final layer of the Mesa Verde Group in the park area. This rock, when eroded millions of years later, formed distinct cliffs that were punctuated by caves with high, vaulting roofs. The Anasazi would put to good use these caves of the Cliff House Sandstone.

The Mancos Shale and Mesa Verde Group were deposited toward the end of the Cretaceous period. At the close of this period, some 65 million years ago, a mountain-building epoch began that was to change

A butte seen from Point Lookout near the entrance to the park.

the face of the West. The land was compressed, folded, and thrust upward. The Rocky Mountains began to rise. Over the next 40 million years, Sleeping Ute Mountain and the La Platas popped up like mushrooms overnight, geologically speaking. The San Juan Mountains were uplifted, gently tipping the surrounding countryside, including the Mesa Verde. These mountains were pushed up by a core of rising molten rock. Erosion was accelerated by the uplifts; the Mancos Shale and Mesa Verde Group, once extending in great sheets in all directions, were whittled down to their present extent at Mesa Verde.

Seen on a map, Mesa Verde is composed of many narrow mesas that run north and south. The mesas are separated by canyons that drain south to the Mancos River. Since the whole mesa tips to the south, canyons that flow in that direction have grown in length much faster than their counterparts that drain to the north. As a result, the south-flowing canyons have cut all the way back to the mesa's great northern escarpment. Geologically speaking, the canyons of the Mesa Verde are being cut deeper and wider at a frightful clip. The two sandstone formations at the bottom and top of the Mesa Verde Group form resistant cliffs that protect the soft underlying shales. Whenever blocks of sandstone are removed by erosion, the vulnerable shales beneath quickly melt away with the next rainfall.

Geology is the study of rocks—nothing could seem more down to earth. But this science lends itself to the consideration of space and time. Sitting at Park Point, one wonders about the birth of this country.

N A T U R A L H I S T O R Y

Climate and Precipitation

Mesa Verde can get mighty cold and pretty warm. Mesa-top temperatures in the vicinity of the park headquarters on Chapin Mesa range from an average low of 18° F in January to a high of 88° F in July, although extremes of −20° F and 102° F have been observed. Summer temperatures can easily plummet 35 degrees after sunset. The dry air of the Southwest will surprise the unprepared visitor. The park's 18 inches of annual precipitation are delivered on a yearly installment plan—divided almost equally between winter snowstorms and late-summer thundershowers.

Both people and animals feed off the juicy fruit of the prickly pear.

Flora

Mesa Verde, the Green Mesa, got its name from the piñon and juniper stands that cover its top. The mesa tops, with elevations of between 6,800 and 7,400 feet, have been called the Anasazi cornbelt by some archeologists. Conditions at this altitude lent themselves to the greatest agricultural development during the Pueblo period. In addition to farming, the Anasazi gathered the wild-growing prickly pear cactus, Indian rice grass, and Rocky Mountain bee plant.

Toward the north end of Mesa Verde grow stands of Douglas fir on the cooler, north-facing slopes. In the canyon bottoms of the south-flowing creeks is found the big sagebrush that is better suited to the dry, warm canyons. Growing in the canyons and on the mesa tops is the versatile *Yucca baccata*, a member of the lily family. Its roots, fruit, and fibers were used by the Anasazi, the fibers to make sandals, baskets, ropes, and other useful items. A fascinating symbiotic relationship has evolved between the yucca and an otherwise nondescript, papery-winged moth. The yucca is completely dependent on the pronuba moth for pollination. In turn, the moth lays its eggs only in the fruit of the blossoming yucca. Without the other, each would be frustrated in its efforts to reproduce.

Above: The Anasazi made sandals, baskets, and rope from tough yucca fibers. Right: Mule deer are browsers, preferring to feed off leaves and twigs of shrubs and trees rather than grass.

Fauna

A surprising diversity of wildlife can be found at Mesa Verde. Rocky Mountain mule deer commonly forage near Morefield Campground around dusk and dawn. Coyotes sing their mournful songs after dark. Cougars, bears, and bobcats are seen on rare and special occasions. Birds are especially numerous within the park. Owls, hawks, eagles, and falcons hunt along the canyon walls and along the mesa's northern escarpment. The canyon wren is more often heard than seen, filling the air with its laughing, descending trill.

SITES, TRAILS, AND TRIPS

Mesa Verde, like an island in the sky, rises 2,000 feet above the surrounding Mancos Valley, Dolores Plateau, and Montezuma Valley. The most important decision, on entering Mesa Verde National Park, is which mesa sites to see.

Park Point. Entering the park from the north, drivers climb the steep shale face of the northern escarpment to the highest elevations of the park. Park Point lies 8,572 feet above sea level. From here the mesa drops sharply to the north and more slowly to the south. The Mancos River, flowing south and then west, holds the mesa in the crook of its arm. Beyond the river, beyond the valley floors at the foot of the mesa, mountains are scattered across the desert. To the north are the Abajos and the La Sals of Utah. To the east lie the La Plata Mountains, and Lone Cone and Mount Wilson of the San Juan Mountains. Shiprock, the Lukachukai Mountains, and the Carrizo Mountains rise up from the Navajo Reservation to the south. Take the time to sit and soak in this country. The wind that always seems to blow here will rustle through the Gambel oak, Rocky Mountain juniper, and Utah juniper. Arrowleaf balsamroot, blooming in June, will turn the hillsides below you yellow. Try to imagine how this country seemed to the people who lived here a thousand years ago.

Far View. The Far View Visitor Center houses an exhibit that illustrates and describes historic Indian life style and culture. A park ranger at the information desk can suggest ruins to visit and trails to hike. Bus trips bound for Wetherill Mesa begin across the parking lot during summer months. One mile to the south, along the road leading down Chapin Mesa, is Far View Ruin, which contains examples of some of the finest mesa-top architecture in the park. The ruin was partially reconstructed by archeologist Jesse Fewkes in 1916.

Chapin Mesa. People visit Mesa Verde to see the cliff dwellings, but it is too easy to see only the *major* ruins and then leave. Take a little time to acclimate to the park. Chapin Mesa offers a number of ways to ease into an understanding of the Anasazi.

The Mesa Verde Museum is an excellent place to begin learning about the ancient people who once lived here. Dioramas depict all the phases of Indian habitation of the mesa. There are displays of pottery, weaving, toolmaking, and jewelry. Dendrochronology—the science of tree-ring dating—is explained in detail. Demonstrations show the native use of plants and animals. The museum can suggest a bit of the richness of Anasazi life.

Next door to the museum is the main ranger station. Here visitors sign up for a hike to either Spruce Canyon or Petroglyph Point. The trails begin immediately below the ranger station; each is a little more than 2 miles long and will take 2 or 3 hours to hike at an easy pace.

The mesa top is covered by the uniformly green piñon and juniper forest that gave Mesa Verde its name. When the Anasazi lived here, much of this forest would have been cleared for cultivation or carried home for firewood. Visible on top is the ever-precious yucca.

Spruce Canyon Trail. Spruce Canyon Trail drops off Chapin Mesa and descends to the bottom of Spruce Canyon. Morning hikers are more likely to be following Rocky Mountain mule deer tracks than those of fellow hikers. Of 600,000 people visiting the park in 1981, only 600 registered to hike this trail. Hikers are likely to have the trail all to themselves.

The Anasazi walked this canyon searching for piñon nuts. The piñon pine bears a crop of nuts once or twice out of every seven years. Many years after the Anasazi, the Wetherill boys stumbled up these canyon bottoms after their cattle, not yet realizing the incredible ruins that lay silent so near by.

Petroglyph Point Trail. The Petroglyph Point Trail is longer than the Spruce Canyon Trail, but it does not descend to the canyon floor. It winds along the base of the Cliff House Sandstone, leading past caves and a small cliff dwelling. Since much of this trail is shaded by the

Overleaf: Decorated interior of an Anasazi dwelling. The figures on the walls are considered to be of religious significance.

Trails of Mesa Verde National Park

Spruce Tree House Trail: Starts and ends at museum; .5 mile round trip; 1 hour; 200-foot ascent; ranger-guided tour in winter, self-guided tour in summer of third largest cliff dwelling (114 rooms, 8 kivas), constructed between 1200 and 1276.

Cliff Palace Trail: Starts and ends at Ruins road loop; .5 mile round trip; 1 hour; 500-foot ascent; largest cliff dwelling (217 rooms, 23 kivas), constructed between 1200 and 1300; narrow, winding, strenuous trail; not accessible to disabled.

Balcony House Trail: Starts and ends at Ruins road loop; .5 mile round trip; 1 hour; 400-foot ascent; ranger-guided tour of cliff dwelling (45 rooms); access by 32-foot ladder, exit by 12-foot tunnel and 100-foot climb up cliff face; open May through September.

Step House Ruin Trail: Starts and ends at Wetherill Mesa Lunchette; .5 mile round trip; 1 hour; 500-foot ascent; ranger-guided tour of pit house/cliff dwelling; very strenuous; access to disabled with assistance.

Long House Ruin Trail: Starts and ends at Mini Trail trail head; .75 mile round trip; 1 hour; 400-foot ascent; ranger-guided tour of second largest cliff dwelling; strenuous, with 50 steps; not recommended for disabled.

Spruce Canyon Trail: Starts at Spruce Tree House; ends at Spruce Canyon picnic area; 2.1 miles round trip; 2 hours; 700-foot ascent; drops off Chapin Mesa to bottom of Spruce Canyon and then turns up canyon; registration at chief ranger's office.

Petroglyph Point Trail: Starts at Spruce Tree House; ends at museum parking area; 2.3 miles round trip; 2 hours; 200-foot ascent; runs below edge of plateau; excellent views of Spruce Canyon and Navajo Canyon; registration at chief ranger's office.

Prater Ridge Trail: Starts and ends at Morefield Campground; 7.5 miles round trip; 4 hours; 700-foot ascent; changes in elevation and vegetation types.

Knife Edge Trail: Starts and ends at Morefield Campground; 1.5 miles round trip; 1 hour; 100-foot ascent; follows old road alignment to Montezuma Valley overlook; excellent place from which to watch sunsets.

Soda Canyon Overlook Trail: Starts and ends at turnout north of Balcony House; .75 mile round trip; 1 hour; three overlooks of Soda Canyon; the southward facing overlook provides only good view of Balcony House.

Far View Ruin Trail: Starts and ends at Far View Ruin; 1 mile round trip; 1 hour; 5 surface ruins of dwellings constructed between 900 and 1300.

Point Lookout Nature Trail: Starts and ends at Morefield Amphitheater; 2 miles round trip; 2 hours; panorama of the surrounding area, including the Mancos and Montezuma valleys, Mount Wilson, the Dolores Peaks, and the La Plata Mountains.

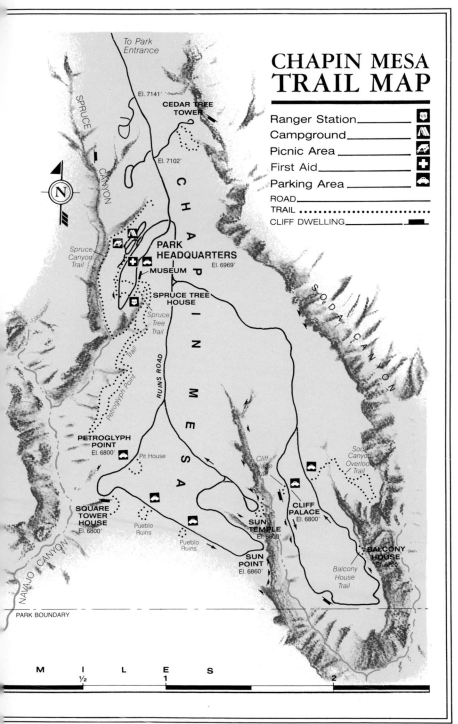

CHAPIN MESA
TRAIL MAP

Ranger Station
Campground
Picnic Area
First Aid
Parking Area
ROAD
TRAIL ••••••••••••••••••••••••
CLIFF DWELLING

To Park
Entrance

El. 7141'

CEDAR TREE TOWER

El. 7102'

SPRUCE CANYON

Spruce Canyon Trail

PARK HEADQUARTERS

El. 6969'

MUSEUM

SPRUCE TREE HOUSE

Spruce Tree Trail

CHAPIN MESA

RUINS ROAD

Petroglyph Point Trail

SODA CANYON

PETROGLYPH POINT
El. 6800'

Pit House

Soda Canyon Overlook Trail

Cliff Palace Trail

SQUARE TOWER HOUSE
El. 6800'

Pueblo Ruins

Pueblo Ruins

SUN TEMPLE
El. 6800'

CLIFF PALACE
El. 6800'

SUN POINT
El. 6860'

BALCONY HOUSE
El. 6720'

Balcony House Trail

NAVAJO CANYON

PARK BOUNDARY

M   I   L   E   S
½
1
2

sandstone cliff, temperatures are lower and the ground is wetter than if it were not shaded, and trees like Douglas fir are able to grow at this 6,700-foot elevation. Also found along this trail is the chokecherry bush, whose fruit was eaten by the Anasazi. Near the end of the trail is Petroglyph Point, where an excellent example of Anasazi rock art can be admired. The trail returns to the museum area along the top of Chapin Mesa.

Spruce Tree House. Spruce Tree House is located directly across from the main ranger station on Chapin Mesa. The hike down to the ruin will take approximately 15 minutes. Just before reaching the ruin, hikers will pass the spring that served the 100 or so people who lived in the 114 rooms of the ruin. The National Park Service has reconstructed one of the eight kivas at this site; visitors are able to climb down the ladder in the kiva roof and view the interior. Kivas are used by men of the modern-day Zuñi and Hopi tribes, thought to be descendants of the Anasazi. Similar use is therefore ascribed to the Anasazi.

Mesa Top Drive. Pit houses constructed during the Basketmaker era (A.D. 575) and an early Pueblo period village (A.D. 950) can be seen along the Mesa Top Drive. The pit houses were built at the beginning of the Anasazi's seven-century occupation of Mesa Verde. There are few places in the United States that allow us to view the systematic evolution of a culture over so long a span of time. Our own European-based culture has not been established in the United States for even half the time spent by the Anasazi in the Southwest.

Cliff Palace. Cliff Palace is the largest, and perhaps the most beautiful, ruin at Mesa Verde. It contains 217 rooms and 23 kivas. Its towers, some four stories high, reach toward but just miss the cave roof soaring overhead. Cliff Palace can be seen in a panoramic view from Mesa Top Drive across Cliff Canyon. Drive along the Cliff Palace–Balcony House Loop to an overlook immediately above Cliff Palace, and hike 10 minutes down to the ruin. A Park Service ranger is on duty to answer questions and *ask visitors to stay off the walls.*

The masonry of Cliff Palace is fascinating. The Anasazi placed small chinking stones in the mortar to prevent cracking. Some walls adjoin others in an ill-fitting manner that suggests sequential rather than simultaneous construction. It is possible to roughly trace the growth of this city room by room as it filled up its cave. Construction of Cliff Palace occurred between 1209 and 1273, dates arrived at by archeologists using tree-ring dating methods on wood found in the ruin.

Because of the protective cave roof, the walls of Cliff Palace have resisted the effects of seven centuries of wind, rain, and snow. Pot hunters took their toll at the turn of this century, but the ruin is now protected. The walls are periodically stabilized to counteract the effects of hundreds of thousands of visitors walking across the base of the ruin each year.

Balcony House. Balcony House is a forty-room dwelling that nests in the cliffs above Soda Canyon. Entrance to the site in Anasazi times was possible only by hand- and toeholds down a cliff and then through a narrow tunnel. No intruder could have hoped to force an entry into this village. Like most other Mesa Verde cliff dwellings, Balcony House was built only in the last few decades of the Anasazi's long occupation of the mesa. Even though Balcony House has an extreme defensive posture, there is no specific evidence that the Anasazi were threatened by enemies.

A ranger-led tour of Balcony House involves a 1-hour hike down to the ruin and back up to the mesa top. Along the way, visitors climb a 32-foot ladder to enter the ruins, and squeeze through the original access tunnel to leave. Those faint of heart or afraid of heights may do well to pass this tour by.

Soda Canyon Overlook Trail. A little farther down the road is the .75-mile Soda Canyon Overlook Trail. It leads past prickly pear cactus (blooming in May and June) to a delightfully quiet view of Balcony House Ruin. Across Soda Canyon lies Moccasin Mesa, which burned in 1972. In many parks, lightning-strike fires are allowed to burn through their natural course, but fires at Mesa Verde are actively suppressed to protect the ruins.

Wetherill Mesa. The science of archeology took a great step forward in 1959 when the five-year Wetherill Mesa Project began. The project's survey documented 800 new Anasazi sites. Taking part in the study, in addition to archeologists, were geologists, meteorologists, biologists, botanists, and ecologists. Even an orthopedic surgeon became involved, examining deformities in the skeletons discovered in the ruins. Never before had such a fully integrated investigation of American prehistory been attempted. The results gave the clearest, most well-rounded picture of Anasazi life ever pieced together.

Wetherill Mesa was opened to the public after the completion of these elaborate excavations. The National Park Service provides a free bus service from the Far View Visitor Center to Wetherill Mesa, where visitors may take a self-guided tour of Step House or a ranger-led tour of Long House, second largest of the park ruins. Each tour is about 1 hour long.

One out of fifteen visitors to Mesa Verde comes to Wetherill Mesa. And because the bus service allows them to temporarily escape the clutches of automobiles, Wetherill Mesa is about the quietest corner in the park. The peacefulness is conducive to soaking in a bit of this land and its history. The Wetherill Mesa Nature Walk begins and ends at the bus parking lot. Along it hikers will see some of the 168 species of birds found in the park—perhaps a violet-green swallow rocketing across the wind, or a prairie falcon or sparrow hawk dropping like a falling star toward an unlucky scrub jay.

Wetherill Mesa is open from about June 1 through Labor Day.

Morefield Campground and Prater Ridge Trail. Morefield Campground, 4 miles past the park entrance, is a funny little town; between May 1 and mid-October, its few hundred residents move in, claim their home-sites, and leave the next morning—a high turnover rate. There is drinking water at the restrooms, and a store and gas pump are up the hill. If you plan to camp at Morefield, the park's only campground, it is wise to choose a site early in the day. Occasionally in the summer Morefield will be quite crowded; certainly the better campsites will be taken by noon. Every summer evening the rangers put on a campfire talk—a National Park Service tradition that Jesse Fewkes began in 1915.

Two trails start at Morefield Campground. The shorter one leads about .5 mile north to the escarpment overlooking the Dolores Plateau and Montezuma Valley—a good walk that can be rewarded by a memorable sunset.

The Prater Ridge Trail, the longer of the two, slants up and to the north along the hill just west of the campground, making a 7.5-mile loop around the cliffs of Prater Ridge. This is the longest, and possibly the prettiest, hike to be found at Mesa Verde. Along the way are extraordinary overlooks of the northern escarpment. Golden eagles patrol the ridgeline; Clark's nutcrackers crash noisily through the oak thickets. Out of the corner of your eye you might glimpse a mule deer raising its head to watch you pass. On the southern end of the Prater Ridge loop, look down into the valleys where a black bear or two is sighted nearly every year. The tranquillity of this trail offers the perfect ending to a day spent in Mesa Verde National Park.

Opposite: Cliff Palace, built in the early 1200s, is protected from bad weather by a steep, overhanging shelf.

PETRIFIED FOREST
NATIONAL PARK

---

*Pebbles and small rocks, washed down from "tepee" formations,
represent final stages of erosion.*

PETRIFIED FOREST NATIONAL PARK, P.O. BOX 217 ARIZONA 86028, TEL.: (602) 524-6228

Highlights: Kachina Point □ Chinde Point □ Puerco Indian Ruin Newspaper Rock □ The Tepees □ Blue Mesa □ Jasper Forest Overlook □ Crystal Forest □ The Flattops □ Long Logs □ Agate House □ Giant Logs

Access: From west, take U.S. 180 from Holbrook to south entrance. From east, leave I-40 at north entrance. See map on pages 278–279.

Hours: Daily, 8 A.M.-5 P.M.; longer during spring, summer, fall. Road closed during bad winter weather. Road open, but facilities closed, Christmas Day. *Note:* Arizona is on Rocky Mountain Standard Time throughout the year.

Fees: Entrance, $5/vehicle; $2/person on buses. Golden Age, Golden Eagle, Golden Access passes available and honored.

Parking: Ample at each public-use point.

Gas, food: In park at Painted Desert Oasis and Rainbow Forest Curios; snacks at DoBell's Curios, park road and U.S. 180. Also in Holbrook.

Lodging: In Holbrook.

Visitor Center: Painted Desert Visitor Center, just off I-40 at north entrance, offers information and 17-minute film on petrified wood every half hour.

Museum: Rainbow Forest Museum exhibits petrified wood and other paleontological features.

Gift shops: At Painted Desert Oasis and Rainbow Forest Curios.

Pets: Permitted on leash, except in public buildings and wilderness areas. Horseback riding permitted throughout park, no grazing; no rentals or stables.

Picnicking: At Chinde Point, Rainbow Forest areas only. No open fires.

Hiking: Throughout park. Water must be carried. Topographical maps advisable outside developed areas. Permit needed for overnight.

Backpacking: Backpack camping permitted in wilderness areas with free permit from rangers. Apply for permit before 4 P.M. Carry water.

Campgrounds: None.

Tours: On limited basis in summer. In English only. Check at Visitor Center, Museum, or entrance station for tour times.

Facilities for disabled: At Painted Desert Visitor Center, 17-minute film and information in large script. At Puerco Ruin, restrooms, summer only.

For additional information, see also Sites, Trails, and Trips on pages 291–298.

T HE PETRIFIED FOREST NATIONAL PARK IS A CURIOUS place. Where once stood tall trees and lush vegetation, there is now arid terrain. Where once reptiles roamed and huge rivers spread their waters, there are now ravens and lizards, dry washes and rivers. The earth has undergone many changes since that time. The area has been weathered over millions of years into sparse shapes and configurations. From the approaching highways, we see no outstanding features—yawning canyons or majestic mountains—that might give the park a familiar identity. Only a marker on Interstate 40 informs us that we are entering one of the most unusual landscapes on the continent.

First wagon trails, then the railroad, and finally, in this century, old U.S. 66 followed by Interstate 40 conducted travelers from east and west across this vast, empty land. The early explorers and pioneers suffered it all—the heat, the lack of water, the endless expanse, the eroded washes and gullies. Today, sealed in air-conditioned capsules,

Banding of badlands indicates different sedimentary layers.

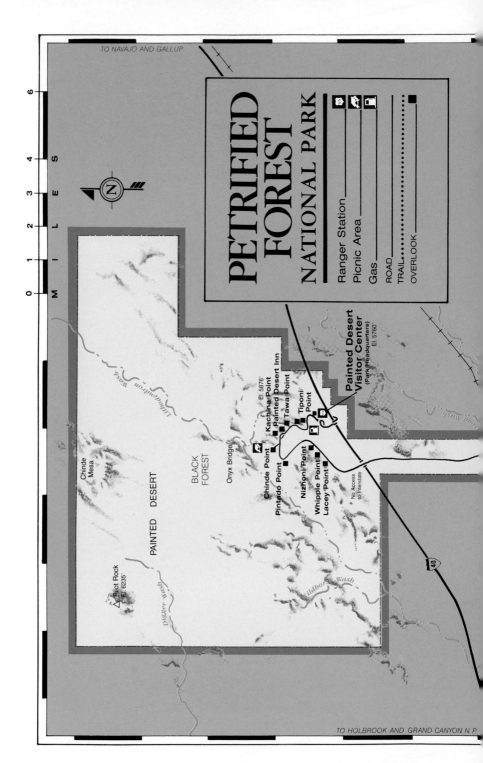

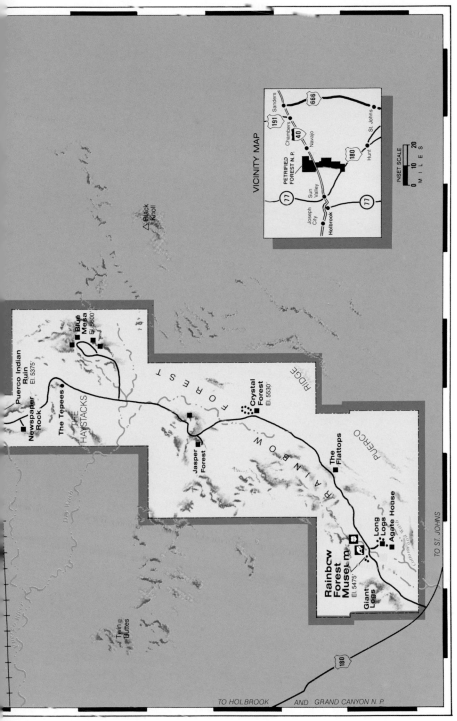

VICINITY MAP

666
Sanders
191
Chambers
40
Navajo
St. Johns
PETRIFIED
FOREST N. P.
180
Hunt
77
Sun
Valley
Joseph
City
Holbrook
77

INSET SCALE
0 10 20
MILES

Black
Knoll

Puerco Indian
Ruin
El. 5375'

Newspaper
Rock

Blue
Mesa
El. 5600'

THE HAYSTACKS

The Tepees

FOREST

Crystal Forest
El. 5530'

RIDGE

Jasper
Forest

RAINBOW FOREST

The Flattops

PUERCO

Long
Logs

Agate House

Rainbow
Forest
Museum
El. 5475'

Giant
Logs

Twin
Buttes

TO ST. JOHNS

180

TO HOLBROOK AND GRAND CANYON N. P.

we speed across the terrain along four-lane highways. To experience a sense of the land, its swoop and roll, and the contours that distinguish one geological marvel from another in the American Southwest, we should follow the older roads that cling to the mantle of the land; or, better still, step out of the car and walk away from the road into the burnished palette of the Painted Desert, into the lunar hills of the Blue Mesa, or among the tangle of fallen logs that marks the petrified forests.

Because it is tucked away in folds and crevices of the desert highlands, Petrified Forest National Park is an easy place to miss. And yet for ninety years, until its full protection as a national park, this remote corner of Arizona was nearly ravaged into extinction by explorers, settlers, and turn-of-the-century entrepreneurs. A land as exposed and mysterious as this is especially vulnerable to exploitation. There are no mountains to guard it or rivers to conceal its treasures or canyons down into which prospectors with picks and shovels must laboriously descend. The accessibility of the land is part of its attraction, as well as its greatest weakness.

H   I   S   T   O   R   Y

Human beings have been present in the Petrified Forest National Park area for at least 1,500 years. Located within the boundaries are more than 300 archeological sites, varying in size from a few potsherd finds to pueblo complexes. It is believed that the oldest ruins were occupied around A.D. 500. Consisting mainly of oval pit houses 9 to 12 feet in diameter, they are scattered on top of a mesa in the southern portion of the park. Ruins of pit houses—with the added features of ventilation shafts and outside storage areas—in the Twin Buttes area indicate a more highly developed culture. Sherds of decorative pottery have been found there, along with sea shells and semiprecious stones, indicating trade with tribes on the Pacific coast and in the heart of Mexico.

The Anasazi

One of the larger ruins, and the one most easily accessible to the public, is located on a windswept hill above the Puerco River. Here, for at least three centuries, resided a people known as the Anasazi (Navajo for "Ancient Ones"), whose civilization at the end of the first millennium of the Christian era extended over the Four Corners region. The Anasazi were one of the most fascinating peoples of this continent. Over an 800-year period, from A.D. 500 to A.D. 1300, they evolved from a tribe of pit dwellers and food gatherers into a culture of sophisticated farmers and architects of complex housing projects like Chaco

Before the park was established, souvenir hunters, attracted by the rainbow colors, removed thousands of tons of petrified wood.

These petroglyphs were carved by the Indians centuries ago.

Canyon and Mesa Verde. They flourished in their Classic phase for a couple of centuries, and then for reasons still unknown, they vanished.

Archeologists estimate that during two occupations in two centuries (A.D. 1100 to 1200 and A.D. 1300 to 1400), as many as 75 rooms were constructed at what is now called the Puerco Ruin. Here perhaps 250 Anasazi cultivated corn, beans, and squash, made baskets and pottery, and lived a remarkably civilized existence in a hostile, arid environment. By 1540, when Spanish explorers first passed through the region, the natives had vanished, perhaps to the north and the heart of the Hopi nation, to the southeast where the Zuñi now dwell, and to the east where they may have resurfaced as Pueblo Indians.

Exploration and Exploitation

The first Spaniards in the area poked around a bit and then moved on. The Indians had left behind no gold, and the petrified wood chips that littered the ground had little monetary value. By contrast, the explorers of the mid-nineteenth century were excited by the petrified wood. A German artist named Baldwin Mollhausen, traveling with the Whipple survey expedition in 1843, wrote that "all the way we went we saw...great heaps of petrification gleaming with such splendid colours that we could not resist the temptation to alight repeatedly and break off a piece..."

The temptation proved irresistible to just about everybody who followed. In 1883, the Atlantic and Pacific Railroad was completed across northern Arizona, and new settlers poured in. Part of the attraction was "Chalcedony Park," as the area was then known. During the 1890s entrepreneurs sawed and polished thousands of tons of fossilized wood into handsome pedestals and table tops, for which people back east were willing to pay high prices. In 1899, Arizona territorial governor N. O. Murphy declared that "the so-called Petrified Forest...is not attractive in the way of natural scenery....Much expense on the part of the Government in creating a reserve for scenic purposes does not seem to me justified."

Establishment of the Park

But also by 1899, a counteroffensive against the exploitation of the Petrified Forest had gained momentum. Charles Lummis, a well-known southwestern writer, reported the depredations in one of his travel books. In 1895, Representative Will Barnes persuaded the Arizona Territorial Legislature to ask the United States Congress to set aside the Petrified Forest as a national park. The request was seconded in 1899 by U.S. Geological Survey paleontologist Lester Ward. The battle for preservation was on, and it was to last until 1906, when President Theodore Roosevelt established the Petrified Forest National Monument. The incorporation included only the Rainbow and Jasper forests in the southern portion of the park. In 1932, a large portion of the Painted Desert and the Blue Mesa area were added to the monument. And in 1962, Congress established the Petrified Forest National Park.

Two hundred million years ago, Arizona was a tropical land located some 1,700 miles closer to the equator than it is today. According to the theory of plate tectonics (better known as the theory of continental drift), all the continents of the earth were once joined together into a supercontinent called Pangaea. Pangaea eventually cracked into blocks that drifted to the positions they occupy as the present-day continents. Thus Arizona shifted north and west, along with the entire North American continent, to its current position. During this long period, the land was shaped and built up by repeated inundations by warm, shallow seas and by metamorphic activity from deep within the earth's molten core.

Sedimentation and Erosion

Chinle badlands.

Mesozoic northern Arizona was a low, flat stretch of country, what today would be called a flood plain, across which rivers and streams meandered, depositing pebbles and sand. Eventually these deposits reached a thickness of several thousand feet and formed a mantle, or covering, called the Chinle Formation. It is the remnants or exposed sections of this formation —denuded by the incessant action of wind and water—that form the topographical features of the park.

Following the era of sedimentary deposition that resulted in the Chinle Formation came yet another that lasted until approximately 70 million years ago. Streams and rivers flowed northward from high mountains in southeastern Arizona toward a sea located to the west of the present-day Colorado River (where southern California is now.) On occasion these streams and rivers formed lakes and swamps, the remains of whose animal life formed deposits of muddy limestone 3,000 feet thick on top of the Chinle Formation. Gradually the weather changed, the climate grew arid, and these sedimentary rock layers above the Chinle Formation began to erode.

During the Tertiary period of the Cenozoic era, approximately 65 million years ago, an uplift occurred in the region that raised the strata of sedimentary rock approximately 7,000 feet. So gradual was this uplift that few faults and folds developed, the land rising with the uniformity of a table top. To the east, the uplift was higher, causing a natural barrier that trapped the waters of the ancestral Colorado River flowing down from the north. Over a long period of time, these waters spread in all directions, forming an extensive impoundment. Sand, silt, clay, and sediments flowed in with the current to create a vast body of water that geologists call Lake Bidahochi.

Some 10 million years ago, an expanding drainage to the west of the lake intercepted the route of the ancestral Colorado and caused it to flow westward, away from Lake Bidahochi. Eventually the lake dried up, and new geological influences appeared. Around 4 million years ago, volcanoes erupted in the area, blanketing the lake bed with lava and volcanic ash. This period was followed by another era of meandering streams and rivers, after which erosion became the dominant geological factor. The mantle of the Bidahochi Formation, laid down by the deposits of the former lake and the ash and lava from the volcanic activity that followed, was swept away. Only a few places within the park boundaries, such as Pilot Rock, remain to indicate the remnants of millions of years of sedimentary and metamorphic activity. The erosion also cut deep into the strata of the underlying Chinle Formation, uncovering the petrified wood and fossils.

Badlands

Nature is full of paradoxes. At Petrified Forest National Park, where there is virtually no water, practically all the landscape has been produced by the action of water and wind. The carving of the Chinle Formation—once a relatively flat series of sedimentary layers—into the gashed and rounded topography of today took many millions of years. The popular term for this kind of terrain is *badlands*, and its creation is the result of a process that geologist William Lee Stokes has called "the principle of differential erosion." Hard rocks, such as sandstone, limestone, and lava, withstand erosion better than soft ones, such as clay and shale. Once, a long time ago, the low, rounded hills of the Painted Desert were protected by layers of hard rock. When this rock disappeared, the softer materials underneath were exposed, and erosion took place at a faster rate, geologically speaking. The hills we see today are composed primarily of soft, porous bentonitic clays. When they are soaked by a summer thundershower, these clays expand to eight times their original thickness. The sun then bakes them, causing the expanded surface to crack and crumble. The next rain washes the fragmented surface into a gully.

To appreciate the natural history of Petrified Forest National Park, we must first look back millions of years and try to visualize what the area once looked like. Two hundred million years ago—during the twilight portion of the Triassic period, early in the Mesozoic era—Arizona was a lush forest of exotic trees, plants, and flowers. Today, that forest is totally fossilized as a result of the effects of time and erosion. This is not to say that there are no plants and animals in the park; indeed, there are. But to truly understand the vast spectrum of natural history represented in the Petrified Forest, we have to reverse our perspective.

Petrified Trees

While walking through the Rainbow Forest in the southern portion of the park, where most of the colorful fossilized wood is located, it is difficult to imagine what the region looked like when the trees were alive and standing. Ninety percent of the fossilized trees in the park are remnants of the cone-bearing *Araucarioxylon*, relatives of which can still be found in parts of South America and Australia. Many of the trees were 200 feet tall, with straight trunks and few limbs. The location and density of the petrified wood have led some scientists to conjecture that the trees grew elsewhere, perhaps to the south and southeast, and that after they fell they were carried into the area by streams and rivers and formed enormous logjams.

But how did these trees harden into fossilized wood? Science has an answer—and a most intriguing one—for that question. After they die, trees and animals usually rot away to renew the cycle of nature. The parts that resist dissolution the longest are the hard trunks and bones. In the case of the towering *Araucarioxylon*, the decay rate was slowed because many of the trees were submerged in silt and water. The water not only excluded much oxygen, which is necessary for the process of decomposition, but also was rich in mineral-laden silica, which soaked through the logs and formed minute crystals of quartz within the cells of the tissues. In some trees, the process of petrification duplicated the original microscopic structure of the wood. In others, the cell walls dissolved as the silica percolated through them, forming amorphous petrifications. Cavities caused by decay or disease eventually filled with large crystals. The various mineral impurities in the silica produced the various colors of the fossilized wood: iron, the reds, yellows, and browns; manganese, the black; other minerals, other colors.

Opposite: The black-tailed rabbit's huge ears help it detect predators.

Fossilized Plants and Animals

Petrified Forest National Park has been described as a "geologic... textbook with the pages not only illustrated in full color, but three-dimensionally as well." While the most extensive chapters deal with the rock formations and the petrified trees, other passages are worthy of mention.

Fossils of more than forty plant species have been found in the layers of the Chinle Formation. The most common of these is the fern, ancestor of the ferns that grow profusely in tropical areas today. Two hundred million years ago, strange insects with wingspans the size of hawks' flew among the trees, but the only insect fossils that have been found are of cockroaches. Plenty of hardened vertebrate remains have been located, however. The most prevalent of these is the *Phytosaur*, an alligatorlike creature that had a narrow snout and bony-plated body. Other fossils include the *Placerias*, one of the largest land animals of its day—a herbivore with a broad, barrel-shaped body similar to that of a hippopotamus. A variety of fish fossils have been uncovered, including the skeletons of the ancient (though not extinct) coelacanth and the lungfish.

Erosion reduces petrified logs to chunks, then to chips, eventually to grains of quartz.

Flora

Despite an annual rainfall of less than 9 inches, a surprising variety of vegetation grows in the Petrified Forest National Park. Prickly pear and cholla cactus are everywhere. Flowers include the mariposa lily, Indian paintbrush, and desert primrose. Sunflowers and asters flourish in the summer, and frequently can be seen from the main park road. Saltbush is found in the Blue Mesa region and throughout the Painted Desert. The tiny salt crystals that form on the leaves help the plant conserve water. Buckwheat, a shrub similar to rabbitbrush, turns a distinct orange-brown in the fall. Cliffrose, with its aromatic white blossoms, can be found along the rim overlooking the Painted Desert.

Wildlife

Because the park lacks significant bodies of water, wildlife is sometimes difficult to detect. The larger animals include pronghorn antelope, coyotes, and bobcats. Porcupines are in evidence, and striped skunks are common. Jack rabbits, cottontails, and prairie dogs are everywhere. The most colorful of the many lizards is the collared lizard. Birds include rock wrens, horned larks, Bullock's orioles, and ravens.

The collared lizard sometimes runs on its hind legs, giving it the appearance of a dinosaur.

The Park's Precious Resources

Animal fossils are difficult to locate in the park, but fossilized wood is everywhere and easy to pick up. This deceptive abundance is the greatest single threat to the park's natural resources. Each chip or piece that disappears into an otherwise honest visitor's pockets leaves just that much less for future generations to enjoy. Today, despite strenuous efforts on the part of the park rangers, small pieces that "will never be missed" are illegally pocketed by park visitors. These "small pieces" add up to an estimated twelve tons every year.

Other threats to the park include tampering with archeological sites and vandalizing petroglyphs. Sites like the Puerco Ruin or Newspaper Rock or Jasper Forest are among the most treasured possessions of our country. They constitute significant chapters in the human and geological history of the continent; when they are vandalized, we are all losers. The history of this country is not to be measured solely by the accomplishments of the pioneers who settled it. There is an older heritage that has nothing to do with our forebears. This heritage centers on landscape as the shaping factor; it relegates humanity to its preindustrial position among the variety of creatures that have inhabited the earth.

An early bloomer, the desert primrose flowers in the unlikeliest places.

SITES,   TRAILS,   AND   TRIPS

There are few trails of any great length at Petrified Forest National Park. Several short trails lead through patches of petrified wood. One trail winds down through the Blue Mesa area, and another leads down a steep flight of steps to Newspaper Rock—but these can hardly be called trails. At sites overlooking the Painted Desert, you can get out of your car to enjoy the view; but even in this area of the park there are few regularly marked trails. And that is really part of the magic. If you choose to hike in the Painted Desert, you can go anywhere. You are free to roam like an Anasazi or a conquistador—to go wherever your feet may lead you.

The Painted Desert. The majority of westbound visitors enter the park at the north gate off Interstate 40. The Visitor Center provides orientation to the park in the form of printed matter and a 17-minute film entitled *The Stone Forest.* A filling station and a gift shop and restaurant are also located at the north entrance.

Once past the gate, the road loops onto a volcanic escarpment that rises over the edge of the Painted Desert. Situated at various points along this stretch of road are overlooks that provide excellent views of the landscape, even from the comfort of a car seat—Tiponi Point, Tawa Point (short sloping path to overlook), Kachina Point (where the Painted Desert Inn is located), Chinde Point (picnic area), Pintado Point (short steep path to the highest point along the main park road; excellent place for taking photographs), Nizhoni Point, Whipple Point, and Lacey Point.

For many, this stretch of road is the grandest in the entire park because the appeal of the Petrified Forest National Park is not just in the shape of its landscape or in the fossilized trees. Spread out below, sweeping north and west, are the incredible colors of the Painted Desert. Various hues of red mingle with crusty alkali patches to create a livid, scaly palette. Red is the predominant color here, varying in degree (depending on the time of day) from a metallic sheen to a dull rust. The presence of iron oxides in the soil is responsible for the distinctive red tones. When the flood plains that originally produced the Chinle Formation dried out, the iron minerals in the mud oxidized. Rarely has a vista been so vividly lacquered by nature. In the late afternoon, the rounded formations cast dark, silky shadows that deepen and define the prominent reds.

Overleaf: The dazzling colors in the Painted Desert result from iron oxides.

Kachina Point. Kachina Point is the starting place for hikes into the desert. A trail leads down the steep face of the escarpment, but it vanishes at the bottom, and the hiker is free to walk anywhere. Pilot Rock, the highest point in the park, is about 6 miles away. Permits are required for overnight backpack camping, which is allowed only in the wilderness areas.

There are many natural wonders to see in that magnificent desolation, though perhaps the most interesting encounter is with the profound and mysterious silence that reigns there. Climbing a cracked and shaly hill, scuffing through a sandy wash, watching the wind kick up spurts of sand brings us into contact with the awesome stillness that lies at the heart of nature in the southwestern United States.

The Painted Desert Inn. The Painted Desert Inn is located at Kachina Point. A classic adobe structure, it was built in 1924 and reconstructed and enlarged during the 1930s by the Civilian Conservation Corps. The inn originally served as a waystop for travelers along old U.S. 66. After World War II, it no longer accommodated overnight guests, but functioned as a restaurant, curio shop, and park museum. Two of the rooms are decorated with murals by Fred Kabotie, the renowned Hopi artist. The inn now is being refurbished as a museum. The National Park Service is installing exhibits that illustrate the human and natural history of the park.

The design of the Painted Desert Inn, and the materials from which it was constructed, make it uniquely representative of southwestern architecture. A mixture of Spanish and Indian pueblo styles, colored a ruddy pink, it is a prime example of how human habitations can blend harmoniously with a landscape.

Puerco Ruin. The main park road slopes gently off the escarpment, heading south. It crosses Interstate 40, the Santa Fe Railroad tracks, and the dry bed of the Puerco River. At the river, the road starts up the incline of another escarpment. A short distance away is the Puerco Indian Ruin, the most easily accessible archeological site within the park. A short paved path leads from the parking lot up a knoll. To the left are the ruins. The right-hand branch of the path has two lookouts from which petroglyphs can be seen. Both paths can be negotiated by wheelchairs.

The walls of the ruins have been ground down by erosion, but it is easy to imagine how they looked 800 years ago. There was perhaps

Opposite: Petrified logs and the Chinle Formation in the Blue Mesa section.

more moisture then, and a variety of small and large game inhabited the banks of the Puerco. Back from the river there were cultivated patches where the Anasazi grew vegetables.

Below the ruin, on the slope of the escarpment, figures have been pecked out of the rocks. One in particular, a large wading bird—an avocet, perhaps—with what appears to be a frog in its beak, rivals in artistry the figures at Newspaper Rock. These petroglyphs are easy to see from the edge of the ruin.

Newspaper Rock. Near the top of the escarpment the road passes Newspaper Rock turnout. To reach the rock, climb down a steep cliff face for 120 steps. The labor is well worth it—Newspaper Rock is one of the finest petroglyph sites in the Southwest. A dense cluster of Indian rock carvings is located here. Presumably, they were carved by the Anasazi. The exact date is difficult to determine; desert varnish forms slowly, and it is impossible to tell from the depths of the incised figures how old they are.

Scholars are still baffled about the meaning of these figures. It has been speculated that some of the marks indicate time periods. Some figures seem to represent animals being hunted or, perhaps, killed in a hunt. Still other figures are hauntingly anthropomorphic, indicative of gods and spirits.

Whatever their significance, the range and variety of the carvings are extraordinary. The Anasazi and those who preceded them had no written language, and these figures are the closest thing to a written language they possessed. Many of the petroglyphs are proving to act as solar calendars. Perhaps the Anasazi equivalent of the Rosetta Stone will be found, enabling scholars to decipher these symbols. We can admire their artistry, and the care with which they were chiseled into the rock. These tantalizing figures deepen the riddle of the Anasazi.

Blue Mesa. Midway through the park the road passes through a fascinating area known as Blue Mesa. It is a severely eroded badlands area, sprinkled with remnants of petrified wood. A 3-mile, one-way, spur road leads to the mesa top, on which are located pullouts that offer a 360° view. Pedestal logs can be found throughout this area. A .77-mile, one-way, paved trail on the north side of the loop leads steeply down into the heart of the badlands formation. To walk down the trail is to descend into some of the most unearthly terrain in the Southwest. Low hills with steep, sloping sides, called "haystacks," are the dominant formation. The haystacks are banded in various colors—blue, gray, red—indicating different sedimentary deposits.

Uncovered by erosion, petrified logs lie scattered and broken throughout the park.

Agate Bridge. This site is a graphic illustration of the bizarre effects that erosion can have on petrified logs. The log here, suspended across a gully with both ends implanted in sandstone, was once photographed with a cowboy mounted on a horse standing on it. Such photographs strike terror into the hearts of park rangers. In 1917, fear of the log cracking led the National Park Service to shore it up and to forbid anyone ever to stand on it again.

Jasper Forest. A short spur off the main road leads to Jasper Forest. The view here, especially to the north and west, is commanding. Chunks and pieces of petrified wood are strewn everywhere. The effects of erosion are especially evident, revealing vast deposits of fossilized wood buried in the Chinle Formation. The Navajos thought that the wood was the bones of Yietso, the great monster their ancestors slew when they first arrived in northern Arizona.

Crystal Forest. A .79-mile paved loop trail winds through the Crystal Forest, one of the densest accumulations of petrified logs in the park. "Crystal" is an apt description for this location, since it once contained innumerable examples of how the wood fossilized into solid chunks of quartz as a result of silica-rich water dissolving its cellular structure. The colors here on a sunlit day are marvelous to behold. It is easy to understand why the wood at the southern end of the park has been described as a "rainbow forest."

Long Logs Trail. The trail is a .5-mile loop, an easy 20-minute walk. Here may be found the largest concentration of petrified wood in the park. The logs are the remains of an ancient logjam that was buried in river deposits of mud, sand, and volcanic ash some 190 million years ago. When the tall *Araucarioxylon* trees that grew then toppled over from decay or old age, they congested together in certain areas—perhaps on sand bars or in shallow lagoons—where they were gradually covered by sediments and eventually petrified. Many of the logs in this section exceed 100 feet in length.

Just off the Long Logs Trail are the remains of an old dwelling known as the Agate House. It is perhaps the most unique pueblo in the Southwest, made out of blocks of petrified wood. Archeologists estimate that it was once a "house" of seven rooms that was last occupied nearly 700 years ago. To give visitors an idea of the original size and shape of the Agate House, two of the rooms were partially rebuilt in 1934 by the National Park Service.

Rainbow Forest Museum and Giant Logs Trail. The exhibits in the Rainbow Forest Museum depict how the tall trees became petrified. The museum also has a mural that shows the variety of unique creatures that roamed northern Arizona 200 million years ago. Behind the museum the .5-mile Giant Logs Trail leads past numerous examples of petrified wood. Due to the uneven terrain, there are many steps along this trail. Located here is "Old Faithful," one of the largest petrified logs in the park. Walking along this path, it is easy to imagine yourself tramping across a "lost continent" where strange creatures once thundered and where jewels lie in mute testimony to the earth's riches.

Opposite: The rainbow colors of a pedestal log in Blue Mesa are produced by the minerals iron, copper, and manganese.

ZION
NATIONAL PARK

The Great White Throne is best viewed from the trails in Zion Canyon.

ZION NATIONAL PARK, SPRINGDALE, UTAH 84767-1099, TEL.: (801) 772-3256

Highlights: Great White Throne □ Checkerboard Mesa □ Weeping Rock □ Gateway to the Narrows □ The Narrows □ Emerald Pools Towers of the Virgin □ Kolob Canyons □ Zion Canyon □ Temple of Sinawava □ Great Arch □ Altar of Sacrifice □ Watchman □ Mountain of the Sun □ Beehives □ Kolob Arch

Access: From west, take I-15 to Utah 17 and 9, or take exit 40. From east, take U.S. 89 to Utah 9. See map on pages 304–305.

Hours: All year, 24 hours daily. Zion Canyon Visitor Center, daily, 8 A.M.–9 P.M. in summer; 8 A.M.–7 P.M. in spring and fall; 9 A.M.–5 P.M. in winter.

Fees: Entrance, $5 except in winter, when waived, camping, $6.

Parking: Ample throughout park except in Zion Canyon during Easter season, Memorial Day, and summer.

Gas: In Springdale, St. George, Kanab, Cedar City, Hurricane.

Food: At Zion Lodge from March to November; off season, in above towns.

Lodging: At Zion Lodge from May to October; off season, in above towns.

Visitor Centers: Near south entrance to park, just north of Springdale, and at exit 40 from I-15; offer information, book and map sales; and a free 12-minute slide show in Zion Canyon.

Museum: In Zion Canyon Visitor Center.

Gift shop: Offers books, posters, cards, film, and maps.

Pets: Permitted on leash in areas accessible by car, but not in backcountry.

Picnicking: At Grotto Picnic Area; at Kolob Canyons Viewpoint.

Hiking: On designated trails. Check with park rangers for off-trail routes.

Backpacking: Permitted with free permit, available at visitor centers. No ground fires allowed.

Campgrounds: Camping in designated areas only. Loop D of the Watchman Campground for tents only. All other sites available for tents and trailers. Full hookups only at Zion Canyon Campground in Springdale. No reservations.

Tours: Daily from late March through October.

Other activities: Rock climbing with voluntary permit; limited cross-country skiing; horseback riding; children's program; annual Folklife Festival in late summer.

Facilities for disabled: Access to restrooms, campsites, parking areas, and most public facilities.

For additional information, see also Sites, Trails, and Trips on pages 317–324, and the map on pages 320–321.

THE DRAMATIC, HIGH-WALLED ZION CANYON WAS CREated by Utah's unimposing Virgin River cutting its way through thousands of feet of layered strata, some as old as 200 million years. Within the 147,035 acres of this beautiful park are four major plant zones, extending from an altitude of 3,666 feet to one of 8,740 feet. Amid the 8 rock formations that compose this incredible landscape, more than 70 species of mammals and 272 species of birds find a home.

Rangers at Zion National Park advise visitors to remain long enough to see the park, especially when it has been drenched with rain. Then waterfalls cascade from every notch and crack and precipice, and the sun, emerging through a break in the clouds, turns the canyon walls into a kaleidoscope of patterns and colors.

The Watchman rises 6,555 feet high at South Entrance. Mormon settlers imagined they could see the face of a "watchman" at the top of the peak.

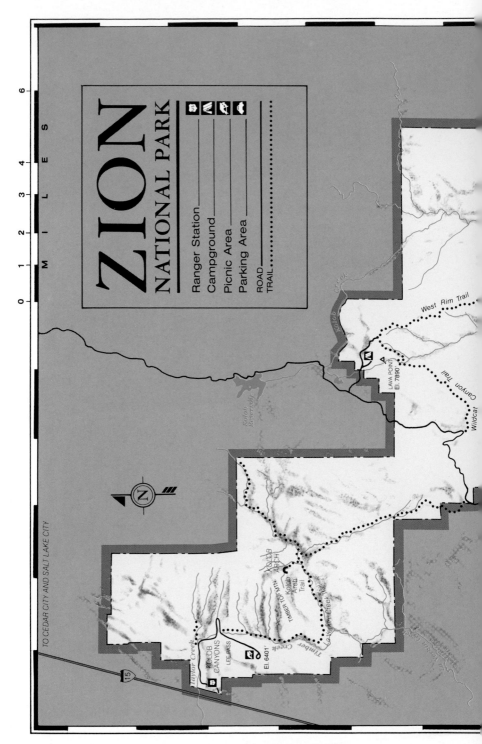

ZION
NATIONAL PARK

Ranger Station _____
Campground _____
Picnic Area _____
Parking Area _____
ROAD _____
TRAIL ••••••••••••

MILES
0 1 2 3 4 6

TO CEDAR CITY AND SALT LAKE CITY

N

Taylor Creek

KOLOB CANYONS

LEE PASS

El. 6401'

Kolob Creek

Timber Creek

Timber Top Mtn

Kolob Arch

KOLOB ARCH

Kolob Arch Trail

La Verkin Creek Trail

Kolob Reservoir

Kolob Creek

LAVA POINT
El. 7890'

West Rim Trail

Wildcat Canyon Trail

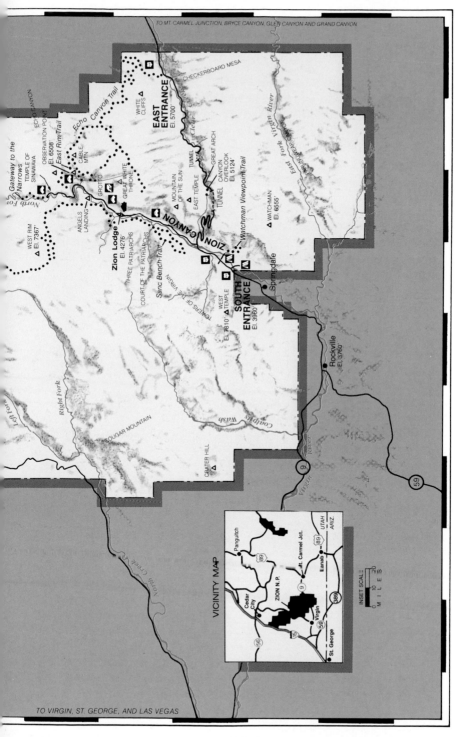

TO MT. CARMEL JUNCTION, BRYCE CANYON, GLEN CANYON AND GRAND CANYON

CHECKERBOARD MESA

EAST ENTRANCE
EL 5700'

ECHO CANYON

Echo Canyon Trail

Gateway to the Narrows

TEMPLE OF SINAWAVA

WHITE CLIFFS

OBSERVATION POINT
EL 6508'

East Rim Trail

CABLE MTN

North Fork

GROTTO

GREAT WHITE THRONE

MOUNTAIN OF THE SUN

EAST TEMPLE

TUNNEL

GREAT ARCH

CANYON OVERLOOK
EL 5124'

TUNNEL

WATCHMAN
EL 6555'

Clear Creek

ANGELS LANDING

WEST RIM
EL 7367'

ZION CANYON

Watchman Viewpoint Trail

Zion Lodge
EL 4276

THREE PATRIARCHS

Sanc Bench Trail

COURT OF THE PATRIARCHS

TOWERS OF THE VIRGIN

WEST TEMPLE
EL 7810

SOUTH ENTRANCE
EL 3960'

Springdale

East Fork Virgin River

North Fork Virgin River

Right Fork

Left Fork

North Creek

COUGAR MOUNTAIN

CRATER HILL

Coalpits Wash

VIRGIN River

Rockville
EL 3760'

9

VIRGIN

59

TO VIRGIN, ST. GEORGE, AND LAS VEGAS

VICINITY MAP

Panguitch

Cedar City

56

89

ZION N.P.

Mt. Carmel Jct.

UTAH
ARIZ.

Kanab

89

15

Virgin

59

389

St. George

9

INSET SCALE

0   10   20
M I L E S

305

The Anasazi

The first inhabitants of Zion were nomadic hunters known as the Anasazi (Navajo for "Ancient Ones"). The magnificent ruins of their dwellings, which were built around A.D. 750, are found throughout the Four Corners area—where the states of Colorado, New Mexico, Arizona, and Utah meet. The remains of one large Anasazi settlement were discovered in the Parunuweap Canyon at Zion.

While the Anasazi were farming the southern part of what is now Zion National Park, the northern part was occupied by people belonging to the Fremont Indian culture. But by A.D. 1200, both the Anasazi and the Fremont had begun to decline. Archeological findings suggest that as a sophisticated architecture developed, an increasing number of trees were used for building and fuel, thus destroying the watersheds so vital for crops, game, and forage food. According to this "ecological suicide" theory, the lack of raw materials and food eventually forced a mass exodus, perhaps as many as 700 years ago.

The Paiutes

During the next several hundred years, the region was visited by small bands of Fremont descendants, but Zion was not permanently populated again until the nineteenth century. We know the settlers as Paiutes, a tribe of Native Americans closely associated with some of Zion's great legends—the pranks of Kai-ne-sava, the God of Fire, who set great flames (lightning) atop the West Temple, and the doings of Wai-no-pits, the Evil One, who invaded the Indian camps with disease. So deeply ingrained were these superstitions and the fears that grew out of them that the Paiutes were of little value as guides to the early white explorers.

Early Explorers

Nephi Johnson, a young Morman missionary and interpreter among the Paiutes, was probably the first white to see the glory of Zion. Ordered by Brigham Young in 1858 to explore the upper Virgin River, he persuaded a Paiute to guide him over the rugged escarpment of the Hurricane Cliffs and up the river. But Johnson's guide refused to go any farther than Oak Creek; Wai-no-pits lurked somewhere in the dark shadows of the narrow canyon called Ioogoon, "an arrow quiver," meaning you "come out the way you went in."

Later explorations soon led to the settlement of Zion and Parunuweap canyons. Joseph Black is generally credited with having been the first to explore the upper area of Zion Canyon. In contrast to the early

A cowboy rides his horse on the wet trail through the Narrows before the park's establishment.

settlers, who viewed the scenery rather calmly, Brother Joseph brought back such glowing accounts of the canyon that it was often referred to as "Joseph's glory."

We owe the name *Zion* to another Mormon, Isaac Behunin. While scraping a living from crops and cattle, Behunin is supposed to have said: "These great mountains are natural temples of God. We can worship here as well as in the man-made temples in Zion, the biblical 'Heavenly City of God.' Let us call it Little Zion."

Although Mormon pioneers farmed and lumbered in and around the canyons, outside expeditions reported Zion's riches to the world. One such expedition was led by the Civil War veteran and surveyor John Wesley Powell, who already was renowned for his exploration of the Grand Canyon. Extending his studies north in 1872, Powell surveyed the Parunuweap ("water that roars") Canyon and Little Zion Canyon, which he named Mukuntuweap ("straight canyon").

Establishment of the Park

Stephen T. Mather, the first director of the National Park Service, was impressed by Zion's beauty and believed the area worthy of national recognition. He and his assistant, Horace Albright, who became the second director of the National Park Service, worked hard to bring it under federal protection. On July 31, 1909, President William Howard Taft signed a proclamation creating Mukuntuweap National Monument. Nine years later, the National Park Service recommended enlarging the monument and changing its name to Zion. President Woodrow Wilson signed the legislation on March 18, 1918, and the following year Zion National Park was established.

Sedimentary Rock

Sedimentary rocks, deposited between 225 and 53 million years ago and forming what geologists call "a staircase of time," are the building blocks of Zion National Park. Today, this staircase is seen in part as Grand Canyon, Zion, and Bryce Canyon national parks. Other "risers" in the staircase are located adjacent to the three parks and are spectacular formations in themselves.

The steps of this great stairway are a series of rock formations that differ from one another in thickness and mineral content. The layered rocks that form the walls of the Grand Canyon were laid down first; the higher layers, those of Zion Canyon, were deposited later; the rocks of Bryce Canyon, the highest layer, are of even more recent origin. Most were deposited by vast seas laden with various types of sediments.

Zion's oldest sedimentary rock is the relatively thick Moenkopi layer, which is composed of sandstone and shale. The composition and depth of these rocks indicate that approximately 230 million years ago the Colorado Plateau was covered by a vast, gentle sea. During the Triassic period (225 to 190 million years ago), as the land began to thrust upward, the sea gave way to shallow rivers that steadily increased in velocity and carried away the rock. Trees toppled, while volcanoes erupted and spewed forth millions of tons of ash. This slow, natural holocaust laid down the Chinle Formation, a remarkable assemblage of shale, sandstone, and petrified wood. The rivers persisted for several million years and, in their wake, left large lakes. Deposits formed the Moenave layer, reddish sandstone in which fossils of fresh-water fish and other creatures are evident, and streams laid down sandstone sediments that would later compose the Kayenta Formation. Dinosaurs plodded through these streams; one track in the Kayenta Formation is displayed in the park Visitor Center.

Late in the Triassic period and early into the Jurassic period (190 to 136 million years ago), the Colorado Plateau became distinctly arid. Sand-laden wind smothered the verdant land and gradually laid the most visible of Zion's formations—the Navajo Sandstone, as much as 2,220 feet thick in some areas of the park. The great temples, towers, and cliffs of Zion Canyon were formed from this sandstone. The Temple Cap Formation is another sandstone layer, some 20 to 200 feet thick,

Opposite: Checkerboard Mesa is one of the strangest formations in the park. The "checkers" are formed by the weathering of horizontal bedding planes and vertical cracks.

with a high concentration of iron oxide that streaks the cliffs red when dissolved by rain.

The most recent mineral layer is the Carmel Formation, deposits of limestone formed by seas that once again flooded the land. Fragments of the Carmel Formation are found high in the canyon on the East Temple and West Temple.

About 13 million years ago, the entire area of southern Utah and northern Arizona began to rise. Pressure on the layered rocks was so great that they broke into great plateaus, seven of which are located in southwestern Utah. Two of these are the Paunsaugunt Plateau, of which Bryce Canyon is part, and the Markagunt Plateau, which encompasses Zion.

The uplift caused rivers to run fast and strong; the Virgin River, for example, began to cut into its present bed. A very powerful process of erosion was quite pronounced 1 million years ago.

Erosion

The steep walls of the North Fork of the Virgin River are the result of water cutting into soft sandstone. So soft is this sandstone and so abrasive is the action of the gushing waters and their accumulated particles, that erosion is quick and decisive. Naturalists call the North Fork an "endless belt of sandpaper."

Zion Canyon is still being formed. Erosion by the Virgin River begins on the Markagunt Plateau at an elevation of 9,000 feet, where the river begins picking up sediment. Downstream, the Virgin combines with tributaries and gathers momentum. Its cuts become deeper, and in some places the river drops 80 feet each mile, a fall ten times as great as that of the Colorado River in Grand Canyon National Park. As it leaves the Narrows, the river opens into a broad canyon at the Temple of Sinawava, where it fans out and loses some of its momentum. Continuing on, it flows southwest for 200 miles until it reaches Lake Mead at an elevation of less than 1,000 feet. Occasionally when the river leaves the Narrows, it floods the river bottom, churning sediments and toppling trees in a few awesome moments. In 1954, its volume increased fiftyfold in fifteen minutes, and the Virgin became an enormous force that ripped through the landscape.

Many other valleys and canyons at Zion also have been carved by erosion, but some have not experienced the force of the Virgin River and have been left hanging, so to speak. These "hanging valleys" stand at 1,000 to 1,300 feet above the river; examples are found between the Mountain of the Sun and Twin Brothers.

The *widening* of Zion Canyon is the result of water percolating

Aerial view of the mysterious and enchanting canyon of Birch Creek. The West Temple rises far off in the distance.

through the porous Navajo Sandstone until it reaches the impervious shales of the Kayenta Formation. Then the water accumulates and flows laterally, forming a natural watercourse that over time erodes the shales, which support the Navajo layer. Once undermined, the sandstone gives way, and the canyon widens. This process is dramatically illustrated near the Temple of Sinawava, where the Narrows of the Virgin River begin.

The percolating action of water also has been responsible for the formation of the Great Arch of Zion, and the cliff along the Weeping Rock Trail. Stream channels, choked with sand, forced the river to meander, removing shales from the Kayenta Sandstone. Eventually, slabs of undermined Navajo Sandstone gave way, and the arch emerged. These forces are still at work, and one day a patch of blue may appear beneath a semicircular ribbon of vermilion rock.

Overleaf: Temple of Sinawava, named after the Wolf-god, a chief deity of the Paiutes. The "temple" is located deep in the canyon where the Paiutes never ventured at night.

Climate and Precipitation

A satellite view of the American Southwest shows Zion National Park situated between the Rocky Mountains in Colorado and the Sierra Nevadas in California. The Sierra Nevadas intercept the moisture-laden clouds that move east from the Pacific Ocean, thus serving as a barrier that puts most of Utah and much of Zion in a rain shadow. The Coalpits Wash area of the park, which is on the edge of an expanse known as the Great Basin Desert, receives only a few inches of rain a year. Precipitation increases in Zion Canyon (4,000 feet), where as much as 15 to 25 inches of rain may fall annually and where temperatures vary between 115° F and −15° F. The high plateaus of Zion (7,000 to 8,000 feet) receive about 25 inches of rain a year.

The mountain lion once ranged from Canada to the tip of South America, but because of its skill as a predator, human hunters have greatly reduced its numbers.

Flora

Because the elevation rises from 3,666 feet to 8,740 feet in the course of a few miles, Zion's landscape changes from desert to boreal forest.

A variety of flowers dot the canyon floor, their appearance stimulated by Zion's alternating wet and dry seasons. The sand buttercup, chorispora, and Indian paintbrush flourish in March and April. May heralds the violet, orchid, sego lily, and columbine. During the drier July and August, day-blooming plants are replaced by night species, such as white evening primrose and the spectacular sacred datura. Reaching a height of 2 or more feet, the datura's trumpet-shaped blossom opens in the evening and then closes in the morning sun.

Where water tables lie near the surface of the canyon floor, groves

Ancestors of the fragile dragonfly once possessed wingspans of more than 3 feet.

Ponderosa pines, with their scaly orange bark, exist in the higher elevations of the park.

of box elder, willow, cottonwood, and ash flourish. Beavertail cactus blooms in the late spring in the dry Parunuweap Canyon, Coalpits Wash, and Huber Wash.

At the higher elevations, nature is not so parsimonious as in the desert, and in some areas plant life is exceedingly luxuriant. Ponderosa pine, piñon pine, quaking aspen, gnarled juniper, white fir, Douglas fir, and, occasionally, sage flats predominate. Dazzling leaves of the radiant aspen transform murky waters of the Virgin River to a golden luster in the autumn. Pines and firs also grow in the side canyons, providing food and protection for wildlife.

Fauna

One delightful animal that can be seen throughout much of Zion National Park is the mule deer. It is particularly abundant in the canyons and occasionally can be spotted sloshing through the Virgin River or leaping a fallen log. So abundant is this animal that it is difficult to believe that its numbers were greatly reduced in Zion at two different times: soon after the establishment of the park, when the National Park Service attempted to reestablish native vegetation; and during the 1930s, when the National Park Service tried to preserve "good" animals, such as the deer and elk, by eliminating "bad" animals, such as the cougar. Predator control was so effective that deer and elk soon overgrazed their ranges, eating themselves out of house and home. Mass starvation became a critical problem. Today, with improved understanding of Zion's ecological system, the deer and the cougar have returned.

Bighorn sheep always have been as much a part of the natural scene as deer, quail, hawks, golden eagles, roadrunners, and kangaroo rats; archeologists know from petroglyphs that bighorn sheep were hunted by Indians. But as the years passed, they became extinct at Zion.

Poaching, construction of the Zion–Mount Carmel Highway, and the inability of sheep to cope with the excessive deer population may have contributed to their demise. Whatever the reasons, the last bighorn sighting in the area, until recently, was in 1953. For the next twenty years, there were no sheep in the park, although biologists believed that Zion could well support them; studies showed that the critical winter range could support a band of 100 animals. In July 1973, twelve sheep from the River Mountain area of Lake Mead, Nevada, were released into a huge paddock adjacent to the Visitor Center. Five years later, acclimated to the environment, the new flock was set free. Some have been seen in Zion Canyon, others in the Poverty Flat country, and still others in the Coalpits Wash area. Whether the transplant will prove successful is still subject to speculation.

SITES, TRAILS, AND TRIPS

Frederick Fisher, viewing the Great White Throne — Zion's chief landmark — declared: "Never have I seen such a sight before. It is by all odds America's masterpiece."

The view from the Visitor Center is magnificent—one of the major features of Zion National Park—but you have barely entered the canyon at this point. A wealth of beautiful geological wonders awaits around the next bend.

Mount Carmel Highway

The Mount Carmel Highway (Utah 9), which enters the park from Mount Carmel Junction, Utah, and U.S. 89 to the east, is a breath-taking engineering marvel, to say nothing of the magnificent natural sculptures it passes as it wanders through one of the lesser canyons in the park. The highway approaches the Virgin River, passing Checkerboard Mesa on the left and the White Cliffs on the right—a dramatic entrance to this exciting country. Then the road begins an abrupt descent, leading first through a 530-foot tunnel and then through the Zion-Mount Carmel Tunnel, which is more than 5,600 feet long and 800 feet above Pine Creek. Piercing the tunnel side at intervals convenient for ventilation are five large, gallerylike windows that look out and down onto the canyon below.

These giant windows were cut first during the early construction of the Zion–Mount Carmel Tunnel; rocks blasted from the internal diggings were then thrown into Pine Creek below. In less than a year, flood waters cleared the entire stream of the boulders.

Then, as the highway squeezes through an area less than .25 mile wide, it plunges toward the great canyon below on a 6 percent grade, covering 1 linear mile in 3.5 miles of broad and safe—but thrilling—road. Six switchbacks take the highway past the Great Arch, and simultaneously offer views of the East Temple and the Beehives. Eventually, the highway leads to the Visitor Center and the south entrance, where the magnificent Altar of Sacrifice, the Towers of the Virgin, the Watchman, and the West Temple can be seen.

The Mount Carmel Highway is intersected by a spur road, the Zion Canyon Scenic Drive, .5 mile north of the Visitor Center. If you bypassed this road on entering the park, it is imperative that you retrace your route to the junction. This canyon drive runs parallel to the Virgin River—passing the Mountain of the Sun, Lady Mountain, the Great White Throne, Angels Landing, Weeping Rock, and The Organ—and ends at the Temple of Sinawava. Few visitors ever complain that since the Zion Canyon Scenic Drive is a dead-end road, on the 6-mile drive back to the junction they must once again view the same features.

Trails

Stopping at overlooks and pulloffs for a view can be an exhilarating experience, but a dozen or so maintained and unmaintained trails covering 165 miles crisscross the park and lead to wondrous, out-of-the-way places that offer a totally different perspective on Zion. Water is scarce, and some trails are steep. But there is nothing fast-paced about exploring the small springs that seep from ledges where Indians once stalked their prey, the sandstone buttes that show millions of years of nature's work, or the isolated pines of a hollow through which have passed bears, mule deer, and bighorn sheep. Stop at the Visitor Center for a free permit if you plan to camp overnight.

East Rim Trail. East Rim Trail is one of the most rewarding—and one of the most strenuous—of the Zion trails. Beginning at Weeping Rock parking area, it switches back and forth up the face of Cable Mountain, through Echo Canyon, and then up sheer stone walls to the plateau and a pine forest, where it levels out and runs on to Observation Point. The trail is 8 miles round trip; 6 hours, 2,148-foot climb.

Opposite: Water spraying down Weeping Rock from openings high up in the Navajo Sandstone brings relief to the visitor on a summer day. Winter transforms the "tears" into icicles.

Trails of Zion National Park

Gateway to the Narrows Trail: Starts at Temple of Sinawava; ends at end of pavement; 2 miles round trip; 57-foot ascent; views of hanging gardens and Virgin River Narrows; wheelchair accessible with assistance.

Weeping Rock Trail: Starts at Weeping Rock parking area; ends at Weeping Rock; .5 mile round trip; 98-foot ascent; views of Great White Throne and Zion Canyon; hanging gardens; self-guiding.

Emerald Pools Trail: Starts at Zion Lodge; ends at Lower Pool; 1.2 miles round trip; 69-foot ascent; views of Heaps Canyon, Red Arch Mountain, waterfalls, and pools; footbridge crosses river; add 1 mile to Upper Pool.

Canyon Overlook Trail: Starts at tunnel parking area; ends at overlook; 1 mile round trip; 163-foot ascent; views of Pine Creek Canyon, West Temple, Towers of the Virgin, and Zion Canyon; easy walking to top of Great Arch.

East Rim Trail: Starts at Weeping Rock parking area; ends at Observation Point; 8 miles round trip; 2,148-foot ascent; views of Zion Canyon, Echo Canyon, Great White Throne, Virgin River Narrows, and Temple of Sinawava; carry water and food.

Hidden Canyon Trail: Starts at Weeping Rock parking area; ends at mouth of

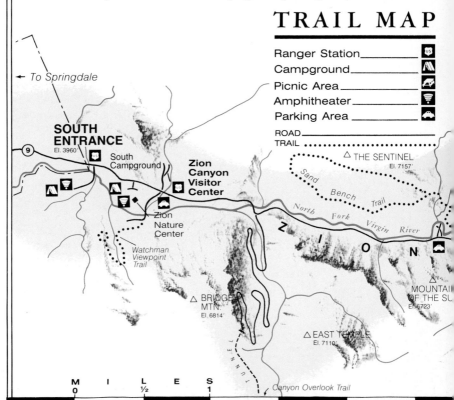

TRAIL MAP

Ranger Station_____ 🇺🇸
Campground_____ ⛺
Picnic Area_____ 🧺
Amphitheater_____ 🎭
Parking Area _____ 🚗

ROAD_____
TRAIL ....

△ THE SENTINEL
El. 7157'

Sand Bench Trail

North Fork Virgin River

Z I O N

To Springdale →

SOUTH ENTRANCE
El. 3960'
South Campground

Zion Canyon Visitor Center

Zion Nature Center

Watchman Viewpoint Trail

△ BRIDGE MTN.
El. 6814'

△ EAST TEMPLE
El. 7110'

△ MOUNTAI
OF THE SU
El. 5723'

TUNNEL

Canyon Overlook Trail

M I L E S
0   ½   1

canyon; 2 miles round trip; 850-foot ascent; views of Weeping Rock and small arch in Hidden Canyon; canyon is good example of hanging valleys; add .5 mile up canyon floor.

West Rim Trail: Starts at Grotto picnic area; 12.8 miles round trip to the West Rim Overlook; 3,070-foot ascent; leads through Refrigerator Canyon and Walter Wiggles to view of the canyon systems; footbridge crosses river; continues through Potato Hollow to Lava Point and Kolob Plateau; carry water and food.

Angels Landing Trail: Starts at Grotto picnic area; ends at Angels Landing; 5 miles round trip; 1,488-foot ascent; view of Angels Landing and of panorama including Great White Throne and Zion Canyon; footbridge crosses river; last .5 mile strenuous; carry water.

Watchman Viewpoint Trail: Starts at South Campground bridge; ends at cliff above Watchman Campground; 2 miles round trip; 368-foot ascent; views of West Temple across Zion Canyon and of panorama of Zion Canyon and arch on Bridge Mountain; recommended for off-season hiking.

Sand Bench Trail: Starts at Court of the Patriarchs; ends under streaked wall; 3.5 miles round trip; 500-foot ascent; views of Three Patriarchs, the Watchman, and Pine Creek Canyon; recommended for fall and spring hiking.

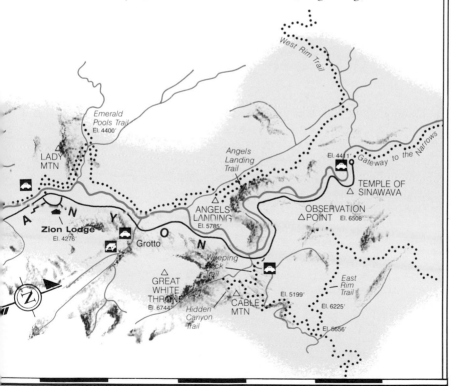

West Rim Trail, including Scout Lookout and Angels Landing Trail. As spectacular as the East Rim Trail, the West Rim Trail is an even more arduous climb to even greater heights. Backpackers begin with an invigorating pull through Refrigerator Canyon; then, before reaching an intermediate point known as Scout Lookout, the trail grows steeper as it passes along Walters Wiggles. (This section of the trail was supervised by Walter Ruesch, who was custodian of the park in 1919, when it was still just a "monument." In those days, 21 switchbacks in 600 feet were necessary to reach a shelf on the cliff!) Park rangers point out that "it is the only place in the world where you can see both ends of a horse at the same time."

At Scout Lookout, you can climb to Angels Landing and peer across to Observation Point or down again into Zion Canyon. The climb on to Angels Landing is an exciting 1-hour hike. Steel railings have been installed to ensure that climbers do not accidentally plummet into the chasms below. Or, at Scout Lookout, you can continue hiking for several days through Potato Hollow, Lava Point, and eventually on to the Kolob Plateau. Wildflowers grow in season all along these trails, even emerging from tiny cracks in the walls. This is the true backcountry of Zion and the area most frequently visited by wildlife—black bear, deer, and, occasionally, a migrant elk.

The trail begins at the Grotto picnic area and progresses upward for 3,070 feet to the highest point, known as the West Rim Overlook. From the overlook, hikers must either return 5.5 miles to the picnic grounds or continue into remote Potato Hollow.

Gateway to the Narrows. One of the most popular short trails is along the Virgin River, from the Temple of Sinawava to the beginning of the Narrows. It is something of an introduction to the much longer and more arduous Virgin River Narrows Route. At the end, the river is but a mere ribbon between canyon walls that run together in a dramatic setting as the door to the backcountry. Those who do not go on can listen to the canyon frogs serenading, and watch the antlion, buried in the sand up to its jaws, snap at unwary insects, preferably ants.

The trail is 2 miles round trip; 2 hours; 57-foot climb.

The Virgin River Narrows Route. The Virgin River Narrows Route is the most demanding of the Zion hikes, and hikers must be in good shape to negotiate the grueling 12.5 miles along the Virgin River. There is actually no trail as such, and in some areas, backpackers have to wade through rather deep waters. In places, the canyon walls close until they are little more than 20 feet apart, with a vertical 2,000 feet to the plateau that allows little sunlight to penetrate to the river.

Registration is required at the Visitor Center before embarking on this trip. It should be done only during dry weather, generally best in late June and late September.

Kolob Arch Trail. Kolob Arch Trail is reached from La Verkin Creek Trail. Side trips into Hop Valley or up Willis Creek, two of the most rugged of Zion's backcountry areas, require a 2- to 3-day trip. Days could be spent exploring these canyons and their beautiful scenery. The spectacular Kolob Arch, the world's largest with a span of 310 feet, is located 6.5 miles from the trail head at Lee Pass. About 15 miles later, hikers reach a road that will take them back to their point of origin, now about 40 miles away. Obviously, advance planning is required as far as logistics are concerned. A trip along Kolob Arch Trail should be planned and then discussed with a ranger at the Kolob Canyons Visitor Center for maximum enjoyment and safety.

Other Trails. Six other trails in Zion National Park lead past waterfalls, canyons, and a myriad startlingly beautiful rock formations. *Weeping Rock Trail* is a lovely, easy, .5-mile walk to a rock that "weeps" with water that has filtered through more than 2,000 feet of Navajo Sandstone.

During a thunderstorm or snowmelt Zion explodes with waterfalls. In Heaps Canyon, the Emerald Pools, with their rich, dark coloring, are fed by several waterfalls.

Weeping Rock is the junction at which water encounters impervious layers of shale, which forces the water to flow outward. As water proceeds along this course, it dissolves calcium, the cementing agent in the sandstone. Once the particles of sand are released and sections of sandstone collapse, the cliff is enlarged. This self-guiding trail has interpretive labels that describe features along the route.

Leaving from the parking area of the Zion–Mount Carmel Tunnel is another self-guiding nature trail, the *Canyon Overlook Trail*. It terminates in .5 mile at the Canyon Overlook and takes about 1 hour to complete. A fairly steep escarpment leads under an overhang before the trail opens to a broad and exciting panoramic view at the Canyon Overlook. All along this trail are excellent views of Pine Creek Canyon, the East Temple, and the west side of Zion Canyon.

Another trail that begins at the Weeping Rock parking area is the *Hidden Canyon Trail*. This rather steep trail ascends 850 feet in 1 mile and leads to a quiet canyon in which the silence is broken only by the occasional trill of a canyon wren. It is a 2-mile round trip and takes about 3 hours.

An arched metal bridge that crosses the Virgin River at the Zion Lodge is the beginning of the *Emerald Pools Trail*. If you are properly dressed in foul-weather gear, this is an ideal area to visit during one of the park's summer thunderstorms. Rivulets of water surge down from every direction and unite to dramatically illustrate the awesome power of nature when unleashed in its fullest force. When the storm is over and the waters quieted, little pools attract a variety of wildlife. Look in the surrounding sands for paw prints. This is a 2-mile 2- to 3-hour, leisurely round trip.

The *Sand Bench Trail* is a 3.5-mile round-trip walk that starts at the Court of the Patriarchs and provides views of the park's main features.

Just a short distance from the South Campground is the trail head for the *Watchman Viewpoint Trail*. It will take 2 hours to hike this 2-mile round trip. This trail ascends to an elevation of about 370 feet in 1 mile and provides views of the Watchman, Oak Creek Canyon, and the town of Springdale. From this vantage point, hikers also will be able to see the rather abrupt change in vegetation as it ascends from the parched desert floor to the relatively moist mountain slopes. This is an excellent site from which to view a magnificent sunset.

There is not a single uninspiring trail in Zion National Park. Some are more strenuous than others; all are rewarding.

Opposite: White Arch, worn away by erosion, looks deceptively small from a distance. It is made up of the surprisingly consistent Navajo Sandstone that is found throughout the park.

ANIMALS & PLANTS

OF THE DESERT SOUTHWEST

This appendix provides a sample of animals and plants commonly found in the national parks of the Desert Southwest. The codes have been used to indicate the parks in which these animals and plants are most often seen.

AR	Arches	CL	Canyonlands	MV	Mesa Verde
BB	Big Bend	CR	Capitol Reef	PF	Petrified Forest
BC	Bryce Canyon	GC	Grand Canyon	ZN	Zion
CC	Carlsbad Caverns	GM	Guadalupe Mountains		

MAMMALS

BADGER
BB, GC, PF

The nocturnal badger is seldom seen in heavily visited areas. Generally a little over 2 ft. long, including a 5-in. tail, it has a flattish body, with short, bowed legs. Its burrow has an 8–12-in. elliptical opening and is marked by a large mound of earth and debris; the badger can bury itself faster than a person can dig with a shovel. It feeds on rodents.

BAT
BB, BC, CC, GC, GM, MV, ZN

Of the 900 species of bats, the big brown bat and the Mexican freetail bat are the most common in the Southwest. The 5-in.-long big brown bat varies from light to dark brown in color and has a plain nose and a tail that extends only slightly beyond the body; it lives in caves, mines, storm sewers, and buildings. The 3.5–4.5-in.-long Mexican freetail bat is dark brown or dark gray and has narrow wings and a tail that extends well beyond the body; it has a snub nose and a face that resembles a mastiff's.

BEAVER
BB, BC, CL, CR, MV, ZN

The beaver is North America's largest rodent; it generally is up to 4 ft. long, including a 1-ft., flat, scaly tail, and weighs 45–60 lbs., but can weigh up to 100. Mainly nocturnal, it is seldom seen; but there is evidence of its work in the dams of small streams. The beaver lives in lodges formed by logs; on major rivers, it lives in dens along the bank. The beaver's diet is mainly the bark of trees, although in summer it feeds on water vegetation.

BIGHORN SHEEP
AR, CL, GC, MV, ZN

Also known as the "mountain sheep" or the "Rocky Mountain bighorn sheep," it is one of the most spectacular animals in the parks. Rams are 3–3.5 ft. in height, 127–316 lbs., and with a horn spread of 33 in. (the horns curve up and back over ears); ewes are 4.25–5.25 ft. in height and weigh 74–200 lbs. Color varies from dark brown to pale tan; generally the belly, rump patch, back of legs, muzzle, and eye patch are white. The bighorn's diet is mostly grasses, sedges, and woody plants, and its habitat is alpine meadows and foothills near rocky cliffs.

BLACK BEAR
BB, BC, GC, GM, ZN

The black bear may be a brownish or cinnamon color, but it can easily be distinguished from the grizzly and brown bear by its straight-profiled face, rather than the dished face of the others, and by its comparatively smaller size (3 ft. at the shoulder, 4.5–6.25 ft. long, 203–595 lbs.) and humpless shoulders. The black bear feeds on grasses, buds, leaves, berries, nuts, bark, insects, rodents, the fawns of deer and elk, and fish, particularly salmon; a scrounger by nature, it will forage near campsites. This is a powerful and potentially dangerous animal, despite its clownlike antics; although primarily nocturnal, it is sometimes seen during the day, sometimes "galloping" as fast as 30 miles an hour.

BOBCAT
BB, CL, CR, GC, MV, PF, ZN

The bobcat is North America's most common wild cat; because it is nocturnal and secretive, it is seldom seen. It is tawny in color, with indistinct black spots, a pale or white belly, and a short, stubby tail with 2 or 3 black bars. It weighs 14–68 lbs. and measures 2.3–4 ft. long; the males are larger than the females. In the late winter, the male may be heard yowling at night, much like a domesticated cat. Kits are born in a den, usually in thickets or under rocks and logs. The bobcat feeds on rodents and especially ground-nesting birds.

COYOTE
AR, BB, CL, GC, GM, MV, ZN

The coyote is the smallest species of wild dog; although resembling a domestic dog, it is often mistaken for a wolf. The coyote is seen fairly regularly in the western parks; its evening "howl" has made it legendary. It weighs about 75 lbs., stands about 2 ft. at the shoulder, and is 3.5–4 ft. long, including a tail of 12–15 in. Its fur is brownish- to reddish-gray—at the lower altitudes more tan and red, at the higher altitudes more gray and black. The coyote has a varied diet of deer, elk, rabbit, rodents, snakes, birds, and insects. A typical den is a wide-mouthed earthen tunnel, 5–30 ft. long, which may be the former residence of a fox or badger.

DEER MOUSE
AR, BB, BC, CL, GC, GM, MV, PF, ZN

There are about 100 species of rats or mice in North America, and probably the most common in the Southwest is the deer mouse. A grayish to reddish-brown mouse about 5–8.75 in. long, including a 2–5-in. tail, it feeds on seeds, nuts, small fruits, berries, and insects. It usually burrows in the ground, though some may nest in raised areas or have refuge burrows.

DESERT COTTONTAIL
AR, BB, CC, CL, CR, GC, GM, MV, PF

The buff-brown desert cottontail is 13–16.5 in. long and can be seen at night sitting on a stump or log watching for predators; during the day, it scampers about feeding on grass and plants. Cottontails usually hop, but they can leap up to 15 ft., and, like all rabbits, they freeze when threatened and then abruptly change direction and flee.

ELK
BC, CC, GC, GM, MV, ZN

The elk is second in size only to the moose in the deer family. Males may weight 600–1,100 lbs. and stand 5 ft. at the shoulders (its graceful antlers may reach another 5 ft.); females weight 450–650 lbs. Mostly nocturnal, elk can be seen at dusk or dawn grazing in meadows on grasses and woody vegetation. Mating season is the fall, at which time occur the legendary fights with clashing antlers.

GRAY FOX AR, BB, BC, CC, CL, CR, GM, ZN

Of the six species of foxes in North America, the gray fox is the most commonly found in national parks; yet, being nocturnal, it is seldom seen. It is gray, with a black stripe running down the top of its tail, stands 14–15 in. at the shoulder, and is 3–4 ft. long, including a 9–17 in. tail.

MERRIAM'S KANGAROO RAT
AR, BB, CC, GM, ZN

Merriam's is the smallest of the kangaroo rats; it is light yellowish-buff and white, and measures 8–10 in., including a 4–6-in. white, side-striped tail. It feeds mostly on seeds. The rat burrows and frequently gives itself a sand or dust bath to keep its fur from matting.

MOUNTAIN LION
AR, BB, CL, GC, GM, MV, ZN

Often called cougar or puma, the mountain lion is a most secretive mammal, living mostly in mountainous areas and seldom seen; it is a rather docile cat, rarely attacking humans, but its scream can be terrifying. Yellowish to tawny, with a long, black-tipped tail, it weighs up to 275 lbs. and measures 5–9 ft., including a 2–3-ft. tail. The mountain lion feeds on deer, coyote, beaver, mice, hares, raccoons, birds, and grasshoppers.

MULE DEER
AR, BB, BC, CC, CL, CR, GC, GM, MV, ZN

The mule deer is a fairly common species of the deer family seen in the western parks, particularly in the early morning and late evening. It is characterized by its large, mulelike ears, from which it gets its name, and white rump, although it should not be confused with the white-tailed deer—also seen in some western parks; it weighs up to 400 lbs. and stands 3–3.5 ft. at the shoulder. The male loses its antlers in the late winter and is generally solitary in its roamings. The mule deer eats acorns, berries, cactus fruits, twigs, buds, grasses, herbs, tree bark, and mushrooms.

PORCUPINE
AR, BB, BC, CC, CL, CR, GC, MV, PF, ZN

Contrary to legend, porcupines *cannot* throw or "shoot" their quills, although the quills are rather loosely attached and may shake off if the porcupine threshes its tail about in self-defense. Classified as a rodent, it is the only quilled mammal. About 3 ft. long, 1 ft. high, and 35 lbs., it lives mostly in coniferous forests, but may also inhabit brushy areas of the Southwest. It survives mostly on a diet of the wood directly beneath tree bark, although it also eats buds and twigs from a number of trees and bushes.

PRAIRIE DOG
BC, CL, CR, GC, GM, MV

Four species of prairie dogs live in the national parks— black-tailed, white-tailed, Utah, and Gunnison's; all four are similar and sometimes difficult to identify. The prairie dog varies from 14–16

in. in length, including a 2–4.5-in. tail, and weighs 1.5–3 lbs. The black-tailed prairie dog builds a 1-ft.-high, volcano-shaped burrow of hard-packed earth; the other three species build burrows ranging from level to 3 ft. high. Several thousand may live in "towns" covering 100 acres or more. Most of its diet consists of green plants or grasses in the immediate area of its burrow.

RACCOON
BB, CC, GM, MV, ZN

The notorious "black-masked" raccoon raids garbage cans in national parks, just as it does in the suburbs; nocturnal, the raccoon can be seen around park campgrounds. It is reddish-brown with black above and gray below, and measures 2–3 ft., including a 7.5–16-in. bushy tail with alternating black and brown rings. Its diet includes grapes, nuts, insects, rodents, turtles, frogs, and birds' eggs; dens are usually in hollow trees, caves, rock clefts, or culverts.

RINGTAIL BB, CC, CR, GC, GM, MV, ZN

The ringtail is a member of the raccoon family, but it has no mask around the eyes and is smaller than the raccoon. The ringtail is yellowish-gray above and whitish-buff below, with a catlike body and foxlike face; it measures 2.5 ft., including a 12–17-in. bushy tail with as many as 16 black bands. A better mouser than a cat, it eats rodents, rabbits, snakes, insects, and fruit. Sometimes found about buildings, it generally makes its den among rocks or boulders.

ROCK SQUIRREL
AR, BB, CL, CR, GC, GM, MV, ZN

The rock squirrel is the largest of the ground squirrels, measuring 16–21 in., with a tail of 6–10 in. It lives in rocky areas, where its grayish-brownish color blends naturally with the terrain. The squirrel feeds on acorns, nuts, and seeds of mesquite, cactus, agave, and currant.

STRIPED SKUNK
BB, BC, CR, GC, GM, MV, PF, ZN

The striped skunk is the skunk that is found almost everywhere in the U.S., except Alaska. It has a narrow stripe of white down its nose, and a V-shaped, white configuration down its back; males weigh 6–14 lbs. and measure 20–31 in., including a 7–15-in. bushy tail. The striped skunk feeds on insects, small mammals, amphibians, and eggs of small ground-nesting birds.

BIRDS

AMERICAN KESTREL

AR, BB, CC, CL, CR, GC, PF, ZN

Until recently, this small falcon was known as the "sparrow hawk." The kestrel measures 9–12 in. from bill to tail and has a wingspread of 22–23 in. It has blue-gray wings and head with a buff breast and nape. The kestrel does not build a nest of its own, but lays its eggs without nesting or borrows another bird's nest in tree holes or building niches. It can be seen perched on trees and telephone poles, from where it swoops rapidly upon its grasshopper and rodent prey.

AMERICAN ROBIN

BB, BC, CC, CR, GC, GM, MV, PF, ZN

Best known of all North American birds, once called "robin," the American robin is gray-brown, with puffed-out, red or orange breast, white throat, and blackish head and tail. It measures 9–11 in. The robin feeds primarily on worms pulled from the ground. In cold weather, the nest is built of twigs and mud and lined with fine material in low, densely leafed or needled trees and bushes; in hot weather, the nest is high in maple or sycamore trees.

ASH-THROATED FLYCATCHER

BB, CC, CR, GC, GM, ZN

The ash-throated flycatcher measures 7.5–8.5 in., has a gray-white throat, olive-brown back, and light yellow underparts. It nests in a cuplike construction that usually includes pieces of shed snakeskin, and it feeds on insects.

BROAD-TAILED HUMMINGBIRD

BB, BC, CC, CL, CR, GC, GM, MV, PF, ZN

Distinguished by a unique musical trill from wings in flight, the broad-tailed hummingbird resembles the ruby-throated hummingbird, but the male is rose, not red, and the tail is rounded, not forked. Both sexes are greenish above, white below, and 4–4.5 in. from bill to tail. It feeds on insects and flower nectar.

BULLOCK'S ORIOLE

BB, CC, CR, MV, PF, ZN

The western species of oriole (eastern is Baltimore), the Bullock's oriole measures 7–8.5 in. Male is orange-yellow, with black crown, nape, and mantle, narrow black eye stripe, narrow black bib, and wings with broad white patch and white edges on flight feathers. The oriole nests in a finely woven basket and feeds on insects, seeds, waste grain, fruit, and small aquatic life.

COMMON NIGHTHAWK

BB, BC, CC, CR, GC, MV, PF, ZN

A slim-winged gray-brown bird, with ample tail, large eyes, tiny bill, and short legs, the common night-hawk measures 8.5–10 in. from bill to tail. Male has white throat patch and white subterminal tail bar. It feeds on nocturnal insects, and by day sits on tree limbs in a "dead-leaf" camouflage.

COMMON RAVEN
AR, BB, BC, CL, CR, GC, MV, PF, ZN

Considered to have an intelligence matching a dog's, applying reason to new situations, the raven is the largest of the crows; it is 21.5–27 in. from bill to tail. It is black, with thick bill and wedge-shaped tail. The raven nests in a large collection of sticks, bones, and soft material on a cliff face or in a tree, and feeds on almost anything.

GOLDEN EAGLE
AR, BB, CL, MV, PF, ZN

The golden eagle, the most majestic of North America's birds, is 2.5–3.5 ft. from bill to tail and has a wingspread of 7–8 ft. It is shaped like a hawk, but with a much greater wingspan when flying. Dark brown with a

"golden" nape visible only at close range, its legs are feathered down to the talons. Its nest is generally a large mass of twigs or sticks on a crag or rocky ledge or high in a tree. The golden eagle's primary diet is rodents and rabbits.

GREAT HORNED OWL
BB, BC, CC, GC, GM, MV, PF, ZN

The great horned owl is common to all of North America, from Mexico to the tree line in Canada. It is 1.5–2 ft. from tail to top of head, gray-brown above, with a fine dark-gray horizontal barring below, large yellow eyes, and ear tufts set far apart. It nests in trees, crevices, or cliffs, often in a nest once occupied by a hawk. The owl hunts rabbits, rodents, ducks, crows, and other owls, and it has been seen capturing a skunk.

HAIRY WOODPECKER
GC, GM, MV, ZN

A medium-size woodpecker, but larger than the downy, the hairy woodpecker has a white head with black crown, eyemask, and "whiskers." Male has red patch at base of crown, and black tail with white outer feathers; female has no red patch. Both are 8.5–10.5 in. from bill to tail. It feeds by pecking a hole in tree bark and, with long, flexible tongue, extracting grubs; it nests in tree cavities.

HORNED LARK
BB, CC, CR, PF, ZN

The horned lark is faithful to its birthplace, where it returns after migration. It measures 7–8 in. long and is pale brown, with black bib, yellow sash on throat and face, and black tail feathers with white margins. The lark feeds on seeds and ground insects, and nests in grass-lined depressions in the ground.

KILLDEER
BC, CC, GM, PF

The killdeer is grayish-brown above, white below, with two black breast bands, and a long tan tail, which is evident in flight. It measures

9–11 in. long. It lays its eggs in a scrape on bare ground in plowed field, gravel shore, roadway, or bald spot in pasture, and is conspicuous for its means of distracting predators from young—by dragging itself along the ground, as though it has broken a wing, until it has led danger away. It feeds on worms and insects.

MARSH HAWK
AR, BB, CL, MV, PF

Also called "harrier," the marsh hawk is a specialized mouser in tall vegetation; its owl-like face directs mouse squeaks to its sensitive ears. It measures 1.5–2 ft. from bill to tail, has slim, long wings, tail, and legs, and in flight shows black wingtips and barred tail. Male is light gray above, with underparts of reddish spotting. The marsh hawk roosts on the ground at night, builds grass nests on or close to the ground, and feeds on rodents.

MOUNTAIN CHICKADEE
BC, CR, GC, GM, MV, ZN

The mountain chickadee is a small, constantly active insect seeker. It is 5–5.75 in. long, gray, with a black cap, white eye stripe, and pale gray sides. The chickadee nests in a hair- or fur-lined natural cavity or woodpecker tree hole.

MOURNING DOVE
AR, BB, CC, CL, CR, GC, GM, MV, PF, ZN

The mourning dove's name comes from the melancholy cooing of the male, generally "sung" from a prominent perch and followed by a courtship flight. The bird measures 11–13 in. from bill to tail; it is light brownish-gray, with a pale buff chest, darker wings with black spots along the inside edge, and an iridescent, light violet neck shield. The central tail feathers on the male are quite long, with sharply tapered, white-tipped outer feathers. Like other species of doves, it feeds primarily on seeds, and nests in trees and bushes.

ROADRUNNER
BB, CC, GC, GM

One of the most famous birds of the Southwest, the roadrunner is named for its rapid actions when surprised; it runs rapidly on strong feet and seldom flies. It measures 20–24 in. long, is brown with a green sheen, streaked with black and white above, buff below, has brown streaks on breast, and a heavy bill. The roadrunner nests in mesquite bush and large cactus, and feeds on snakes, lizards, insects, scorpions, and rodents.

ROCK WREN
AR, BB, CC, CL, CR, GC, MV, PF, ZN

The 5.25–6.25 in. rock wren has a gray body and rust-colored rump. It feeds on insects, and nests in crevices in rocks and walls. The wren can be identified by a trail of rock chips leading to the nest, a behavior presumed to be "decorating" its territory.

RUBY-CROWNED KINGLET
BB, CC, CR, GM, MV, ZN

A small, Old World warbler, the ruby-crowned kinglet measures 3.75–4.5 in., is olive gray above, shaded white below, with white wing bars, and is conspicuous for its "broken" white eye ring. It nests in small cups in bushes or trees, and feeds on insects.

RUFOUS HUMMINGBIRD

BB, BC, CC, CL, CR, GC, GM, MV, ZN

The male rufous hummingbird is identified by distinctive black throat and white collar below; the female is greenish above, whitish below. Both are 3.5–3.75 in. from bill to tail. It nests in a feltlike cup in shrub or tree, and feeds on insects, spiders, and flower nectar.

SAY'S PHOEBE

BB, BC, CC, CR, GC, GM, MV, PF, ZN

A flycatcher that is about 7–8 in. long, the Say's phoebe has a dusky body, with dark wings and black tail. It feeds on insects and berries, and nests in a cup or bracket of mud, grass, or moss on an elevated ledge, rock wall, or building.

SCALED QUAIL

BB, CC, GM, PF

The scaled quail has a white, cottony topknot, with pale unstreaked gray head, and black-edged bluish-gray feathers on breast and mantle. It measures 10–12 in from bill to tail. The quail feeds on insects, seeds, buds, and berries, and nests in a grass-lined hollow under a bush.

SCRUB JAY

AR, CL, CR, MV, ZN

A robin-size member of crow family, the scrub jay has a blue head, wings, and tail, a brown back, gray underparts, and a white throat. It measures 11–13 in. The jay nests in a twiggy cup in dense shrub or tree, and feeds on nuts and has been credited with helping regenerate forests—burying more acorns than it eats.

SHARP-SHINNED HAWK

BB, BC, CR, MV, ZN

Recognized by its short, broad, rounded wings and long, thin, cross-barred tail, which is often notched, the sharp-shinned hawk is slate blue above, white below, with rusty cross-barring. It measures 10–14 in. long. The hawk nests on a twiggy platform in dense conifers, and feeds on small mammals, reptiles, and insects.

WESTERN KINGBIRD

AR, BB, CC, CL, CR, GM, PF, ZN

The male western bluebird has a deep-blue hood and upper parts, and a rust-red breast, to warn off aggressors and rivals and to attract the female; it measures 6–7 in. The bluebird feeds on insects, worms, snails, berries, and fruits, and its grass nest is generally in a tree hole.

WESTERN KINGBIRD
AR, CC, CL, CR, GM, PF

Formerly called the Arkansas kingbird, the western kingbird is found throughout the West. It measures 8–9 in. from bill to tail, and is olive brown above and yellow below, with a light gray breast, dusky wings, and a blackish tail with white margins. The western kingbird nests in trees, bushes, or buildings, and feeds primarily on flying insects.

WESTERN TANAGER
BB, CC, CR, GC, GM, MV, PF, ZN

The male western tanager has a brilliant red head,

bright yellow body, and black back wings and tail; the female is yellow-green above and yellow below. Both measure 6–7.5 in. It makes a shallow saucerlike nest of woven weed stalks, bark strips, and rootlets, usually in the fork of a horizontal branch of Douglas fir, spruce, pine, or oak.

WHITE-CROWNED SPARROW
BB, CC, CL, GC, MV, PF, ZN

The white-crowned sparrow has a crown with alternating 5 white and 4 black stripes; a white stripe over the eye, and a black stripe through the eye; face and nape are grayish, and breast is pearl-gray. It is 6–7 in. long. Its grass nests are on or near the ground, and it feeds on seeds, insects, and small fruit.

BLACK-NECKED GARTER SNAKE

AR, BB, CC, CL, GM

The 1.5–4-ft. black-necked garter snake is olive gray or olive brown, with 2 large black blotches on the neck separated by a stripe down the back that may be wavy and orange in neck region, yellow or cream toward tail. Pale side stripes occupy second and third rows of scales; 2 rows of black spots are between the back and side stripes; and the top of the head is gray. Active during the day, the snake swims on the surface of water and feeds on frogs, toads, and tadpoles.

BLACK-TAILED RATTLESNAKE

BB, CC, GM

The unaggressive black-tailed rattlesnake can be seen during the day basking in the sun. It is 2–4 ft. long, greenish, yellowish, or grayish, with irregular light-edged and light-centered crossbands, and black tail. The snake feeds on small rodents.

BULLSNAKE

BB, GM, MV, PF

Large and powerfully built, the bullsnake measures 4–8 ft. and has a small head. The yellowish snake has at least 40 black, brown, or reddish-brown blotches on back and sides. Active during the day, it consumes large numbers of rodents.

CANYON TREE FROG

BB, CR, GC, ZN

The canyon tree frog is small, brown or olive-gray, with a blotched or spotted dark-brown or olive camouflage pattern (sometimes no pattern) and a cream belly, grading to yellow on the hind legs. It measures 1.75–2.25 in. and feeds on insects.

COACHWHIP SNAKE

AR, BB, CC, CL, GM, PF, ZN

The coachwhip is perhaps North America's fastest snake; when cornered, it will coil and strike out. It is 3–8 ft. long, and a patternless yellow, tan, brown, gray, or pinkish. The coachwhip hunts during the day for cicadas, lizards, grasshoppers, small rodents, and other snakes.

COLLARED LIZARD AR, BB, CC, CL, GC, MV, PF, ZN

The collared lizard is aggressive and will bite. It has a large head, a conspicuous black and white collar across the back of its neck, and a yellow-brown to green body with bluish highlights. It is 8–14 in. long. When fleeing danger, it lifts its body and tail and dashes on its hind legs. The collared lizard feeds on insects and other lizards.

COUCH'S SPADEFOOT TOAD

BB, CC, GM, PF

The Couch's spadefoot is a plump toad, with long, sickle-shaped spades on hind feet, a bright greenish-yellow to brown body, and a white belly; it measures

2.25–3.5 in. The nocturnal spadefoot lays eggs on plant stems in temporary pools, lives in underground holes, and feeds on insects.

CREVICE SPINY LIZARD
BB, CC, GM

The crevice spiny lizard is elusive and hides among stones and in crevices. It is 8.5–11.25 in. long, with large rough scales on its drab olive to reddish body, a prominent white-edged black collar, dark crossbands on tail, and blue patches on its throat and belly. It feeds on insects and occasionally on blossoms.

DESERT TARANTULA
BB, GC, ZN

Despite bad publicity, the tarantula is not dangerous; its venom is no more poisonous than that of a bee, and it is reluctant to attack humans. The male measures 2–2.5 in. and the female, which can live for 20 years, 2–2.75 in. The tarantula's body is gray to dark brown, its abdomen is brownish-black, and its legspan is 4 in.; it nests on the ground and feeds on

insects, lizards, and other small animals.

DESERT TORTOISE
BB, GC

An endangered species, the terrestrial desert tortoise has a domed shell and round, stumpy hind legs; it is 9.25–14.5 in. long. Its small head is reddish-tan; upper shell, horn-brown; and lower shell, yellowish. The desert tortoise feeds on grasses in early morning and late afternoon.

GRAND CANYON RATTLESNAKE
GC

The size and color of the Grand Canyon rattlesnake vary. Generally 1.3–5.3 ft. long, it has brownish blotches down midline of back, edged with dark brown or black, and often surrounded by light color. Aggressive, it feeds on small mammals.

GREAT BASIN GOPHER SNAKE
AR, BC, CL, CR, GC, MV, PF, ZN

The 4–8 ft. Great Basin gopher snake is light-colored, with black, brown, or reddish-brown blotches on back and sides, and wide, black blotches on forepart of body. Active during the day, it feeds on rodents.

LEOPARD FROG AR, BB, BC, CC, CL, CR, MV, ZN

The leopard frog is gray or dull-green, with a dorsal pattern of well-defined oval or round dark spots with pale borders; it measures 2–5 in. The frog frequents springs, creeks, rivers, and ponds where there is abundant aquatic vegetation, and feeds on insects.

RED-SPOTTED TOAD
BB, CC, GC, GM, PF, ZN

The small, flat, red-spotted toad is olive to grayish-brown, with reddish warts; it measures 1.5–3 in. It is active at twilight, can be seen as far as 1 mile from water, and feeds on insects.

SIDE-BLOTCHED LIZARD

AR, BB, BC, CC, CL, GC, GM, PF, ZN

The small side-blotched lizard measures 4–6.5 in. It is brown, with blotches, spots, speckles, and stripes on its scaly back, and a single dark blue to black spot on each side behind the foreleg. The lizard feeds on insects.

SOUTHERN PRAIRIE LIZARD

AR, CC, CL, GM, PF, ZN

The terrestrial southern prairie lizard is 3.5–7.5 in. long; color varies according to geography—generally gray to brown or rusty, with wavy, dark crossbars on back and blue patches on belly and throat. The lizard shelters under bushes and feeds on almost any insect, spider, centipede, and snail.

TIGER SALAMANDER

AR, BC, CC, CL, CR, PF, ZN

The tiger salamander is the world's largest land-dwelling salamander; it is 6–13 in. long. It has a broad head and small eyes. Often seen at night after heavy rain, the tiger salamander lives beneath debris near water. It feeds on earthworms, large insects, small mice, and amphibians.

TRANS-PECOS RAT SNAKE   BB

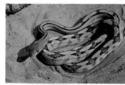

The 3–5-ft. Trans-Pecos rat snake has large "bug-eyes" separated from upper lip scales by a row of small scales. It is yellowish-tan or olive green, with a series of dark-brown, H-shaped blotches. It feeds on small mammals, birds, and lizards.

TREE LIZARD   AR, BB, BC, CL, CR, GC, GM, ZN

The tree lizard spends much time on rocks or in trees, from which it sometimes can be seen hanging head down. It measures 2–2.25 in. and is dark brown, tan, sooty, or gray, with small scales. The tree lizard feeds on insects.

WESTERN SPADEFOOT TOAD

AR, BB, CC, CL, PF, ZN

The western spadefoot is a stout, 1.5–2.5-in. toad, with wedge-shaped spades on hind feet; its body is dusky-olive to brown or gray, with irregular light stripes, random dark blotches, and a white belly. A nocturnal toad, it feeds on insects.

WOODHOUSE'S TOAD   AR, BB, BC, CL, CR, GC, PF, ZN

The Woodhouse's toad is large, with a light stripe down the middle of its back; it is yellow to green or brown, and measures 2.5–5 in. The nocturnal Woodhouse's toad feeds on insects.

FLOWERS, SHRUBS, AND TREES

BLAZING STAR
AR, CL, PF, ZN

This member of the stick-leaf family is called blazing star because of barbed hairs on its leaves that stick to fabric. Many large, starlike blooms are on branches at the top of a stout, satiny, white stem; flowers 2−5-in. wide bloom from June to September; 4−12-in. leaves are very rough, with large, irregular teeth. It grows 1−3 ft. high.

BOX ELDER
AR, CL, CR, ZN

Classed with maples, the small to medium-size box elder has a short trunk and a broad, rounded crown of light-green foliage. It grows to a height of 30−60 ft. and a diameter of 2.5 ft. Its leaves are 2.4 in. long; flowers are ³⁄₁₆ in., with small, yellow-green calyx of 5 lobes. Plains Indians made sugar from box elder sap.

COLUMBINE
AR, BB, ZN

The columbine is a bushy plant, with white and blue flowers that tip upward at end of stem. The 5-petaled flowers are shaped like sugar scoops, and bloom from June to August.

CLIFF ROSE
AR, BC, CR, GC, MV, PF, ZN

The cliff rose is a stout shrub, with shreddy bark and small, pinnately lobed leaves; its flowers have 5 light yellow or white petals.

ENGELMANN ASTER
AR, CR, GC, MV, PF, ZN

The Engelmann aster is one of a number of tall asters. Stems are leafy; flower heads have a yellow disk about 1.5− 2.5 in. around and are surrounded by about 15 rays of white or pinkish petals. It grows to 1.5−5 ft. and is found in open places.

FREMONT BARBERRY
AR, BC, CL, CR, GC, GM, ZN

The barberry is a shrub with compound leaves and clusters of bright yellow, fragrant flowers; the evergreen leaves are spiny. The Fremont grows up to 4 ft., and is frequently seen on dry slopes south and west of Zion.

FREMONT COTTONWOOD
BC, CL, CR, PF, ZN

Named for its discoverer, John Charles Frémont, this

cottonwood is a tall tree, with a broad, flattened, open crown of large, widely spreading branches. It is 40–80 ft. high, 2–4 ft. in diameter, with 2–3-in. leaves. The cottonwood grows in wet soil and indicates permanent water. Hopi Indians carve kachina dolls from cottonwood roots.

GAMBEL OAK
AR, BC, CC, GC, GM, MV, ZN

The Gambel is the common oak of the Rocky Mountains, and abundant in Grand Canyon. A tall tree with rounded crown: 20–70 ft. high, 1–2.5 ft. in diameter, 2–6-in. leaves, egg-shaped .5–.75-in. acorns. Foliage eaten by deer and livestock; wild turkeys, squirrels, and other wildlife, as well as livestock, eat acorns.

INDIAN PAINTBRUSH
AR, BB, CC, CR, GC, GM, MV, PF, ZN

The flower resembles a crimson or scarlet paint-

brush, thus the name Indian paintbrush. Usually found in clumps of several stems in sagebrush areas, it grows to 1–3 ft. and flowers from May to September. Indian paintbrush parasitizes other plants through connecting roots.

MONKEY FLOWER
AR, BB, CR, ZN

The monkey flower is a leafy plant ranging from spindly and tiny to large and bushy; it can grow to 3 ft. Its yellow, bilaterally symmetrical flowers measure .5–1.5 in. on slender stalks, and bloom from March to September.

OCOTILLO
BB, CC, GM

The funnel-shaped ocotillo has several woody, spiny, straight stems with a cluster of red flowers at the tip of each branch. It is leafless most of year, with leaves appearing only after rain and then withering when the soil dries; it flowers from March to June. It grows to 2.5 ft.

PENTSTEMON
AR, BB, CR, ZN

The name pentstemon comes from the Greek *pente* (five) and *stemon* (thread) and refers to its slender fifth stamen. The slender, scarlet flower hangs slightly in a long open cluster on sparsely leafy stems that grow to 3 ft.; its 1–1.5 in. flowers bloom from June to September.

PIÑON PINE
AR, BB, BC, CC, CL, CR, GC, GM, MV, PF, ZN

The piñon pine is a slow-growing, small evergreen, with spreading, rounded, gray-green crown; it is often shrubby. The pine is 16–30 ft. high, and 1–1.5 ft. in diameter, with stiff, sharp needles and egg-shaped, dull yellow-brown cones. Large, edible, mealy seeds are sold as piñon nuts and used as staple food by some Indian tribes.

PONDEROSA PINE
BB, BC, CC, CR, GC, GM, ZN

The most widely distributed and common pine in North America, the ponderosa pine is a large evergreen with a broad, open, conical crown of spreading branches. It is 60–130 ft. high, and 2.5–4 ft. in diameter, with stiff dark-green needles and 2–6 in. cones. It is the most commercially valuable western pine.

PRICKLY PEAR
AR, BB, CC, CL, CR, GC, GM, MV, PF, ZN

The prickly pear is a flat, nearly oval cactus, 3–6 in. high. Its bright yellow or bright magenta many-petaled flowers are 2–3 in. wide and bloom in late spring.

QUAKING ASPEN
BB, BC, ZN

The most widely distributed tree in North America, the quaking aspen grows to a height of 80–100 ft. Its leaves are 1.25–3 in. long and nearly round, shiny green above, dull green beneath, and turn golden-yellow in autumn before dropping; the "quaking" comes from leaves that tremble in the slightest breeze. The bark is the favorite of beaver and rabbits; deer, elk, moose, sheep, and goats feed on twigs and foliage.

RABBITBRUSH
AR, BC, CL, CR, MV, PF, ZN

Rabbitbrush is a shrub found only in North America. Its erect, slender, flexible branches are covered with dense, matted hairs; it has narrow leaves and small yellow flower heads in dense clusters at ends of stems. It grows to 7 ft. Rabbitbrush flowers from August to October, and Navajo Indians use the flower heads for yellow dye.

ROCKY MOUNTAIN MAPLE
GC, GM, MV

This maple is a shrub or small tree with short trunk and slender, upright branches. It grows to 30 ft., 1 ft. diameter, with leaves 1.5–4.5 in. long, flowers .25 in. wide, with 4 greenish-yellow petals. Deer, elk, cattle, and sheep browse foliage.

SACRED DATURA
AR, BB, CL, CR, GC, ZN

The sacred datura is commonly called jimsonweed, a corruption of Jamestown weed. Its large, trumpet-shaped, white flower blooms at night and is usually withered by morning. It has coarse foliage, with rank-smelling, spherical fruit 1.5 in. in diameter, with a prickly surface. The datura grows to 5 ft. and flowers from May to November.

SAGEBRUSH
AR, BC, CL, PF, ZN

There are several varieties of sagebrush in the western U.S. They are silvery shrubs, with rigid black trunks and persistent leaves, whose heads are small and yellowish when in bloom. Sand sagebrush at Zion is 2–3 ft. tall, with narrow, threadlike, silvery leaves.

SQUAWBUSH
AR, BC, CL, CR

Also known as lemonade sumac, squawbush is a rank-smelling, sprawling shrub with greenish flowers.

SUNFLOWER
CC, CL, CR, GC, GM, PF, ZN

The common sunflower is a tall, coarse, leafy plant with a hairy stem that grows to 2–13 ft. Its flower head has a central maroon disk surrounded by many bright yellow rays; it flowers from June to September.

UTAH JUNIPER
AR, CL, CR, GC, MV

Junipers are also called cedars. This short tree, with upright trunk, low spreading branches, and rounded open crown, is 15–40 ft. high and 1–3 ft. in diameter; the leaves are 1/16-in. long. It grows slowly and becomes contorted with age. Indians used juniper bark for cordage and sandals.

YUCCA
AR, BB, CC, CL, CR, GC, GM, MV, PF, ZN

Of the several species of yucca, the banana yucca is the most common. It has rigid, spine-tipped leaves in 1 or several rosettes, and a long cluster of large whitish flowers on a stalk; flowers are 2–4 in. long in spring. The yucca grows to 5 ft. Baked fruit of banana yucca tastes like sweet potato.

PHOTO CREDITS

288: ©David Muench
289: ©John Running
290: ©Roy Murphy
292–293: ©Russ Finley/ Holiday Films
295: ©David Muench
297: ©Russ Finley
299: ©Russ Finley/Holiday Films

300: ©Jeff Gnass
303: ©Ed Cooper
307: New York Public Library Picture Collection/Photograph by Eyre Powell
309: ©David Muench
311: ©Collier/Condit
312–313: ©Jeff Gnass

314: ©Dr. E.R. Degginger
315, left: ©Sonja Bullaty; right: ©Stephen Trimble
317: ©Ed Cooper
319: ©Michael Collier
323, 325: ©Jeff Gnass

Appendix of Animals and Plants Photo Credits

328, col. 1, top: ©Roy Murphy, bottom: ©R.C. Simpson/Tom Stack & Assoc.; col. 2, top: ©Larry Thorngren/Tom Stack & Assoc., bottom: ©G.C. Kelley/Tom Stack & Assoc.; col. 3: ©Roy Murphy.
329, col.1,both: ©Roy Murphy; col. 2: ©Joe McDonald/ Tom Stack & Assoc.; col. 3, both: ©Roy Murphy.
330, col. 1, top: ©Bob McKeever/Tom Stack & Assoc., center: ©Stephen Trimble, bottom: ©Roy Murphy; col. 2: ©Rod Planck/ Tom Stack & Assoc.; col. 3, top: ©William R. Eastman III/ Tom Stack & Assoc.,bottom: ©Robert C. Gildart.
331, col. 1, top: ©Roy Murphy, bottom: ©C. Summers/ Tom Stack & Assoc.; col. 2, top: ©Phil & Loretta Hermann/Tom Stack & Assoc., bottom: ©Robert C. Gildart; col. 3: ©Joe Branney/ Tom Stack & Assoc.
332, col. 1, top: ©Christopher Crowley/Tom Stack & Assoc., bottom: ©Stephen Trimble; col. 2, top: ©John Gerlach/ Tom Stack & Assoc., bottom: ©Stephen Trimble; col. 3, top: ©Anthony Mercieca/ Tom Stack & Assoc., bottom: ©John Shaw/Tom Stack & Assoc.

333, col. 1, top: ©G.C. Kelley/Tom Stack & Assoc., bottom: ©Joe Branney/Tom Stack & Assoc.; col. 2, top: ©Stephen Trimble, bottom: ©Rod Planck/Tom Stack & Assoc.; col. 3, top: ©Anthony Mercieca/Tom Stack & Assoc., bottom: ©Rod Planck/Tom Stack & Assoc.
334, col. 1, top: ©Keith H. Murakami/Tom Stack & Assoc., bottom: ©Anthony Mercieca/Tom Stack & Assoc.; col. 2, both: ©Roy Murphy; col. 3, both: ©Anthony Mercieca/Tom Stack & Assoc.
335, col. 1, top: ©Alan G. Nelson/Tom Stack & Assoc., bottom: ©G.C. Kelley/Tom Stack & Assoc.; col. 2, both: ©G.C. Kelley/Tom Stack & Assoc.; col. 3, top: ©Robert C. Simpson/Tom Stack & Assoc., bottom: ©Anthony Mercieca/ Tom Stack & Assoc.
336, col. 1, top: ©Anthony Mercieca/Tom Stack & Assoc., bottom: ©Larry R. Ditto/Tom Stack & Assoc.; col. 2: ©Anthony Mercieca/ Tom Stack & Assoc.
337, col. 1, both: ©Bob McKeever/Tom Stack & Assoc.; col. 2, top: ©C. Summers/Tom Stack & Assoc., center: ©Stephen Trimble, bottom: ©Steve Elmore; col. 3, top: ©Stephen

Trimble, bottom: ©Bob McKeever/Tom Stack & Assoc.
338, col. 1, top: ©Wayne A. Lea/Tom Stack & Assoc., bottom: ©Bob McKeever/ Tom Stack & Assoc.; col. 2, top: ©Michael Collier, center: ©Stephen Trimble, bottom: ©Bob McKeever/ Tom Stack & Assoc.; col. 3, both: ©Stephen Trimble.
339: All ©Bob McKeever/ Tom Stack & Assoc., except col. 3, bottom: ©J. Cancalosi/Tom Stack & Assoc.
340, col. 1, top: ©Rod Planck/Tom Stack & Assoc., bottom: ©Stephen Trimble; col. 2, top: ©Frank Mendonca/Tom Stack & Assoc., center: ©Michael Collier, bottom: ©Stephen Trimble; col. 3, top: ©Stephen Trimble, bottom: ©Roy Murphy.
341, col. 1, top: ©Jeff Gnass, bottom: ©Roy Murphy; col. 2, top: ©Michael Collier, bottom: ©Roy Murphy; col. 3, both: ©Stephen Trimble.
342, col. 1, top: ©Stephen Trimble, bottom: ©Michael Collier; col. 2, top: ©Tom Stack/Tom Stack & Assoc., bottom: ©Stephen Trimble; col. 3, top: ©Ed Cooper; bottom: ©Michael Collier.
343: All ©Stephen Trimble, except col. 2, bottom: ©Ed Cooper.

INDEX

Numbers in italics indicate illustrations.